MW00338220

PRAISE FOR

"With admirable candor, the author chronicles . . . the longing to return to Israel, which 'waxes and wanes' for her as she becomes more settled in her new home in Pittsburgh. Sasson's account is often stirring, and she intelligently discusses the enormous power exerted by the allure of home."
—Kirkus Reviews

"A moving tale of two homes, told by a gifted storyteller who helps you live in her moments. Dorit Sasson captures the heat of Israel and the snow of Pittsburgh, the sense of belonging and the loneliness of newness . . . You learn how she creates a true home for herself and her family by reaching out to her community even while she plunges into her heart to find peace of mind and believe in God."
—Dr. Judy Siegel Henn, retired English teacher and lecturer

"This unusual coming-of-age story is a moving testament to the courage of those who must live in two cultures at once."
—Pat Schneider, author, *Writing Alone and With Others* and *How the Light Gets In*; and founder, Amherst Writers & Artists

"*Sand and Steel: A Memoir of Longing and Finding Home* is a richly woven emotional tale about one woman's attempt to reconcile and find home. From Israel to the United States, Sasson unpacks the richest kind of homelessness, of being untethered and knowing your roots while feeling very far away from both."
—Laurie Wagner, writer, teacher, and host of *27 Powers*

SAND
AND
STEEL

www.mascotbooks.com

Sand and Steel: A Memoir of Longing and Finding Home

©2021 Dorit Sasson. All Rights Reserved. No part of this publication
may be reproduced, stored in a retrieval system or transmitted in any
form by any means electronic, mechanical, or photocopying, recording
or otherwise without the permission of the author.

For more information, please contact:
Mascot Books
620 Herndon Parkway #320
Herndon, VA 20170
info@mascotbooks.com

Library of Congress Control Number: 2020914984

CPSIA Code: PRV0321A
ISBN-13: 978-1-68401-885-7

Printed in the United States

To Haim, my everything

To Ivry and Ayala, my finest creations

SAND
AND
STEEL

A Memoir of Longing and Finding Home

May 2021

Dear Lisa — Here's to finding
home and deeper connections!
From Dorit Sasson

DORIT SASSON

A NOTE FROM
THE AUTHOR

To write this book, I delved into the memory of this event and time of my life and supplemented the process with research, personal journals, and notes. At times, I changed names to preserve anonymity. There are no made-up events or characters in this story. Many people and events that had no impact on the truth of the story have been omitted.

CONTENTS

1

WAR

The dust still hasn't settled on either side of the fields by the time we pull onto Road 90 en route to our kibbutz in the Upper Galilee of Israel on August 21, 2006, but something tells me it's safe to return. *As long as we don't leave again.* A breeze passes through our green Volkswagen. Cotton plants in the near distance wave in the hot air. How can it be that these fields haven't been burnt by rockets and Scud missiles? What kind of war is this?

I've never known before what it feels like to have to leave a home suddenly, against your will. But for the past thirty-four days, I've been tested; I've had to stay courageous and resilient in the face of a psychological war that will determine my family's economic security and my own commitment to staying in Israel for the long haul.

When I was eighteen years old, I left my home in New York City and my fearful mother, who couldn't stand the thought of me trading college life for the battlefield, to volunteer in Israel for the Israel Defense Forces. I was desperate to escape and saw the IDF as my path to emotional freedom.

During those two and a half years of service, I not only reinvented myself as a soldier, but also as a female immigrant to Israel trying to assimilate into a militaristic, male-dominated culture in which I often felt voiceless. And ultimately, I achieved the emotional freedom I was seeking.

For Israelis like myself (it took me three years to claim that status), who are constantly confronting threats of terrorism, the only way to escape the madness of political unrest is to live in the moment. This kind of living is difficult for Americans—most of whom are focused planners preoccupied with their own agendas—to understand.

When things are peaceful, I'm pretty good at being in the moment, but when threats loom large, like right now, the New Yorker in me resists and resents the situation I've been thrown into. This state of constant worry, which for Israelis is a never-ending reality, has become my new normal, and I don't like it one bit.

We cross the narrow "Yosef" bridge, and then drive through the automatic gate (which now stays open) and past the factory and water tower before reaching the right fork in the road that brings us to the single paved road leading to a small group of Spanish stucco houses—some of which, ours included, were just renovated. Anxious to know if our home is still intact, I rush out of the car and down the path, just enough to catch a glimpse, while Haim is still unstrapping our son from his car seat.

There it is. Untouched.

Thirty-four days as "refugees." Thirty-four days listening to Kol-Yisrael, "The Voice of Israel" hourly news station, from Pardes Hanah, a small city an hour north of Tel-Aviv, where we holed up with our old friend Tamar and her two kids in a tiny two-bedroom apartment just a few minutes' drive from the beach. Thirty-four days of fretting over how close rockets shot from Lebanon might land near our home.

The day we left the kibbutz, tanks and encampments from different Israel Defense Forces units were hunkered down in the fields outside our bedroom window.

Now, finally, they are gone, and we are home.

※

When Haim, my Israeli-born husband, and I decided to leave the kibbutz a couple of days after the war started, I felt secure in that choice. As the mother of a young son, my first priority was to protect him; our kibbutz was under attack, and for our own sanity, I knew we had to leave. I didn't yet know the difference between leaving a home for good and leaving to save my sanity.

I also knew that what lay outside our self-contained kibbutz nucleus wasn't an unknown or hostile world. As a young immigrant from America, I thought Israelis were arrogant, rude, and pushy, but I eventually learned that they are simply direct and honest. Israel is a very small country whose population is like one big family. This is a state seeded with survivors of the Holocaust; a strong trauma binds us to one another, not just in the kibbutz, but everywhere in the country. We protect one another with fierce loyalty. Everywhere you go in Israel, you sense how important it is to Israelis that we look out for each other.

Historically, cities have always been major targets during Israel's wars. Who would think of aiming a missile at an army base in the desert, or at a relatively isolated beach, when the Hezbollah could kill thousands of civilians and soldiers in the city? At Tamar's home, we'd often visit the beach—but somehow, the waves, the open sand, and the three flashing electricity company towers in the distance often made me feel more vulnerable than anywhere else I'd been since the war began. I tried to enjoy the moment, knowing there were bomb shelters nearby if we needed them. But why leave the kibbutz for this? True, at the beach we didn't have to hear the sirens signaling falling rockets and Scud missiles—but that didn't stop my feelings of helplessness from overwhelming me. Plus, we were completely in the dark about what was happening to our home.

Haim couldn't understand how new and scary our current situation felt to me. I'd never lived through a war. The Persian Gulf War in 1991 didn't count—I was just a nineteen-year-old soldier serving in the Arava desert at that time. Now I was a thirty-six-year-old mother who'd been living in Israel for seventeen years. *This war is real, and it isn't stopping. Day in, day out, the same routine. How long can we go on like this?*

I boarded the train from Binyamina to Tel-Aviv to run some errands. I set out with an unwashed face and bad breath from having stayed up all night trying to get comfortable sleeping on the beach. Before allowing us into the railroad car, the conductor gave us a stern warning not to push each other; an unprecedented number of travelers were on board. I hugged my bag.

This train ride was about to test my comfort zone. Signs of danger were everywhere. Security personnel hopped on and off in a steady stream. With terrorist attacks and bombings, the recent norm on busy railroad cars and buses, I was going to have to let go of any pretense that I was in control, and trust that my country would support, protect, and help me even in desperate situations.

In every respect, I'd earned my social status as an Israeli; I'm a citizen like any other here. But it was only when I happened to sit down next to an abandoned open newspaper on that train did I realize the degree to which I'd fully integrated into this country. There in the newspaper was a picture of a former student of mine: Sergeant Haran Lev, age nineteen, killed in ground operations on Saturday— the thirty-second day of what would turn out to be thirty-four days of fighting in Lebanon. My throat closed. I was fed up with these feelings of helplessness, and now a boy I'd known and taught was dead.

I held the newspaper in disbelief.

Haran Lev.

The Haran I knew was a scrawny ninth-grader who liked to saunter into the classroom after the bell. He often got up without permission and laughed at jokes his friend Yakir made. He made my life hell. He forced me to raise my voice constantly to get his attention. He didn't care about learning English, and I never figured out how to reach him. I found out later that he was dyslexic. He needed a mentor, not an English teacher—but I didn't know how to be that person. Now that I was a mother, I understood.

And now he was a statistic, a combat soldier killed in the line of duty. I peered again at Haran's picture. His boyishness had been replaced by sharp, masculine features. In the photo, he wore a red beret that hugged his head, and his hands hung at his sides. I realized that only now, seventeen years after moving to Israel, I had been indoctrinated into this country in a new way. Now I understood the pain and suffering Israelis felt when hearing the name of a loved one who had died at the special ceremony for the annual day of remembrance for the fallen soldiers and victims of terror.

Until this moment, this intimacy with death hadn't been part of my experience. Though I was familiar with the concept of national mourning—the fact that in Israel grieving is a public act—I hadn't been touched personally by death before now.

In Israel, one needs to adjust one's expectations constantly and adapt to new situations. You have to be amenable, moldable—like sand. So unlike America, where a strong will and firm resolve are prized. Where Israel is sand, America is steel. For me, because of my New York City roots, adjusting to Israeli culture is a constant work in progress. Straddling two different cultures, languages, and mentalities is challenging, and yet in other ways, this is perhaps inevitable. So long as our home is in Israel, I want and need to consistently maintain a lifeline to these sandy qualities that will allow me to thrive here, and yet the American in me struggles to let go fully of the inflexible, steely qualities that were driven into me by my upbringing. Mine is an identity in flux—and this war constantly tests my ability to adapt.

On the way back to Tamar's home from Tel-Aviv, thoughts of Haran flooded me. I left my sunglasses on and turned up the radio in our car after getting off the train. A news story broke into the monotony of music that was playing—a song by a new American pop band called the Backstreet Boys.

Beep. Beep. Beep. It was time for the hourly news.

More casualties. I zoomed past unlit paths and through a roundabout, parked in what was now our unofficial parking space, fumbled with the gate, and walked gingerly up the steps to Tamar's house.

I took in my new landscape: weeds peeking out from scattered houses of various styles dating back to the period of the British mandate before Israel became a state, and unpaved roads with the occasional blossoming almond and olive trees growing at their edges. I've spent most of my post-army years on a kibbutz, which only now I realize has given me a strong sense of peace that life in a big city in Israel, with all its accompanying social and financial struggles, would not.

Tamar's house was filled with dirt and sand. I fumbled my way to the bathroom. No lightbulb in our bedroom. Smells of incense, baby powder, and soiled sheets. Healing crystals on bookshelves. We were now six people living in a one-bedroom home. No one was particularly focused on cleaning up.

Haim flicked on a flashlight. "Don't worry, *Motek*, sweetheart. I've got it."

I gave up groping in the dark once he turned on the light. I was trying yet again to go with the flow, but I found myself frustrated by the chaos. We had gotten two messages from a good friend who stayed behind that all was well, and then nothing. Three days had passed since the last message. I just wanted reassurance that our home was okay.

⁂

This morning—two weeks into our stay with Tamar and before the sun even had a chance to reveal the thick line of dirt on the green patio furniture outside—I ask Haim when we could go home.

"Not tomorrow," he said.

"Well, when do you *think* we can go home?"

"I don't know.

I took a deep breath. "Is our house okay?"

"I don't know."

"I'm worried."

He shook his head. "Don't be."

I wanted to wash my sandals in our own bathtub. Dry myself with our own towels. Water the flowers in our own garden.

"This is going on forever," I complained.

He shrugged. "It will be over soon."

I wanted to scream, kick, yell, and run, but words stayed bubbling in my throat. Patience, *savlanoot*, is how Israelis get through these tough moments.

"Another attack happened last night," Haim said after a long silence.

"On our kibbutz?"

"Yes."

Why isn't he reassuring me? Just a few minutes ago, he told me not to be worried. I imagined a kibbutz member's home with a gaping hole through the ceiling and a ray of sun streaming in revealing twisted wire and metal, like a robot's intestines. "Whose house was bombed?"

"Yael and Hanouch." He gestured with the kettle. "More tea?"

"No." I sipped at the Israeli-style tea Haim had made from mint leaves, lemon, and a few dried-up tea bags. "Nothing's going to be the same now."

"Probably not."

I willed myself to believe it was better to stay where we were, far away from the blasts, rumbling walls, and crying babies. But I longed to return to our kibbutz home.

"You know how it is," Haim said. "We can be here for a while. A person can't sit on two chairs. Be in two places, I mean."

I was very familiar with this concept. After all, isn't this what any expat grapples with—not being able to be in two places at once, the experience of two homes? My home was apparently here, in Israel. But how loyal was I to this country that kept testing my ability to thrive? This country whose political turmoil was threatening our very stability.

Haim gathered the tea things. I wrote in my journal while Ivry played. My pen hovered above the page. The words I wanted to say didn't come, so I just sat and watched and waited.

<hr />

To stay positive during times of adversity, you have to activate positive thinking—also synonymous with *savlanoot*, or patience. When Israelis need to "keep it together," they band together. They walk hand in hand with the fear.

In the States, we don't have the daily pressures of an ongoing war, and due to America's vastness, we are far-flung; our distance separates us, both in space and in values. It's easier to deal with feelings of stress, and perhaps even denial, privately. In Israel, people reflect the reality of their hardships. They are direct and to the point, and less prone to chitchat and pleasantries. But the cultural

DNA of Israelis compels them to be socially enmeshed with one another, which is what keeps them tethered together as a nation undergoing hardships.

Each day for the past few weeks, I'd watched how the waves rushed in—each one a little stronger than the last. I'd fingered grains of sand, trying to find that soft spot among the coarser ones. I'd refrained from asking Haim whether it was safe enough to go back to our kibbutz, afraid of coming across as too needy. *Flow, flow. Go with the flow.* I'd smiled at how Ivry gurgled with excitement each time the water gathered around his beach toys.

Each morning, on the beach, Haim appeared in a wrapped *tallit*, mumbling morning prayers. He wrapped the traditional prayer shawl around his bowed head as he recited the holy prayer of the *Amidah*, and I sat back and watched. He was a glowing, spiritual silhouette against the Mediterranean Sea. *Pray for me. Pray for us. Pray, pray, pray.* Each time he bowed, Ivry laughed with delight.

Prayers done, Haim scooped up our son, and there I was, alone again. The waves seemed to shoot an answer: *Let it all go. Give up control. Just let it go.*

Twenty-seven days into the war, I found myself again at the sea, noticing this time how it ran parallel to my feet. Seagulls landed in a puddle, squawking at the sound of my feet splashing in the water. A few minutes later, a strawberry sunset swirled into orange and cracked open into a golden yellow. From the top of the tall towers in the distance, three white lights flickered.

You are afraid. You are fearful of losing your beautiful home in a kibbutz you claim as your own in a country where you've worked so hard to build roots. A home that's now part of your identity and heritage. And who you've become.

I thump-thumped my feet and kneaded the sand with my toes. The plastic clip holding my brown, salty seaweed hair fell onto the sand.

I didn't want to go back to Tamar's. I wanted to stay at the beach, curled up in the sleeping bag stashed in the car. The beach had become our home. I imagined going back to the kibbutz—but what quality of life waited for us there?

Waves continued lapping at the shore.

Stay open to the flow. Be in the moment.

※

I looked up at Haim from the pile of dirty breakfast dishes I was cleaning. The kitchen clock said twelve noon. The hourly news on the radio announced that the war was over. Thirty-four days of ground fighting had ended. We could go home.

An hour later, we started packing up. I was surprised to discover that I was now torn.

"Are you coming?" Haim asked, resting a hand on my shoulder. Ivry had fallen asleep in his arms.

I brushed the sand from my sandals, packed up our things, and said good-bye to our beachy home.

※

And now, four hours later, we've arrived home, just like that. Before we can even lift Ivry from his car seat, a kibbutz member sees us from afar and approaches. I quickly look around to assure myself all is well. The kibbutz resembles a ghost town since most of its members with young children have fled—about one hundred in all. But lights soon flicker on, bicyclists appear, and members start appearing on their porches.

"*Ahalan*, Haim, *mah-inyanim?*" our friend asks, giving my husband a hearty *chapha* on the back.

We're home.

2

THE DECISION

It's our second day back at the kibbutz, and Haim leaves in the morning for the *butkeh*—guard's quarters—where he works as a security guard pushing an on-off button to open the gate to the entrance of our kibbutz. It is one of several positions kibbutz members refuse to automate due to security issues, given our proximity to the Israel–Lebanon border, and it pays less than $800 a month. On our newly privatized kibbutz, it is one of the few blue-collar jobs available. With my $1,500-a-month salary as an English teacher, we are just barely able to stay afloat.

Since the kibbutz voted to privatize in 2003, we have each become financially responsible for food, education, and other necessities the kibbutz previously covered. When the kibbutz was a "commune," the classical agrarian model of a kibbutz, members enjoyed three full meals at the dining room, and the kibbutz was in charge of education. Holidays were celebrated together. Laundry was taken care of. Haim worked as a buyer and procurement manager for the dining room and later as a researcher for a media company, one of the jobs he loved. But when the company shut down, he was forced to work on the factory's assembly line, and then as a security guard. Now that this war has hit, this region of Israel has become economically depressed, and the possibility of Haim finding any kind of "dream job" has fallen through completely.

Now, almost every kibbutz member owns a vehicle, and in some cases, two. Almost every family is expanding their property, building second and even third floors. Instead of working to support the common good of the kibbutz, members are now pushed by greed— to work more to get more—the opposite of Karl Marx's theory of socialism, upon which the classical principles of the *kibbutzim* were founded. Bit by bit, we're seeing this historical vision crumble before our eyes.

It's our first Friday afternoon back home. I pick up Ivry from daycare and go for a bike ride around the perimeter of the kibbutz. Hope lingers in my heart. Just this week, I faxed Haim's resume for the two hundredth time to a company advertising a buyer and procurement position. This time, we've opted to look as far south as the city of Beersheva. I am willing to see him only once every few weeks if it means he doesn't have to work as a security guard.

So far, we haven't heard back from a single job we've applied for.

Snow-capped Mount Hermon sits in the distance, basking in the fiery, reddish glow of the sunset currently announcing the Shabbat. A gentle breeze tousles my hair. Ivry reaches out to grab some strands and coos with delight. On a last-minute whim, I circle my bike back to visit Haim at work.

Haim fumbles with the coffee pot the minute I appear. Black bags under his eyes are shadowed by his baseball hat. His tan stops at the bottom hem of his shorts. He is strongly built, and today he is wearing one of his favorite, well-worn T-shirts showing an image of John Lennon and the word "Imagine." Complete with his well-worn blue shorts and flip-flops, his dark hair and brown eyes take me back to our early courtship and the young man he was when we first fell in love.

I unstrap Ivry from the bicycle seat and lean my bike against the fence. I am meters away from the Jordan River Promenade, the site of our marriage ceremony. Also known as Shvil Ami, or Ami's Trail, the Jordan River Promenade is a delightful, paved walkway that follows alongside the flowing waters of Israel's most famous stream.

Since we returned from the beach a week ago, Haim has worked the night shift three times and now is set to do so again on our first Shabbat back home. Instead of eating home alone tonight, I will spread out our home-cooked Shabbat dinner on the grass next to the *butkeh*, picnic-style, feed Ivry, and watch Haim approach each car as it enters the gate. While other members are sitting around the Shabbat table with family and friends, Haim will work.

After dinner, I will take Ivry home and tuck him into bed, wondering how long Haim will continue to work a job where he is unappreciated and undervalued—seemingly the only job left for him to do, due to the fact there are so few jobs available. I will wake up in the middle of the night comforted by the rise and fall of his chest, a moment that will remind me of our pre-marriage and pre-privatized days when we'd sleep until nine in the morning in our one-bedroom apartment and I'd snuggle in closer to his side of the bed, intending to throw an arm around his back, only to discover he was in the kitchen whipping up a stunning concoction of whipped eggs and leafy green vegetables too pretty to eat. My heart will continue to break for this forty-four-year-old father, one of the smartest men I know, who served in the intelligence division during his army and reservists days and still fiercely believes in the classical kibbutz model, despite having been relegated to being a mere security guard.

☼

On this first Shabbat back at the kibbutz, over forkfuls of coleslaw and potato salad, Ivry and I share three pieces of chicken schnitzel and a garden mosaic salad of peppers, tomatoes, and cucumbers spiced Israeli style—a touch of lemon juice, a dash of olive oil, and salt.

For the next hour, I watch how Haim chats with the kibbutz members coming through the gate. Encounters start and end in the same fashion: they roll down their window and shout, "*Ma-yan-nim?*" and Haim bends down and chats with them for a few minutes until another car approaches. Sitting here on the blanket, I hear pieces of conversation spilling out the windows: "What the heck are you doing here at the *butkeh*? Why are you working here? This isn't a job suited for you!"

These seemingly jocular comments, often tinged with cynicism, incense me. How dare they poke fun of Haim like that, knowing we've reached the end of the road and can't find him a better-paying job? I know Israelis don't champion each other's success, as it's usually seen to come at the expense of their own, but my temper flares at their insensitivity. It's almost too much for me to put up with.

A memory surfaces. The day before we left the kibbutz, when the war had just broken out, I showed up at the gate with a packed lunch.

"When do you finish?" I asked Haim eagerly.

"In another four hours," he said. "Why, what's up?"

"You're not picking up your phone and I need to finish packing. We're leaving tomorrow, remember? What else do I need to bring?"

"Take my *tefillin*."

"Okay."

"And *tallit*."

"Will do," I told him. "No problem." But as I biked home, I thought, *Why does he need those religious items if we're going to be at the beach and, most likely, a bomb shelter? What's the point?*

Now, watching Haim at his post, I'm finally beginning to understand. He prayed every day at the beach for himself. For us. For all of Israel. And for the kibbutz. He asked me to bring his *tefillin* and *tallit* because, even before we left, he already knew how bad it had become.

Over the next few days, Haim and I send out resumes for jobs all over the country. In the meantime, a position for a buying and procurement position opens up on our kibbutz. We jump at the possibility, hoping this could be our lucky break—but soon discover that Haim not only didn't get the job but that it has gone to someone outside the kibbutz.

Again, I am furious. "They gave it to someone else—*outside* of the kibbutz?" I shout. "There seems to be no way out of this mess."

He isn't the only kibbutz member to have applied. Another woman, too, has been rejected. This doesn't help my sense of injustice.

He turns up the corners of his mouth and stares into the distance.

"I refuse to let them treat you like this," I spit out. "It's humiliating to watch how they speak to you." Relief washes over me as I say these words. It is liberating to finally name the injustice I've been witnessing for months.

"The kibbutz is dead," Haim says. His voice becomes low, and his brown eyes gradually soften.

I look up at him in shock. For the first time, I sense how fed up he has become, too. I never thought he'd express his deep frustration and pain with our kibbutz's new social system.

What will become of us now?

"I know how dedicated you are to the kibbutz system," I say delicately, "but I cannot let you work like a security guard anymore. I cannot let a man I love continue to do this kind of work."

"Okay," he says, "but what else am I supposed to do? Do you see a job waiting for me?"

We have already used our six months' worth of *reshet bitachon*, a monthly allowance the kibbutz gives to its struggling members.

We go on our usual evening stroll around the kibbutz, and we walk past the job bulletin board. The lingering sun illuminates the outlines of the new neighborhood. We turn back to the new main road, trying to pinpoint a familiar house or even a face. It occurs to me how caught up we have become in the divide of social change. To our right are houses symbolic of the old generation, including our own. To our left is the kibbutz's new, upscale neighborhood, filled with former city dwellers who can afford the high price tag of land and construction.

Stay abreast of the forces of social and economic change, despite the injustices. This is the voice behind the need to stay adaptable—to be malleable and open. To be sand.

"What about that opening for a sales associate at Zol Poh?" I ask. "The one we just saw on the bulletin board? Do you want to apply for it?"

"They're not going to hire me," Haim says, shaking his head. "What am I supposed to do—clean floors?"

My heart breaks for him yet again. I pine for the days when we didn't have to struggle so hard to make ends meet, and when this kibbutz fit the classical version of one big, happy family. *Biyachad.* Together.

And yet the classical kibbutz model is now flitting back into my life like some wannabe friend. Other kibbutz members who are still attached to the old kibbutz way of life are now openly expressing their anger. I'm still struggling to accept the changes, and yet my anger is catching up with me, too. I don't want to tough it out anymore. I don't have the energy to be strong. I am not up for a long-term fight. But as a wife of a kibbutz member, I don't have the "right" to speak out about some of the social injustices. I struggle to accept the situation. It makes me feel pathetically helpless.

I turn to look at my husband's glazed-over expression. "Nobody cares about you here," I say quietly. "Don't you see what's happening?"

Silence.

In the months to come, I will avoid acting too impulsively for fear that my emotions might get the better of me. Right now, though, I want him to feel the urgency of the situation. I want this patient *sabra* to realize that if we wait too long, we might end up getting stuck here, and he might have to work as a security guard until pension age. I can't afford to let that happen.

Today, we make our way to the sandy curb of the pavilion that stretches beyond the gate leading to Ami's Trail. My heart aches. Am I really ready to leave after all these years? We have had such a strong sense of belonging within this close-knit community, and yet now that feeling seems to be crumbling. I feel nostalgia for what has been, but don't see how we can possibly resurrect what we once had. Everything is different now. To leave the kibbutz means pulling Haim away from a community that once took him in, and to leave Israel means saying good-bye to a country I've grown to love. But what alternative do we have but to go?

"We have to leave," I whisper. "As in, leave the kibbutz. There's just no other way. Do you see yourself working as a security guard here forever? You're worth way more than that. I know that with your qualifications and experience, you are going to be successful in America. This system can only take us so far."

For the last few weeks, I've mulled over the possibility of moving to America, and I've decided it's the only answer to my prayer of finding a decent job for Haim. The more I've witnessed the way the kibbutz is treating my husband, the more fueled and driven I've become to prove we won't let ourselves be the victims of a crumbling kibbutz system. To prove that Haim doesn't have to be silenced professionally, that we can find economic success. But it is a now-or-never decision. The longer we stay, the harder it will be to go.

I dare to think of what this move would mean for both of us professionally. I start by checking both sides of his face for a sign of excitement. It is often hard to tell, as Haim acts nonchalant about many things. It will take me years to reach the soft, pulpy interior *sabras* are known for. Today, I yearn to find a sign that will affirm we are both on the same page.

Haim's lips twitch. His brown eyes soften in a way that affirms he is taking in the power of my words. I feel a stab of pain when I think of what this will mean for us. When Haim deserts his home country, his family and friends will call him out on it—and when they see they can't go very far with him, they'll soon move to me. But right now, I try putting that out of my mind. We aren't traitors; we're a humble couple trying to make a difficult decision in the face of an uncertain future.

You've got this, Dorit. Breathe in and out. It's just you and Haim now. You've both got this. Trust in the power of your bond and in your ability to make a sound decision with your head and heart.

"Nu?" I reach for his hand. "What do you think? We can always come back if it doesn't work out."

"Okay," he says, lacing his fingers through mine. "Let's do it."

3

TRAITOR

The timing of our request for an indefinite leave of absence from the kibbutz, just five weeks after the start of the war in 2006, makes me feel like a traitor. Leaving for a year—which is what we are planning, even though we've purchased one-way tickets—is a big deal. Former Israeli Prime Minister Yitzhak Rabin (who was assassinated in 1995), said on Israeli TV in 1976 that Israelis who left were *"nefolet shel nemushot,"* which translates roughly to "leftover weaklings." These words echo in my mind. Our request feels like a cop-out.

Nevertheless, Haim and I take our fate into our own hands and write a special letter to the kibbutz committee in charge of requests like ours. We are determined to pave a new path; we tell ourselves we deserve economic success, even if that means leaving. Since my emotions have taken hold of me, I have Haim write the official letter of request. His words are concise and to the point and fill me with hope:

I, Haim Sasson, a long-time kibbutz member since 1987, am requesting a year-long leave of absence in the United States. I've devoted many years to working in the fields of agriculture and education, and finally as a buyer and procurement manager in the dining room. After studying for a certificate as a buyer and procurement manager in Tel-Aviv, it's become clear that I won't be able to find suitable means of employment, especially since the kibbutz has become privatized. The only answer is to find a job in the United States that fits my skills.

To ask permission for an indefinite leave of absence means giving up on an ideology both Haim and I were drawn to in our youth, and which has carried us into adulthood. For Haim, it means giving up on a way of living, a movement that has served him for years, ever since being released from the Israel Defense Forces. For me, it means giving up on a support system that had been invaluable to me as a new mother. As we prepare to deliver our letter, I can't help but wonder whether the kibbutz will remember Haim's devotion over these many years. The children he has accompanied on all those field trips. The many meals and budgets he's overseen. Soon, just like that, we'll be gone. Will anyone even care?

As we wait for a response from this special committee in the fall of 2006, the dining room, which in the past hosted so many communal meals, is taken over by subcontractors offering lunch only at a premium price. The communal laundry, too, is subcontracted out, and members who had never been used to doing their own laundry start purchasing machines to take these tasks upon themselves to avoid another charge. The race is to save money. Nobody seems to care about social relationships. The orchards are taken over by foreign workers. Contractors begin to build new houses for families coming from big cities who crave a more peaceful existence in the once-empty fields adjacent to our home. Capitalism has finally caught up with this formerly socialist enclave, and greed is quickly taking over. The familiar rat race from America has set in.

During these final countdown months, I look at our one-way tickets as a way to get out of the mess. Yet in many ways, our decision terrifies me more than Haim, who continues to silently support and even pray for his economic success beyond our kibbutz walls. Steel is impervious to outside forces such as water and heat, but it loses strength at low temperatures. I consider this concept as I feel my own resolve weaken. But I try to keep my tough bravado going during these fragile moments. The kibbutz is no longer taking care of Haim, and we have to come to terms with this new reality.

Still, I can't yet see our move as positive. Perhaps this is an opportunity to elevate ourselves, an idea illustrated by the concept *yeridah l'tzorech aliyah*—leaving Israel for the sake of ascent—which is one of the most important paradoxical principles in Chassidic thought. But who could escape the sentiment that we are turning our backs on our country? That leaving is on par with being a traitor? Everything about making this decision has been complex and awful, and my constant obsessing can't change the reality of what we'll have to go through to actually get to the other side.

Toward the end of October 2006, we receive notification. Our request has been approved. My heart flickers in the way a candle does when it tries to keep its flame in the face of a gust of wind.

But the hope I'm trying to hold on to does not accompany me when I walk into the kibbutz supermarket the day after receiving the news that we're free to go.

"An Israeli never leaves his country," a member shouts in one of the aisles with a victorious look.

In a tight-knit community like a kibbutz, gossip and other news travel fast. The supermarket is mostly empty. Silence reigns at the cash register. I am face-to-face with a proud, second-generation female kibbutz member I've avoided since we made the decision to leave.

In this accusatory moment, all I hear is, "Traitor, traitor, you're a traitor." I traded American college life for the IDF battlefield, taught English to Israeli schoolchildren, and served on military bases, settlements, and kibbutzim, and yet now my fears of not belonging here are being made real.

Without saying a word, I pay for my groceries and walk out. I am too stunned and hurt to even look up at the cashier. Anger mounts in my throat. I know that if I try responding to this woman in Hebrew, emotions will get the better of me and I'll end up regretting my words. I want to leave on a positive note; this moment is testing my resolve to get through this moment and go with the flow. I know she is picking on me instead of Haim because I'm a woman, not a member who's invested years into the system. I want to defend myself—to tell her how the kibbutz has let us down by not helping Haim. But none of that will matter to her.

A few hours from now, I will sit in our house and stare blankly at our son until, unable to hold in the emotions any longer, I call Haim at the guard's quarter. He will listen with compassion and put my feelings into perspective. He will describe past examples of how this member undermined his work as a procurement manager during the old days when the kibbutz operated as a commune. Once again, I will be uplifted by his kindness and his reminder of how to be like sand in emotionally unpredictable times.

Letting go of your home, or anything near and dear to you, requires the courage to go through the emotional terrain of the unknown despite naysayers. Intuition becomes your inner GPS. You have to distinguish between your enemies and mobilize your inner army. Right now, I'm not familiar with Dr. Brene Brown's work, but later, I will come to see her work as indispensable to this experience. You can become strong by embracing vulnerability, and you dare more greatly when you acknowledge your fear. You can set your course on being more courageous, connected, engaged, and resilient by finding a wiser way to your inner world, even when fear and self-doubt sabotage your plans. During times of uncertainty, you need an inner road map.

To attempt to defend our decision to those around us would stifle our ability to go ahead with our plans. I have to protect myself emotionally, even if it means being called a "traitor."

Haim appears out of nowhere with a map of America that he spreads on the floor. It's been years since I've looked at a map of my former home country, and my eyes have to readjust to the size. I start feeling heart palpitations. He breezes through the moment, pointing to various states. I look at him quizzically. *What kind of crazy idea is this? Are we really trying to find a new home by opening a map of the United States?*

Years from now, I will laugh with friends about the "research" we did to choose our preferred state, but for now I am panicking. The vastness of America feels foreign after more than eighteen years away, living in a country the size of Delaware.

In our living room, I finger the Hudson River on the map. Memories of biking alongside the West Side Highway down to Battery Park as a teenager rise in my mind. Compared to the Hudson, the Jordan River, which loops along the side of our kibbutz, seems like a small stream. That huge city. This tiny village. Big and small. I left the United States as a teenager with one suitcase, feeling so very small yet so determined to serve in the Israel Defense Forces. Now, eighteen years later, I will be returning as a wife and mother—perhaps "big" with experiences, but once again feeling "small" in the face of our decision.

I'll soon learn that when you're an immigrant to the States or even a returning American, everything feels big, bigger than you. You try not to focus on it, but America's vastness will not let you forget.

Our kibbutz, by comparison, with its total of a little over four hundred residents, has everything we need within a 360-degree radius: doctor, supermarket, post office, neighbors, dining room, old-age home, car mechanic, bike shop, orchards, gas station, Thai restaurant, pizza parlor, dentist, and even a massage and hair salon. I feel protected. The only time I ever actually need to "leave" the kibbutz is for my teaching job at the nearby high school. To get there, I bike every day alongside the Jordan River, and if I want to do any "mega shopping," I go to the neighboring town of Kiriyat Shmona.

It isn't just the convenient lifestyle we'll be giving up that unnerves me, but the emotional security of having a home. To start afresh feels unsettling. I look down to where Haim is pointing. The state of Pennsylvania.

"So the way I see it," he says, "we can either live on the East Coast . . ."

"To be close to Mom," I say. She has Alzheimer's, and I know she is slowly withering away. A part of me feels obligated to be near her, but another part dreads the idea of being back in New York City—the city in which I was raised, the city from which I escaped.

"You've got to be a crazy millionaire to live in New York City," I protest. "The New York City of 2006 is not the New York City of 1989. It's gotten way too expensive now."

I think quickly. New Jersey could be an alternative, but it's still too pricey for our Israeli pocketbooks. California, too. After years of living on a kibbutz, we aren't used to the American standard of living.

During our honeymoon in 2003, relatives took Haim and me to Gettysburg, Pennsylvania, for a historical tour. As an avid student of American history, Haim peppered the tour guide, who happened to be a professor of history, with questions.

In the car on the way back to where we were staying, we reached for each other's hands. As newlyweds, excitement landed in our laps like a trembling autumn leaf in late summer; that encounter had enriched us culturally forever. We were training for a new form of biculturalism. He was experiencing my culture; I was experiencing America through new eyes with him. I was no longer a runaway. I no longer had to wrestle with Mom to prove myself. I was no longer that eighteen-year-old who'd felt compelled to escape. We were starting a fresh chapter.

We both look again at the map.

"So what about Pennsylvania?" Haim cracks a smile.

My heart beats faster. Pennsylvania. Rolling hills and fields of green. A place where I have no roots. No history. What do I know about Pennsylvania? The Liberty Bell, yes. And the Amish.

"But Pennsylvania is so far away from Mom," I muse, knowing that this could be the better choice. I'd still be close enough. Certainly closer than I am in Israel.

"It's a pretty state. So much history," Haim enthuses.

I'm not about to challenge him, but I'm not eager to choose a state for its beauty. I'm far more practical than that. "Yes, but a big one," I say, marveling at the size of everything in comparison to Israel, which is, in contrast, a speck on the map.

"They're all big," Haim says. "What did you expect? Israel?"

"So we're going to bet our cards on a state where we had a nice conversation with a tour guide?" I balk. "What kind of logic is that?"

Back and forth we go. Economics would clearly rule Pennsylvania in our favor. Living with Mom is not even a possibility; even the thought of living too close to her unnerves me. And Pennsylvania is much more affordable than New York.

Maybe it's not the worst idea after all.

Some days later, we zero in on the community of Squirrel Hill in Pittsburgh, after an Israeli-born pulpit rabbi approaching the end of his sabbatical in Squirrel Hill with his family recommends it. He can't praise the multiethnic town enough; he calls it a "nurturing home." The portrait he painted was quaint: a small kibbutz in the Diaspora, like an oasis in the desert. My interest was piqued. Squirrel Hill has a fairly large Jewish community, with lots of Israelis. New York City is the only US home I've ever known. Now, I am eager to tell myself a new story of what life can be there, despite my fear of the unknown.

Tonight, I hug Haim tightly after putting our son to bed.

"Honey, I'm scared about this move," I whisper. I find myself taken aback by my own words. Intuitively, I know that the Diaspora will be a cold place. Even with all the negative changes happening in our kibbutz, this move is already pulling us out of our comfort zones a thousand times over.

Haim grabs my arm and tucks it under his, a gesture meant to comfort me. What I want is for him to embrace me, to tell me we'll be okay. But he is deeply lost in his own thoughts, dealing with his own uncertainty about the long road ahead of us. It's difficult to be comforted when you too need comfort. I try to remind myself of this, but for now, I feel like we are strangers in the same bed.

His back is still turned to me

"Haim?" I ask.

Silence.

It's January 2007, seven months before we'll leave Israel for good, and Haim and I are at the US Embassy in Tel-Aviv, dealing with a wave of interrogation.

"What kind of employment will you have there?" the clerk asks.

Haim tells him he'll work for the US government as an Arabic linguist, being that his mother tongue is Arabic, and he knows four dialects. At first, I am surprised by his response, as he has never floated that kind of work as an option, but then I understand: so much is at stake with the green card application process, especially with the events of September 11, and he needs now to put his best foot forward.

"We certainly need people like you," the clerk says eagerly. "There are lots of opportunities for that kind of thing."

I watch patiently as the clerk and Haim speak for the next five minutes about the US government, history, and the need for Arabic speakers. A friendly conversation—one I hadn't anticipated. This is another piece of the hope puzzle.

The other piece will be my first and only upcoming sabbatical from teaching, which will start once we arrive in the States. I've been envisioning a personal development book for teachers for instructing at-risk English language learners, and it's been approved by the Ministry of Education in Israel. I am tickled by the fact I can essentially write this book from anywhere in the world; I feel that doing so will comfort me about our exiled status.

My heart swells with pride at the thought that Haim could potentially have employable skills. The American dream. I turn around and look back at the nervous crowd behind us, which only confirms my anxiety. Nothing about this is straightforward or easy. But things are looking up.

As we exit the building and head home, I turn to Haim. "Perhaps it won't be hard to find a job. It seems that way, doesn't it?"

He nods and holds my hand even tighter.

Look, we're already changing our trajectory, I think. This feeling of optimism, sparked by Haim's conversation with that clerk, would never have come to us on the kibbutz.

A new path. A new narrative.

Hope.

4

THE HUNT

August in Pittsburgh is particularly humid, but that doesn't stop me from walking the three long blocks to Murray Avenue in August 2007, four weeks after arriving in Squirrel Hill from Israel. Our new, multiethnic neighborhood feels like a good fit. Today, I asked a woman for directions to the nearest supermarket. I was struck by her accent and the way she pronounced the words "Giant Eagle" like one big drawl. Coming from New York City, I didn't anticipate the slower pace of life we'd find here, including the way people speak.

I feel small walking these long streets. After eighteen years of living in Israel, everything now feels supersized. And yet, just as was the case back on the kibbutz, everything we need is right here on one long, busy street. There's just a lot *more* of what we need.

The heat of August makes me breathless. It slows my movements and turns my brain to mush. It reminds me of childhood: summer camps, city pools, Italian ices that melt all over you. The same sticky heat I left as a teenager heart-bent on escaping my mother.

I walk down the tree-lined streets, open-mouthed, entranced by the exquisite yet mammoth homes in this neighborhood, only to find myself disoriented by the size of everything. These elephant-size vehicles make cars in Israel look like dog cages. Here a blossoming garden that could easily grace the cover of a glossy magazine, and there a mansion so enormous I can't see where it ends in the back. When I finally muster the courage to ask a mother at a nearby park what "SUV" stands for, I realize just how culturally displaced I really am.

I reach the end of the street, and all I can think of is our small, modest kibbutz garden and the five awkwardly sized cement footprints I placed in the tall, straw-like weeds surrounding it when we first moved into our house. How tickled I was by the plot of land that was "stamped" with my own footprint. Now, at the corner, I try not to dwell on how inconsequential I feel here.

In a country so vast, there's a certain anonymity. The States feels like a vast unknown. It's intimidating. I have yet to discover the community that makes up Squirrel Hill, Pittsburgh, and how it will replace our kibbutz home. All I know is, as of now, I don't belong here.

Clearly, having been away from the States for eighteen years requires me to navigate a new way of being. It won't occur to me until 2017, after reading an entry on the US Department of State's website, that what I'm experiencing right now is "reverse culture shock"— the cross-cultural adaptation stress associated with reentry of one's mother country.

While the phenomenon of cultural shock is widely accepted, reverse culture shock is not nearly as recognized or understood. It only took me twenty minutes of walking down a street in my new neighborhood to realize that I am in fact a "stranger" in my own country.

For the last eighteen years, my concept of "home" in Israel has been tested. I worked hard to build a connection in Israel; to become an "insider," however, is not an easy thing to do when you are up against the brusque *sabra* mentality. The super convenience of kibbutz living was something I loved right away, though joining the kibbutz far from guaranteed connection and belonging.

The biggest challenge during those years was putting aside the expectation that my native-Israeli born peers *should* pay attention to me and my individuality. I was bringing my impatient American mentality to the table, wanting to be seen and accepted among them without realizing that I first had to earn their respect. In time, though, I did. I adopted the "wolf pack" mentality that defines the Israeli culture. Being part of a group in this way created emotional safety, and over time, it also filled a void I'd harbored since childhood. The worrying and catastrophizing I'd inherited from my mother gradually melted away.

Now, the pressure is on me to build that same sense of community here. Problem is, I know no one in Pittsburgh. We do not have jobs or friends or family. Here, I am expected to start afresh.

In Israel, I built familiarity, routine, communication, and identity—the key variables that affect stress after reentry into one's mother country, which is something I will read about years from now in Craig Storti's *The Art of Coming Home*. In a city like Pittsburgh, finding a similar community is going to be a challenge. It's too early to know for sure if I will succeed in planting roots and building relationships here. I feel intimidated by the giant cars, unfamiliar street names (written in English, no less), and lack of self-contained residential areas.

During these trying and scary moments, I wonder if it is even possible to make a home here.

For the time being, I am set up in a cozy one-bedroom apartment in an airy attic inside a renovated twentieth-century home. The owners, a Jewish family, live downstairs. A kind rabbi set up a three-day homestay with them to give me time to find an apartment. Meanwhile, I've sent Haim and Ivry to New York City to stay with Mom, knowing I'd get more done on my own.

The summer of 2007 is winding down, and college students are scrambling for last-minute apartments. I worry that three days will not be enough time.

Now I'm approaching the second day of the homestay visit, and I haven't found anything yet. I experienced seismic emotions at the sight of the first apartment I visited on a quiet fifth-floor walk-up. An enormous swarm of flies surrounded a tower of pizza boxes. Filth and dirt were everywhere. Never mind that the building manager offered an apology and suggested we look at another unit. It was too late. The seeds of doubt had been sown. Did I give up our pastoral kibbutz home for this?

In desperation, I call that same rabbi, who kindly offers to drive the long city blocks to help me gather names of other management companies. Names like Hobart and Shady Avenue sound just as foreign to me as Costco and Target, but I force myself to stay open and curious. *Be vulnerable. It's okay.*

I'm hardly the first or only person in the world to be dealing with the unknown. Whether you're an immigrant, a returning American from a hiatus abroad, or simply a person moving to a new city to start a new job, you have to deal with the unease of inhabiting a new environment and the ambiguity of not knowing. In these circumstances, you must accept that you are new. You have no history in this new place. Facing loneliness and the lack of any sort of roots, you must muster an inner strength. For me, this strength was now firmly represented by the quality of steel that I'd come to associate with the United States in general. I resolved to get done what needed to get done.

Every sight here strikes me as so different from our secluded pastoral kibbutz home. There are no roundabouts breaking up noisy streets. There's no separate supermarket for kosher food. No outdoor markets or drive-thrus for banks. No falafel stands at various corners. No fragrant smells of burekas and chocolate-filled croissants wafting from bakeries, particularly during lunchtime and early morning. These are things I didn't realize I'd miss as much as I do now. The kosher falafel that the nearby Jewish Community Center sells is dry and tasteless and reminds me of the cold world that makes up the Diaspora, and again of what I've given up in leaving Israel.

In Pittsburgh, most people avoid eye contact. There is nonstop traffic on Friday evenings, as opposed to the way traffic came to a grinding halt in our neighboring town of Kiriyat Shmona back home, as people stopped everything in anticipation of Shabbat.

I am plagued by doubts. What have I done? Even though Haim willingly came along for this adventure, it occurs to me now that I've yanked him away from everything familiar. Will he suffer from the stress of all this newness even more than I will? Will Ivry be worse off growing up here? We were so anxious to have our travel plans approved, I didn't allow the magnitude of this move to sink in before we left. Now, the ramifications of the choices we've made are weighing heavily upon me.

The kind rabbi and I circle back to Shady Avenue.

"You see?" he says. "All streets circle back to Shady. Shady runs parallel to Wightman."

He shifts to second gear, and the van suddenly jerks forward. Soon, we come to a grinding halt. Down the hilly street, eight more rental signs are scattered in between garbage cans. To my left is Shady. To my right is another foreign-sounding side street. I quickly jot down names. I notice how jittery I feel.

The rabbi remains steady throughout, reassuring in the face of my frenzy. "You'll find a place," he tells me. "Don't worry." He holds himself with an air of confidence. A youthful energy belies his trimmed beard, brown peppered with grayish tints. We talked earlier about his many trips to Israel. He spoke of family in Jerusalem, and I saw that he understands my predicament. He understands how it feels to straddle two cultures. I feel less alone as we drive around together, momentarily comforted by this kind man who's taken it upon himself to help me, in no small part because we are part of the same tribe. I am grateful for that and am trying to hold on to that feeling.

"But I head back to New York City tomorrow," I say, telling him something he already knows. I recognized this anxious self so well, and know of her pitfalls, but I am in default mode. So, instead of asking myself questions that might calm my racing mind—*Why am I feeling so anxious about settling in Pittsburgh? What do I need to do to feel more settled? Is it possible to feel hopeful about finding a home in Pittsburgh?*—I sink into despair. I feel like I'm being punished. That I'm deserving of punishment. That the decisions I've made are responsible for this hardship being imposed upon my family. And to make matters worse, I feel like a traitor. We abandoned our kibbutz home and community, our country—and for this!

In short, I'm catastrophizing. For now, getting absorbed in the struggle of finding a home is easier than asking myself why it feels so difficult.

This morning I was up early, invigorated by an eight-hour sleep. But in no time, I found myself overwhelmed by the task in front of me. I'm going to see apartments that look promising before I leave for New York today. *How am I going to sign a lease in a city I don't know? What if we don't like the neighborhood?*

Now, as I head out the door, I remind myself to stay focused and in the present. I remember myself as a sixteen-year-old, hiking in the Catskills with my best friend's parents, afraid to go one more step up the mountain. Quaking, I said, "I'm scared, I'm scared." The mother bent down close and whispered, "Dorit, don't look too far ahead. Just go up one step at a time." I feel fortified by this idea today and try to hold on to it. Each time I get too carried away by worry, I tap into these words of wisdom.

I arrive at my appointment on the corner of Hobart and Wightman Street at nine o'clock. The property manager, a tanned-looking girl named Tenisha who looks like she's in her early twenties, arrives ten minutes late, sending me into a tailspin of anxiety. She apologizes, and I remind myself to stay calm and will myself to be gracious.

She stretches a hand toward me. "You're Dorit, right?"

"Yes, that's me." I watch her fish into her purse for the keys to the main entrance.

"So this is a two-bedroom apartment, right?" I ask her as we enter the three-story brick apartment. I rummage through my bag, looking for my pad of notes. Tick-tock, tick-tock. Time's running out.

She gingerly leads the way, step by step, up the well-worn, stained lavender carpet covering the stairs, up to the second and third floors. I trail behind her like a timid child. One step at a time, Dorit.

From the second-floor hallway window, I see black-hatted young Yeshiva students scurrying like mice across the street. In Israel, I never paid much attention to them, but here they are a welcome sight against the buzz-hum of the hallway lights, another unfamiliar thing. *Take the next step. One foot in front of the other.*

Number eight is in the far corner. A barely visible mezuzah seems to have been painted over many times. At the door, Tenisha continues fumbling with the keys. Fumbling and apologizing.

Finally, she pushes open the door and we walk in. A police siren wails in the distance.

I walk around quickly, taking it all in, trying to imagine if this place could be home—and as luck would have it, the apartment has the elements I'm looking for. It's a second-floor walk-up in a central location in a small residential neighborhood, above an art supply store, and next to a dry cleaner and nursing home. Living in this area, we won't need to buy a car for a while—a welcome savings. I take in the details: carpet, windows, pre–World War II fixtures, walk-in closets, ceiling fans, two bedrooms, both the same size. But it has the closed, boxed-in feel of apartment living, so different from the open airiness of our kibbutz home on the banks of the friendly Jordan River. Can I even get used to these confining spaces? What am I thinking, comparing this apartment to our kibbutz?

"So this is the only one left?"

"Yes, ma'am."

The sense of urgency I've been feeling all weekend surges to new levels. Is this the one?

The hot pink and black tiles in the windowless bathroom remind me of my grandmother's Far Rockaway apartment. They now seem tacky compared to our cream-colored tiles back at the kibbutz. I could get by with the fixtures, the concrete, the carpet—all but the bathroom tile in this windowless bathroom with a bathtub that can fit only half my body.

I tell myself not to be too picky. I try to see the positives. The walk-in closets are particularly delightful—something I never had growing up in a loft in New York City. I eye the proximity of the garage parking lot from the living room window, and immediately notice a bit of moss growing there. A tenant from the floor below is currently climbing out of his window to access the roof below, and as I watch him, a memory surfaces of my father at his studio on one of the rooftops of our childhood home. His studio contained commissioned works of stained glass, and the neighbors who shared access to the same roof created a "garden" from flower boxes and grass. I wonder about the possibility of closing the real spaces of time between childhood and adulthood. I see that this "roof" above the garage has potential. It's immense, and I feel a flicker of hope. I wonder if we might turn it into a garden someday, like the luscious green of our kibbutz garden. It occurs to me that doing this would be the equivalent of creating something from nothing, an apt metaphor for our lives right now.

That I might walk down one flight of stairs and immerse myself in a kibbutz "garden" that others in the apartment might participate in caring for brings me some semblance of calm. This could be the home away from home I've been looking for.

I circled back to the property manager at the entranceway, who is by now eager for an answer.

"Okay," I say. "We'll take it."

"Wonderful. I'll let the office know," she says, handing me her card.

We say our good-byes outside the main entrance and she marches off, keys in one hand, purse in the other, a startling case in the study of human effervescence. Only when she has jumped in her car and sped off do I glance at the card. *Tenisha Williams, Myers Management.* My first professional interaction as an adult living in the States.

I'm really back.

5

COMING AND GOING

Already in the early morning hours, Squirrel Hill roars, screams, clangs. Police and ambulance sirens; the garbage truck backing into the driveway, upending the dumpsters across from our building, shaking them a few times, and finally dropping them again onto the asphalt.

Our building funnels noise oddly: muffled footsteps in the apartment upstairs, loud shouts from the adjoining apartment building, a chorus of front and back doors slamming, voices trailing up and down the back entrance stairs. I'm amazed each time my son sleeps soundly through all the commotion. For the last few weeks, ever since we moved here, the humidity has been sticking to the sheets. The air conditioner only manages to cool anything within a few feet of it.

I throw open the window, stick out my head, and shout in Hebrew to Haim—directly but as quietly as possible (I don't want to wake up our son, who's asleep in the adjoining bedroom)—"Your clothes!"

A dark-faced stranger immediately turns around, and suddenly I feel self-conscious.

Still, I persist. "How can you go to a job appointment with a career counselor looking like that?"

"Nu, what's the problem?" he shouts back.

Haim's career counselor, herself an immigrant, told us when we'd first met with her that his buying and procurement experience in the food industry on the kibbutz would be an asset in the US. And there it was—the validation I'd been waiting for. He's employable in the US! Now all we have to do is sit back and wait for doors to start opening. But how will anyone hire him if he dresses like this? Doesn't he realize that first impressions count, especially in a country like the United States?

I look at those old black pants with the knee hole and his flip-flops, worn down from walking through airports and over hot sidewalks, and I start getting jittery. "You're not going like that . . . Come on up and change!"

He shouts back, "It's okay. Don't worry!"

To say I'm frustrated is an understatement. Haim just doesn't understand how things work here in the States. Never mind that most Americans don't understand him. Never mind that he dresses like a camp counselor. Part of why I felt we could leave the safety and security of our kibbutz had to do with the professional opportunities I thought we'd find for him here. Is his nonchalance going to jeopardize our success?

A slight breeze tousles the John Lennon T-shirt he's worn nearly every day since we arrived. Unkempt salt-and-pepper hair flies every which way. He's in desperate need of a haircut.

Haim's style has always been to let things roll off his back, and I embrace that aspect of him; in part, that's what first attracted me to him. Back at the kibbutz, he was well-versed in the system and knew who to approach about various problems and issues. But in Pittsburgh, he has become dependent on me when it comes to figuring out bureaucracy and other cultural nuances. In Israel, when I aired my concerns to him, I appreciated how he would reassure me that the worries and concerns I'd concocted in my head weren't worth getting upset over. But here it is different. Here, I know how things work, and all I want is to start fresh.

⁓

I've decided to document our transatlantic move by blogging about it, so I open a library account that gives me internet access our first week here. I've called the blog *Pieces of Me*, and I write in it about the emotional process of settling into our Pittsburgh home. I write about how I hoped we'd feel more connected to this strange place called Squirrel Hill. I'm surprised when a blogger I've just befriended remarks on my posts, "Be gentle on yourself. Give yourself time to readjust to life back in the States."

Time.

Time we don't have. We're living off funds from the sale of our car, and my modest sabbatical stipend won't be enough to make ends meet, even here in Pittsburgh.

For years, I have been an American minority immigrant teaching in rural areas of Israel. Before that, I was a lone American-born IDF soldier adjusting to the Israeli mentality. My success depended on learning to stretch myself emotionally. Because I wasn't born into the Israeli culture, it was a challenge to assert myself aggressively in Hebrew, Israeli-style, complete with hand gestures, body language, and, of course, rising intonation. Compared to most Israelis, I was an introvert, forever lost in my head and in the moment, always questioning and reevaluating my own intentions and actions, and, generally, trying to figure out how much I was willing to sacrifice my inner voice for an outer, unfamiliar one.

Staying amenable enough to adjust to another culture is necessary if you expect to live as an expat, but it's also pertinent to returning to your birthplace after a long absence. Right now, I'm stuck in an in-between place, between Israel and America, between what I love about Haim and what I need him to be now that we're here, in my homeland.

I've been straining to stay adaptable, but I'm wearing thin. This in-between space has become jarring in so many ways. I worry constantly: Will we have enough to make ends meet here? Will Haim find his dream job? Will we get incredibly homesick for Israel and end up going back? Is my determination enough to see us through to the finish line?

⁂

I watch Haim from the window for a moment longer before going to check on my son, with his flushed pink cheeks and huge red ringlets plastered to his face. He's awoken from his nap, and I am thrown back into the here and now.

The heat has been unbearable and has caused Ivry to have sporadic attacks of inexplicable terror. In these moments, I long to wheel him onto the shaded roads of our kibbutz. Our walks to the park down the street offer little relief from the heat of our boxed-in apartment, and retreating to an air-conditioned mall isn't an option—the nearest one is too far away.

I try to console him first with a toy, then with singing.

I figure Haim has gone, despite my insistence that he change, but when I return to the window, I'm surprised to see him chatting in Hebrew with a black-hatted yeshiva *bochur* with a milky-brown complexion.

Their chatter rises like bubbles. Ivry points his stubby finger at the window and yells out, "*Abba*, Daddy!" arms flailing forward.

I'm bowled over. It's the first time he's said something recognizable as a Hebrew word. I didn't plan on prioritizing passing on Hebrew to our son when we arrived. I only want him to fit in.

But now I am reminded that the only way he'll acquire listening Hebrew vocabulary is if we intentionally speak Hebrew to him. Language encompasses culture and identity.

As he rap-tap-taps on the window, I make a mental note: speak more Hebrew with Ivry.

I listen in on the conversation below from my perch at the window. The men are talking about children—a favorite topic among Israelis, even in the Diaspora.

In a few months, when we're invited to our first Shabbat meal, Haim and I will push Ivry's stroller a few streets down to a three-story red brick home framed by topiaries. This *bochur* Haim is currently speaking to, who is some years older than my husband, will emerge from his front door hand-in-hand with a blond-haired child and say in Hebrew, "*Ahalan, begatem!*"—Hey, you made it!

But for now, that *bochur* is still a stranger. As Haim parts from him, he gives his new friend a *chapcha* on his back and they shake hands heartily, and then he strides away. Ivry and I watch together until he's out of sight. I consider the man with whom he's been talking—someone I would refer to in Israel as a *Shasnick*, a religious Israeli, by virtue of the affiliation to the religious party *Shas*, which dominates mainstream Israel politics to this day. We'd see *Shasnicks* in outdoor markets or pass them on the streets. They were always in the backdrop, forever the subject of the media, though mainly in terms of social divides, contentions, and rifts. Because they held so much political power, they were often scrutinized, especially since the rabbinical hierarchy in Israel is fraught with controversy.

As affable as he is, Haim has never been one to cozy up with the religiously observant, but maybe everything is different here. What is he doing talking to a *Shasnick*? Doesn't he know better?

Members of our kibbutz had no interest in embracing Jewish spiritual practices. Like many secular Israelis, in Israel we were "cultural Jews," attending ceremonies for Holocaust Remembrance Day and participating in Chanukah festivities in the dining hall. We were Israelis first, Jews second, which is the case for many Israelis under the Law of Return. In the nearly twenty years I lived in Israel, I entered a synagogue just a handful of times. My already loose sense of spirituality fell apart like an old house in need of repair, though it was never fully intact to begin with.

Now, as I watch this *Shasnick* lingering in the sunlight, checking his phone quietly, I wonder if maybe the lesson to be learned from being in the Diaspora is the courage to be Jews again. To learn how get in touch with my spirituality and attempt to give new meaning to those impressions I had when I first arrived in Israel of what it means to be a Jew in Israel, which ultimately left such a profoundly bitter taste in my mouth. Perhaps our move to the United States will give us a more tolerant and pluralistic way of viewing spirituality—one that was inaccessible in Israel.

Today we get notice that our shipment of things from Israel is finally due to arrive at 3:00 p.m. Eastern Standard. I am so relieved, especially because it means we'll all have better wardrobes and I'll be able to stop bearing down on Haim about his worn pants and shirts.

For most of the morning, Haim and Ivry play with a bunch of empty boxes and suitcases in the apartment. We currently have a mattress, a few cooking utensils, a bookshelf, and a few chairs, but the apartment still feels bare. I stare at my shipping papers—detailing the terms of the shipment in both Hebrew and English—and worry. Will our things arrive intact? Will the driver get accurate instructions about rerouting our shipment from New York City to Pittsburgh, a change I requested a few weeks ago?

I pretend to be calm. I go to the library and work on my blog to kill time.

We've been here twenty-one days and still I feel lost in a daze.

For twenty-one days, I've looked longingly at the photos of our kibbutz I taped to a piece of poster board covered with saran wrap and hung on our bedroom wall. We have one yellow potted plant from a new Israeli friend that resembles an impressionist painting. I like the yellow of it. It helps me to stay hopeful. It helps me to stay grounded and to move past the various frantic moments I encounter each day, as I try to find words to replace the longing that's consumed me for our home back in Israel.

I'm at home again, watching the clock, waiting for 3:00 p.m., when a Canadian neighbor, an immigrant himself, tells me to mark the street off with chairs and a sign.

"You'll need space for the semi-trailer," he tells me. "Pittsburgh streets are narrow."

One hour later, chairs appear in front of our building. As a kind gesture, he'd done this task for me. I'm not alone.

Thirty minutes before the truck's anticipated arrival, I am greeted with yet another waft of heat, this time accompanied by humidity so extreme and oppressive I feel like I'm stuck in a sauna. Coming from the dryness of our area in Israel, I'm not used to this.

It's almost three. I make my way down the steps to direct the movers. The back door to the building leads to a driveway lined with four garbage bins strewn with litter and peppered with bursts of hot air from the dry cleaners next door. All I can think about are our olive and pomegranate trees; I keep hoping they'll magically appear here.

Here, our windows have no screens. There is no patio. You flush the toilet with a metal lever. Laughter from the nursing home workers on a smoking break from the adjoining parking lot often catches me off guard. Shouts seem an octave higher. Conversational English fades in and out. Even the lemons we buy at the local supermarket for our hummus smell different, having lost some of their essence from long days of travel.

"The ache for home," writes Maya Angelou, "lives in all of us, the safe space where we can go as we are and not be questioned." Our Pittsburgh flat is no substitute for the kibbutz home I grew to love. It feels as if the body of ocean I just crossed has swallowed me whole and spat me back out. I wake up each morning a stranger in my own land on a borrowed mattress, with only my memories to convince myself and others of my deep connection to Israel—the connection I worked so hard to earn and cultivate.

I remember the semi-trailer that arrived outside our kibbutz to pack our things. It made an obtrusively loud engine sound—*vroom-vroom-vroom*—followed by a high-pitched screech, a loud moan, and, finally, a hiss. Then, silence.

By the time the movers entered our living room, I was so shaken up I couldn't think straight. Within an hour, in soldier-like fashion, slowly and silently, they had emptied the house of all its contents. I almost sensed they were happy to rid my place of its things, to remind me of my outsider status in their actions. I wasn't one of them, and I was going home. Neighbors gathered, and I mustered my inner strength. It took everything I had to hold onto that steely part of me that had the resolve to leave with my head held high, to believe in the possibilities those boxes held for us. I grasped on to the hope they symbolized for myself and my family to start anew, away from this group of onlookers.

I learned that day that the journey of an immigrant doesn't start on the plane, but at home, in front of a bunch of movers who are staring and waiting for your next set of instructions.

Now, in Pittsburgh, I wait. I wonder how a semi-trailer one-third the size of a football field will manage with such a narrow entranceway. The idea of unloading our precious cargo into this boxed-in space threatens to upend any sense of calm I've managed throughout the day. It's a twisted logistical nightmare, but perhaps not mine to worry about.

For the next thirty minutes, I stay perched on the sidewalk alongside the two chairs my neighbor spaced about ten feet apart, joined with a rope, and adorned with a sign saying, "Do Not Park, September 15, 2007." The sign flutters in a hot breeze. Seven or so cars are parked at and around the dry cleaners. Mechanical hissing follows us to the sidewalk.

I wait outside for thirty minutes. Just when I've started contemplating calling the moving company, my cell phone rings.

"Is this Dorit Sasson?"

He's got a New York City accent.

"Yes, who's this?"

"I'm the driver with your shipment. I just checked the GPS and the street where I'm supposed to pull in is really narrow. I've been driving in circles for the past thirty minutes. It doesn't look like I'm going to make it through with this semi-trailer. So I'm heading back to New York City. You'll have to . . ."

Anger and fear threaten to overwhelm me. I walk away from the curb and shout into the phone, "You can't do that! I rerouted that shipment from New York City to Pittsburgh. We *need* that shipment! That's our stuff from Israel! And we need it *now*."

After back-and-forth shouts for nearly twenty minutes, I finally convince the driver to turn into the narrow driveway. Not a small feat.

Back at the curb, I try to calm down. I am surprised by my sudden ability to be assertive here in the States, a trait I associate with the Israeli me. As a teenager, I was introverted and intimidated by my talented peers, all of whom seemed, to me, to speak boldly and with confidence. Perhaps Israel has changed me. Perhaps my strength is being tested. Perhaps I *can* show my firm resolve. Could it be that the very characteristics I associate with the States were cultivated and nurtured all those years I lived abroad?

∽⊱⊱

Rosh Hashana eve, our first Jewish New Year in Pittsburgh, looms, and cool rain pounds on the dumpsters. I hobble from one room to the next, poring over checklists for my first shopping trip to Target—baby wipes, cleaning supplies, a stroller rain cover. Because it hardly rains in Israel, I never bought a stroller rain cover there, but now, suddenly, it's necessary that I have one.

I again pretend to be calm. Two days after our shipment arrived, we attended a Shabbat dinner at an Israeli rabbi's home, and while we were there, I twisted my ankle. We don't have health insurance, and the bill came out to nearly $1,800—twice as much as we have on hand from selling our car.

On crutches, and in excruciating pain, I've only been able to unpack an average of two boxes a day since I hurt my ankle. Between that and changing Ivry's diapers, I'm exhausted. I frequently check responses to my daily blog posts in hopes of feeling a connection with the outside world.

The sun slowly descends, and masses of people come from various directions, dressed in their finest, to enter the Yeshiva for Rosh Hashana evening services. People greet each other, voices rise, cars wait deferentially. I hobble to the window to watch my husband and son enter the building. Our first Rosh Hashana in the Diaspora; I opted to stay home. The pain in my ankle is unbearable, even with the painkillers I'm taking.

When I think of Rosh Hashana, I remember new beginnings— our pomegranate tree, the challah bread made at my son's daycare. I see kibbutz members gathering at a special service to ring in the New Year, and fondly remember the Rosh Hashana song I taught in English to young Israeli schoolchildren to the melody of Michael

Jackson's "Heal the World" during my first year of teaching.

Today is Thursday, tomorrow is Friday.
Friday is the New Year.
It is Rosh Hashana. We eat apples and honey.
It's a special time for you and for me.

More clearly than anything else, I see a family gathering with my in-laws at their home in Haifa after a long day at the beach. My son, just barely nine months old, slurped milk from a cup for the first time. Sun-tanned and happy, he grinned at the camera in our first family shot of the New Year.

Whatever Rosh Hashana meant to me then, it's hardly clearer now. Here in the Diaspora, stuck between concrete buildings, I feel terribly alone. Spaces and distances upend me. As a Jew in Israel, I was familiar with the sights, tastes, and sounds of Rosh Hashana—the cry of the shofar piercing the air, the sweet sensation of honey on my tongue, the rhythmic swaying of the congregation in prayer. But as an American Jew in the Diaspora, I am a castaway at sea. All I feel is loss, and a longing for Israel. I write about all of this on my blog.

I know I'm complaining when an American-Jewish blogging acquaintance who lives in Israel comments, "We're celebrating the same holiday and looking up at the same sky." For a moment, at least, those words are of some comfort and consolation.

An hour after Haim leaves with Ivry, there's a loud rat-a-tat-tat on the front door. Thinking it must be Haim, I shout to him from the bed that my foot hurts.

"Did you forget your keys? Could you please open the door?" I struggle to move. My foot throbs.

No one responds.

Again, a knock, this time stronger than before.

"Who is it?" I call out.

"*Shana Tova* and *Chag Sameach*. Happy New Year. Your husband said you had sprained your ankle and you wanted to hear the shofar," a male voice pipes up.

I am touched by this act of generosity, but at the same time I question this man's motives. Why would anyone want to go to a stranger's home to blow the shofar—the ram's horn—on Rosh Hashana? It doesn't make sense, especially since we've only been in Pittsburgh for three weeks. We aren't members of any synagogue. We hardly know anyone. I conclude that there must be some kind of ulterior motive. "Do you want to hear the shofar?" he asks, politely but loudly.

"Yes, but I can't move from the bed." In actuality, I am too embarrassed to hobble to the door and show my face.

And so, from behind a locked door, this male stranger unexpectedly fills our second-floor hallway with a magnificent sound that reverberates with its *tekia* and *terua*, as if he's unleashing herds of wild animals.

"Have a very sweet New Year, and feel better," the *bochur* says kindly from behind the door when he's done playing.

"Thank you so much!" I shout. Sunlight streaks from the living room and gradually makes its way to the foot of the mattress.

The floor creaks with his lingering steps as I listen to him retreat. I am touched and curious: Who is this person I can't see? And why did he feel called to blow the shofar for a stranger?

Years from now, I will come to understand that these Chabad *bachurim* carry out a strong religious mission based on personal outreach and love for fellow Jews. But for now, I'm just conflicted. I've been longing for nothing but connection, so while this encounter should fuel me, it does not. I'm too full of distrust based on my previous experiences to be able to accept this act of kindness.

Each time I enter a conversation with myself about the chances for our success here, I sense a need to put my faith into action or into the doctrine of *bitachon*, trust in God, which the Chassidic master Rabbi Menachem Mendel of Lubavitch distilled into the

Yiddish adage *Tracht gut, vet zein gut*—"Think good, and it will be good." This positivity would be reassuring, but it would not sustain me for the long term in this country where I still feel like a foreigner. For now, the gap between being a cultural Jew and a spiritual one is too great.

Months from now, I will come to understand that what this *bochur* gave me tonight was a first taste of what it means to be Jewish in the Diaspora. It will take a while, however, before I'll muster up the courage to get past my own prejudices and sail into a place where I can leave the distrust behind and put faith into action.

6

FINDING A JOB

The date for Haim's interview—his only interview so far—looms.
I make a last prep call to Rachel, Haim's career counselor, buy him
a prepaid cell phone for ten dollars, and get him his first haircut.
Rachel is used to spouses calling, and I take advantage of her being
"unemployment central"—a person with whom we can actually
interact, a person who humanizes the job-seeking process for for-
eigners like us.

At our last meeting with Rachel, I asked for recommendations for
where to buy nice clothes and she quickly waved her hand and gave us
a black garbage bag full of new men's attire, dressy and classy clothes.
At home, Haim rummaged through. For the interview, he will don a
classic white Ralph Lauren button-down with faux pearl buttons and
pleated black trousers. Tonight, he lets me cut his outgrown toenails
and give him a pedicure. I trim his bushy salt-and-pepper eyebrows
and toss aside his worn-down flip-flops. His groomed appearance fills
me with hope. *Trust him to communicate well in English during the
interview. Trust that he will pull through for us.*

Later, when both Ivry and Haim are in bed, I look at my to-do list and fret. *What if he doesn't get this position? Then what? Do we go back to Israel?* Everything is riding on this one position.

Known for its astronomical prices and wide array of gourmet items, the supermarket caters to an upscale clientele. I can imagine Haim in a job like this, and I'm happy that Rachel has this place on her radar for him too. *Finally, someone who believes in him. Finally.*

Haim told me about his last visit with Rachel, where she engaged him in a brief mock interview. She was impressed by his knowledge of the food industry and instructed him about cultural expectations in the workplace. I feel that she's all in, that she's on the journey with us. Having her in our corner in this way makes me feel less alone in this endeavor. I allow myself to believe that Haim will succeed. I breathe and try to remind myself to take things one day at a time.

The night before the interview, we don't talk about it. Instead, we walk hand-in-hand to a nearby park and enjoy the way Ivry squeals with delight as we push him higher on the swing. An Israeli couple arrives with their toddler son, and both of our redheads chase each other until we are worn out. We coax Ivry home for dinner, but he collapses on the couch before we even get a chance to enter the kitchen.

We relax to the sound of Alex Trebek bellowing on the black-and-white television we picked up from the dumpster. Ivry's toys are strewn every which way. As we sit there, a bowl of uneaten cereal tips over my knee soaks through the fabric of my pants and drips onto my legs, but I don't reach down to straighten it for fear I will wake Ivry, who has just fallen asleep.

We have managed to secure an interview for Haim in less than a week. During that time in Israel, we couldn't have even applied for a job. Everything works so much slower there—mainly due to the fact there are fewer jobs for limited niches and industries. It's far easier to get a job here in the States. America, the land of opportunity. It's certainly earned its reputation. In Israel, Haim faxed two hundred resumes out over the course of two years and didn't receive a single response. Here in America, it seems, companies value a person's years of work experience more than his age, while in Israel someone with more work experience is valued less than a younger person just starting out. Perhaps it's because Israel is a young country and thrives on young blood; what's more likely, though, is that they do not want to pay more for someone with more experience.

Although I've had my doubts about our move, tonight I allow myself to hope against hope. We don't know what will come of Haim's interview, but I feel an expansive sense of freedom and hope. As Socrates wisely said, "The secret to change is to focus all of your energy not on fighting the old, but on building the new." Fighting the old. How long did I wait for the kibbutz to change its attitude toward members like Haim? To treat him with the respect I felt he was due? But it was all for nothing. Our own home let us down.

Here, though, we have the power to change our karmic patterns by changing the way we make our choices. After all, fighting the old can only take you so far—and lamenting over what you can't change only leads to bitterness and resentment. Ultimately, I'll find my way around this—by having the courage to surrender.

⁂

Thirty minutes after Haim's interview ends, I call him on his cell phone from the library, but he doesn't pick up. Heaviness weighs on my heart. It's my default mode to expect the worst. Why wouldn't he answer, unless he believes he flubbed the interview? I consider how back on the kibbutz, there was no such thing as not being able to connect with my husband. In that way, the self-contained unit always had my back. People knew the whereabouts of their neighbors, which instilled a sense of emotional security. Plus, I could almost always reach Haim at the guard's *butkeh*; he was stationed there five to six days a week for eight- to ten-hour shifts, after all. Here, though, we are strangers, still unsure of our place, and not being able to reach him only reinforces that for me.

My ego has always wanted to know all the details ahead of time: *Where, exactly, are we going? How long will it take? Will we be safe and comfortable and enjoy ourselves?* And, of course, the big question: *Will we succeed in creating our desired outcomes?* I want certainty, though of course, this isn't possible. I try to keep focused on the big picture, the real reason why we decided to move to the States in the first place—but the truth is, I wasn't mentally prepared for the extent of the changes we were about to subject ourselves to when we left Israel. The reality is, there is no cure for reverse culture shock. You just have to wait it out.

What I want to do is curl myself into a ball. Everything here is too big. Even here at the Carnegie Public Library, where every book is in English and where one might expect me to feel safe and secure, I feel out of place. Hebrew is nowhere to be heard, and I feel adrift. English is my mother tongue, but Hebrew is my language of preference in so many ways. I'm stuck between cultures, having spent nearly two decades of my life trying to be an Israeli, trying to make my way and be accepted, and now suddenly finding myself part of the majority.

From time to time, a grey-haired security guard passes by. Each time, I glance his way. Occasionally, he looks at the makeshift office space I've set up: books for my research on how to support EFL learners in a heterogenous classroom in one pile, notes in another, and my cell phone set to vibrate. On either end, surrounding me, are endless rows of library books on topics ranging from World Wars I and II to the Bible, none of which are relevant to my research.

After two hours of scribbling, I get no writing done and feel useless.

Finally, just when I'm feeling like I've been stalking him all day, Haim appears.

"Why haven't you been answering your phone?" I whisper when he approaches my table. I can't hide the irritation in my voice.

He pulls out his phone. We finally discern that his ringer was inadvertently set to silent, but that doesn't excuse him in my eyes. He's late, and he's being his usual, nonchalant self. It's clear to me right now, as it so often is, that we have very different expectations of one another.

"Nu? So, how did it go?" I ask, trying to discard my irritation.

He leans toward me. "I got the job, Dorit. Peggy hired me on the spot. Rachel said she had never seen anything like that."

I want to run to the bathroom and cry, but instead, I cup my hands in his as he looks at his brightly polished black shoes. Could it be that we're on our way to the American dream?

"Wow," I exclaim. "Oh my goodness. I can't believe it. This is so amazing." This feels both too easy and like vindication. I allow myself to trust again. We've made the right decision. We're going to be okay. We're on our way.

True to his character, Haim remains calm, unruffled.

"So when do you start?"

He smiles. "Tomorrow."

It's September 2007, just one week into Haim's new position, and I'm sitting on a barrel of hay on a tractor at a local farm festival, where we're having some much-needed family time. Ivry, clad in a warm crimson shirt, steadfastly holds on to the metal bars of the wagon and looks ahead with fascination at the tractor pulling us, his red curls bobbing up and down.

I see apple trees in the distance. Cranberry, amber, magenta, and ruby leaves gently rustle under a cobalt blue sky. Golden light glows on the leaves, illuminating their veins. The air is unusually moist and warm. It smells vaguely of cabbage. For the time being, I'm letting go of the "to-do" lists centered on Haim's job hunting process. Now is the time for the three of us to bond.

Haim's thoughts, however, seem to be elsewhere as he looks into the distance. I clasp his muscular hand in mine and recall a fall from my own upbringing. I go far back, to crisp apples and the butternut squash–colored leaves I gushed over as a freshman at the State University of New York at Albany. In one memory, the camera lens zooms in to catch fading tints of ruby and pumpkin. The images are vivid, but the memories themselves are lifeless, lonely, transient. What good are beautiful images without an emotional context? It gets lonely sometimes, living my life hearing two different voices from two different linguistic settings, always trying to remember where I come from.

In Israel, you never have to work hard to feel connected, for the country won't let you be disconnected. That energy is missing from this remote American landscape. Nothing in this picturesque scenery can make up for my nostalgia and displacement.

Haim and I are on this lonely ship together, traveling in and out of the darkness and fog of words, culture, and time zones. Each day feels like a brain exercise. *Are you okay? Yes. Do you need anything? No. Do you miss your family in Israel? Of course, I do, but not the kib-butz. I miss the kibbutz that used to be.*

What drives one to remember?

And what comes first—the willingness to forget or the willing-ness to remember?

The tractor brings us to the top of a hill. I am still in the habit of looking for signs in Hebrew indicating the direction the Jordan River lies in. I remind myself where I am.

We pull Ivry down the rows filled with enormous pumpkins—

some twice as big as my head. He tries to climb over one while I walk along, taking everything in like a child: the smooth yet rough exterior of the pumpkins, the nearby apple orchards, the wide expanse of the farm below.

Strangely enough, I start saying things like *dla'at*—pumpkin— and *bo lishkol*—let's weigh it. I notice how I switch back to Hebrew to express things that are important to me. Speaking Hebrew feels like home and family. I realize that my language ties me to something I've struggled for—my hard-won fight to be an Israeli, to the extent that they'd let me. And as one who is raising a child in America, I can't shake the idea that without Hebrew, my Israeli identity will be lost. Language is inextricably connected with identity. Not only am I a Diaspora Jew, I am also an Israeli-American. Until this moment, I've never owned that part of my identity in quite this way.

For many of us, finding a sense of belonging has not just to do with the realm of memory, but also with the moment. Here in the pumpkin patch, I'm connecting with a childhood moment, reliving it through Ivry's eyes. He's going to grow up here. He's going to have a life much different from his father's.

We carry our bulky pumpkins back to the tractor and I'm flooded immediately with memories of carving jack-o'-lantern and participating in the famous Ralph Lee's West Village Halloween parade in New York City. Ivry looks at me in delight, and I say, "Ivry, it's your first hayride!"

Soon other parents catch on and shout out to their kids, "First hayride, buddy!"

"And after this, I'm going to go on another hayride!" Ivry grins with pride.

As parents chatter back and forth about topics like insurance and liability against the screeching and clanging of the tractor, I am stuck figuring out which memories we're making right now will be long-lasting, and despite my efforts to stay in the here and now, what I long for most right now is Israel. This "farm" I'm visiting sends me back to our kibbutz, quietly nestled in the Hula Valley region of the Upper Galilee in Israel, some thousands of miles across the Atlantic Ocean, where my heart still lies.

7

WOMAN WARRIOR

I'm standing at a busy intersection in Squirrel Hill, just a few streets away from our home. Within five minutes, ten students, each one absorbed in a cell phone, gather along a stone wall perpendicular to the adjacent houses elevated on tall pillars of earth. Joggers, dog walkers, and mothers with strollers become silhouettes in the early -morning light, elevating them to the point of holiness. Dozens of trees soar like crowns. I'm in awe of the sequoias' stately appearance. I never expected Pittsburgh to be a living garden—moss in the sidewalk cracks, mulberry trees sashaying in front of various homes, turn-of-the-century homes streaked with ivy, wild-flowers sprouting from cracks everywhere. I even see a thatch of mint growing from a crack in a stone wall next to a post-box.

I'm staring at a wild bed of tangled, thorny roses when the bus pulls up. Their beauty amidst all the chaos feels symbolic to me— expressing promise, new beginnings, and hope. A native-born Israeli or *sabra* has an association with another prickly, thorny plant: Israel's national, cactus-like fruit, also known as *sabra*. Though spiky on the outside, the plant has a pulpy and sweet inside. I marvel at how plants, like humans, express this self-protective instinct.

As I contemplate the twisty nature of the thorns before me, I think back to all the years I spent fine-tuning my own understanding of what it means to be a *sabra*, to the point that I started to feel pride in being able to own the identity. I wanted to assimilate and survive as a *sabra* at all costs, no matter how difficult the challenge. But here in the multiethnic community of Squirrel Hill, the life and identity I nurtured in Israel doesn't have an obvious place. I feel vulnerable. There's no need for that kind of assimilation here, where everyone else is absorbed by his own world.

The driver nods when I show my ticket and chirps to the convoy of students behind me, "Morning! All aboard!" He motions for us to move back, but no one already on the bus seems open to the idea of making room.

Starting today, for the next two semesters, Fall 2008 and Spring 2009, I'll be an instructor of adult ESL students, temporary student visa, and green card holders at the Community College of Allegheny County (CCAC). There is no organized ESL department at CCAC, just a random offering of ESL academic classes sprinkled throughout the English curriculum, designed to help the adult ESL student acquire some kind of written and reading proficiency, so they can enter mainstream classes as soon as possible. I'm eager to hear from my fellow instructors about strategies for reaching these ESL students effectively, but so far everyone appears overworked and uninterested. I'm shocked to discover that some of my colleagues are teaching as many as eight classes per semester!

There are eighteen students on my list, none of them Israeli. I share a tiny office consisting of three desks, a bookcase, a corner filing cabinet, and an old push-button beige phone. On one side are narrow, six-foot-tall, tightly locked windows. Across the street is another marvel: a gothic arch to another building on the campus, a tree-lined sidewalk, and a perch with a view over the entire North Side Park.

As the bus passes the Carnegie Public Library and a slew of university buildings, I consider how my much-desired sabbatical has actually created a disconnect for me where teaching is concerned. We are not going back to Israel, especially now that Haim has secured a job. Reinventing myself as an ESL teacher has come as a bit of a surprise, but this is a transferable experience, and I landed a job fairly easily. I consider what I can bring to this experience from my time teaching in Israel, and all that occurs to me is to serve my students above all else.

Are you ready to do this? I ask myself, to which I answer, *I think so.*

To get to campus, I have to take two buses—one downtown and a second to the North Side—followed by a ten-minute walk past the park. The last part is a trek, but it will be a welcome one after this crowded bus ride.

When the driver lets me out at my stop, I look up in the sky and see a chopper. Then there's a series of sirens. I pretend to be calm, but in Israel, these noises would mean some sort of threat, like a terrorist attack.

The chopper is similar to the kind I used to see often from my beach perch in Israel. Nobody seems to even notice its incessant noise. On the street, people are moving about their day, plugged into their cell phones, crossing the street like zombies. The scenery around me is oddly calm. It's like watching a movie where everyone is going about their business while threatening music suggests everything is not okay. But the part that's not okay here is just in my mind, in my associations. To the passersby crossing the street here in Pittsburgh, it's just another grey Monday morning.

I find myself awaiting the four beeps that would typically indicate the hourly news of *Kol Israel*, "The Voice of Israel," announcing a *pigua*—some kind of terrorist attack—but it doesn't come, and I'm forced back to my current reality. I'm back in America. Nothing is wrong. No one here is panicked by the noise of a helicopter overhead.

Just two summers ago, my family and I had to leave our home

to seek refuge from war. In America, war is a spectator sport, something far away that you watch on the news. In Israel, it's a constant reality; the war is never truly over. And I acclimated to that. It strikes me that maybe I don't have what it takes to return to "normalcy." Watching the news cycle obsessively, always being on guard to hear of any casualties or mass destruction on our kibbutz or other settlements in the area, living on pins and needles about the welfare of our friends and our home—all of this was normal in Israel. That taught me to stay flexible. In Israel, too, people go about their lives despite the constant threat. They drink tea with fresh mint and honey, eat vegetables and cheese *bourekas* for breakfast, shop for sixteen-spice *halva* from the Mahane Yehuda *shuk* for Shabbat, jog through pointed arches, float in the Dead Sea, eat olives with beer, wish each other *Shabbat Shalom* beginning from Wednesday night, and sit under olive trees munching on fresh tomatoes and cucumbers. And at the same time, you can hear in people's voices the deep, frantic need to live. To never stop living. This is how you live in such a pressure cooker of a country. You live for the moment, in the moment.

In her book *Legion*, Lori Goodwin notes that "even in times of trauma, we try to maintain a sense of normality until we no longer can. That, my friends, is called surviving. Not healing. We never become whole again . . . we are survivors. If you are here today . . . you are a survivor. But those of us who have made it through hell and are still standing? We bear a different name: warriors."

As the chopper continues to make wavy circles under a grey-blue sky, I consider the appellation of "Warrior."

I say it out loud and decide I like it. It suits me.

Now on the second bus, on the way to CACC, past the feelings of trauma evoked by the helicopter, my heart feels empty, unsure, unclear. I'm following my calling to teach, but I have doubts about what kind of impact I'll make. I think about my students back in Israel, grappling with whether I made a difference in their lives. I'm afraid my anger will get the better of me just as it did with Haran—my former student, now dead—when he challenged all the classroom rules. After all, managing a classroom, no matter what level, is equivalent to Anger Management 101, a class within itself that I've had to learn entirely on my own.

In front of me on the bus, two redheads are texting and snapping their gum. "Whaaaaaat did you say?" one says to the other in a defiant tone.

I remember how, at the sound of the bell, I'd ask Haran to take his seat, and how, instead, he'd float around the room and then, from a faraway corner, turn his hand in an upward sweep Israelis are known for, signaling defiance. There was no question it was a rude gesture. My efforts to teach him felt thwarted, useless, and undervalued. I was so frustrated one day, I let out a scream. Some of the ninth graders stopped what they were doing, but he continued to jeer and talk. "Watch out, Haran," Yakir called out. "Dorit's getting mad."

Clearly, I had lost the battle.

It took ten minutes before Haran finally took his seat, and by then my day was already shot.

Although he was clearly a tough student, I wish I'd used a more personal touch with him, instead of raising my voice each time he challenged me. But I was a young, inexperienced teacher and I wanted to prove my authority. Now I want to tap into that voice of intuition, that kernel of deeper understanding, that will guide me toward deeper clarity and manifestation. That's the "third eye" I'm looking to embrace now.

Learning to trust your intuition is a process—and that process begins when you start paying more attention to your voice of intuition. It takes courage to hit the "reset" button, but I'm ready to try.

I'm moments away from my second stop. I look out the window at a cauliflower-like cloud. A sudden rainstorm bellows in from the east. The last archway of the bridge opens to a street buzzing with cars. As we pass by what I think is the Andy Warhol Museum, the rain starts coming down hard.

In less than an hour, I'll be teaching my first class. I've been told that adult ESL students are motivated to learn English. I've had time to prep and meet some of my colleagues, who've told me that based on the stories I told them about what it's like to teach English in Israel, I will have a much easier time teaching in the States by comparison. Still, I worry about not fitting in. I've been told that my ESL teaching skills are "transferrable" since I've taught extensively abroad, but the doubt still creeps in.

In 2000, I found a letter in Hebrew in my box from the school guidance counselor informing me that Haran had been diagnosed with dyslexia, along with some recommendations. Some days later, during one of the breaks, I found some books about dyslexia so I could brush up.

Despite my curiosity around the subject of dyslexia, I didn't know how to be that "softer," less interrogative, and demanding teacher with Haran. Didn't understand that I needed to be more patient and personal if I wanted to succeed with him. That reading about dyslexia was just half the battle. I had to get out of "student mode" and remember that I was dealing with the real world of teaching. As long as his jeering laugh irritated me, I would only continue to lose the battle. He'd continue closing himself up like a fan.

I sobbed deeply into my pillow some nights, praying for help. I almost gave up.

I discovered that Haran had died six years after I had him as a student. There was his portrait in the newspaper that lay open on the train heading to Tel-Aviv. It was a grainy black-and-white photo, but the image was unmistakably Haran. The Earth kept turning on its huge axis until I got off. I raced across the street, whizzing between buses, and started up the stairs to the Azrieli Center, a complex of skyscrapers in Tel-Aviv, for a career appointment. Soldier after soldier headed down the escalators of the large shopping mall, milling about in open spaces. The cool breeze of the air-conditioning offered relief from the heat outside. On the third floor, I looked out of crystal clear, fifteen-foot-high windows. The horizon of the city basked in the ghostly haze of August heat and yet Tel-Aviv was stark and defined, until it gave way to distant mountain ranges.

Haran, I thought. *Haran Lev. Why? Why you?*

Then everything went dark again—the clouds knitted together, the distant haze sucked back into a silhouette sinking into shadow. He was gone. Forever. And I'd never really connected with him. I hadn't been ready to reach him in a real way when I was his teacher.

Now, as a mother, I understand something I couldn't as an unmarried teacher just fifteen years older than my oldest students: Haran needed someone who could listen to him deeply. Someone who cared enough to see past his shenanigans with compassion and patience.

I wish I'd been that person.

I walk the ten minutes to the campus in the rain. I have an umbrella, and I hear the tap-tap-tap of rain coming down as I walk briskly.

Haran, Haran. His name echoes in my mind.

"Let's have a seat," I imagine saying. "How's it going? Come . . . I want to talk with you."

In my mind, he sits with me, and instead of arguing, we engage in conversation. He tells me about his life. It's one of many fresh starts.

I cross the street to campus, wiping my eyes with the back of my sleeve. My heart knows better now. It knows what to do.

‑‑‑

I take the escalator up the two flights of stairs to my office, hurrying down the long, black-carpeted hallway on the second floor, past dozens of closed doors. Behind them are tenured faculty of various departments. Already the office is brimming with instructors preparing for their first day. I'm hoping for some quiet to finalize my own preparations for my class. I plop my books on a corner table and strike up a conversation with a fellow instructor. *Fresh start*, I remind myself.

I ask him about his first day.

"I haven't started yet," he says, chuckling. "But I'll let you know how it went."

A half an hour later, I'm in class. As an ice-breaker, I give all eighteen students ten true and false questions about myself. I share my own history of having lived in Israel on a kibbutz. I hope sharing openly about my background will allow for building trust and community in this foreign cultural classroom.

The front of my desk does not scrape against other desks like it did in Israel. No need to battle for territory with hips and elbows, wedging my wheeled carry-on through tight spaces.

"I come from a family of ten," I say, reading from one of my true-or-false statements. An Asian student wearing a Steelers sweatshirt smiles in the seat directly across from me. "That's not true!" he calls out, and I laugh.

Another student whispers, "That's me!"

I deeply appreciate how easy it is to connect when we consider our similarities rather than our differences.

When I first told the principal at our kibbutz school that I wanted to go to the States to write a book, I told her the truth—that my mother's health was declining due to Alzheimer's. That I wanted nothing more than to be closer to her. That admission shifted the principal's energy from suspicion to empathy. In Israel, the word "family" is holy.

Now I ask my new students to share true and false sentences about themselves with a partner, using the categories of work and family as a model. They chuckle and get to work. I can tell they are tickled by all the possibilities of what they might write.

A *fresh start*. I'm on my way.

Eyes are fixed on me when bits and pieces of my truth come out— that I'm a former New Yorker, that I served in the Israel Defense Forces and actually shot guns during that time. That I've taught Israeli learners struggling to learn English. This exercise is pushing me out of my comfort zone, and yet I can feel how engaged the students are. Learning about me prompts them to share even more about themselves.

We get to talking about their writing experiences and their academic goals for the semester. Some have never attended an American college class, let alone a writing class; some have just a rudimentary understanding of academic writing and reading. But clearly, they all want to be here. There is no reason to return to their home country. We are all here for the same reason: to get a fresh start in a new country that we've all claimed, for now, as our home.

Bearing the new "me" in mind, I attempt to stay in the present. As Rabbi Hillel writes in the ancient Jewish text *Ethics of the Fathers*, "If I am not for me, who is for me; and if I am (only) for myself, what am I. And if not now, when?" This passage has always spoken to me, but never more so than now, as I'm attempting to find a sense of belonging as an American Israeli, dealing with reentering her native country after nearly two decades.

As I wait for my bus this afternoon, I run into the Asian student in the Steelers sweatshirt. She waves to me as she opens her car door—and then, before taking off, takes a few steps toward me and says, "Thank you for today's lesson. I learned a lot today about you." She is dark-eyed and curly-haired, beautiful.

"Let me know if you need anything," I say. I'm conscious of the way Hebrew seems to linger in my mouth.

"Oh, I am doing okay," she says. "But thank you." She pats her pocketbook shut. Her eyes are far away.

I consider what my role is with these students. I am a teacher, not a friend. I want to connect with them, but the ease I felt in the classroom vanishes here on the street.

8

THE LANGUAGE OF HOME

It's the summer of 2011, our first family trip to Israel since arriving in Pittsburgh four years ago. I finger my Israeli passport in my pouch. Ten hours ago, I boarded an EL AL plane with Haim and Ivry at JFK airport in New York City. We're all anticipating a sweet homecoming with family and friends. Between Haim and me, I'm the only one missing the kibbutz. Still, I don't want to deal with any confrontations there that might remind me of the days I was called out as a traitor.

I also know Haim is not crazy about visiting the kibbutz because when I asked him a week ago how he felt about it, he was clear: "Dorit," he said in a serious tone, "I miss the kibbutz that used to be."

Still. I managed to convince Haim to go—even to spend a few days there.

The pilot announces that in an hour's time we'll be descending into Israeli airspace. My heart pounds. The airplane hurtles through the troposphere at six hundred miles per hour. Ivry sleeps in a mound of blankets between us.

Over the past four years, I've time-traveled in and out of familiar images and words in an attempt to consummate my longing for Israel. When you leave a country or familiar place, all you have to anchor you is your memory. The depository of sights, sounds, and words in your brain is accessible at any given moment in time, bridging past and present. But then there comes a time when memory pulls you in the other direction—in the physical direction of your old home. I call it "longing materialized."

I reach for Haim's hand and watch the screen in front of me, fixated on the plane icon that hovers over Western Europe.

"Getting excited? We're almost there. Home." I lace my fingers through his.

He smiles and squeezes my hand. "Yes."

He sustains the squeeze and I take a mental snapshot of this moment. I've been longing for this for so many years. *We're here. Take it in.*

Though he hasn't expressed it, I know Haim's been craving face-to-face family time. I start playing out in my mind the chats he and his sisters will have about the differences between the Israeli and the American ways of life.

For the last five hours, we have chatted with the passengers on either side of us. Only on a plane bound for Israel can you get to know your entire aisle of the plane without the need for formalities or pleasantries. Israeli people are tethered and connected everywhere they go, and even more so on this EL AL 747. This notion pulls me even deeper into the vortex of longing for the place in my heart where I feel I have always belonged.

This was never a given. It took me years to find what Dr. Brene Brown calls "the courage [that] starts with showing up and letting ourselves be seen," beginning from the days of arriving in Israel as an American immigrant in 1989, carrying shame and self-doubt in my suitcase. So different from present-day Dorit, who can talk with any Israeli, in Hebrew, about a multitude of topics that are indigenous *only* to the country and culture at large.

Stewards shoo men who steadfastly stand in the aisle with their tallits—making their last attempt to pray for a safe homecoming against warnings of turbulence. We have crossed from North America to Israel in the time it takes to watch three full reruns of *Casablanca*. The outside temperature is -60 degrees Fahrenheit. We are nearly home.

An airport *sherut* taxi drops us in front of my in-laws' four-story complex in a neighborhood known as Shprintzack, located at the lower level of the three-tiered city of Haifa. The driver shouts to us in Hebrew, "That's it, your stop." After an hour of nonstop conversation, he shakes my husband's hand and slams the double doors of the nine-seater passenger van shut. To me he vivaciously says in English, "Welcome." I'm always frustrated by this. I lived in Israel for two decades, yet I'll always be seen as an outsider.

My in-laws live in a working-class neighborhood minutes away from the beach. The first thing I notice as we walk to the door of their complex is how much louder everything is here compared to Pittsburgh. Buses and ice cream trucks that seem to stop every five minutes; kids and passersby shouting from either side of the street. People are interrupting each other and talking over one another. Such is the intensity of the Israeli culture. No time to waste.

We pass through a rusty gate that clangs as we swing it open and walk up to the entrance. Just inches above our heads hangs an array of pink and red sheets and towels. We lift our bulky carry-ons and suitcases up the two flights of stairs. The walls are scratched in a thousand places; papers are strewn everywhere. At first glance, it seems as if the place has gotten dirtier, but perhaps I have simply gotten more accustomed to the American way of life. Doors slam up above. Voices of children call out. I hear cats yowling, truck brakes squealing, neighbors shouting to each other from various floors. I'm on edge.

The door to my in-laws' apartment opens straight into the living room, and the first thing I notice are my mother-in-law's forever tangled gold necklace strands. She shakes with excitement in her pale pink nightgown as she slowly gets up to extend her hand, but I ignore the hand, grab her, and quickly peck each of her two cheeks in the traditional Israeli greeting. Haim and Ivry pile into the living room behind me with the rest of our bags.

The tiny two-bedroom apartment is exactly the same as it was four years ago: the fake green vines trailing the shellacked shelves, the low ceilings, the comfy, tan leather sofas and chairs, the brown tile floors shined to perfection, the delicate row of spotlights above the kitchen. The same glass bowl of fake apples, pears, and bananas sitting on a laced doily. I'm comforted by the fact that nothing has changed.

The apartment's jewel is the partitioned-off verandah facing the sea, accessible through a sliding door on the farthest side of the kitchen, where my in-laws keep their washer (no dryer, as is typical in Israel). I walk out to the verandah, lean over the empty clothesline, and look past the various rows of hot water heaters on roofs to the fine blue horizon hovering over the sea. At nine o'clock in the morning, the air is unusually warm for this time of year, and the sun beats down on my head and arms. Cooler air awaits me inside the apartment, but still, I lean over. I'm relieved that the long trip is behind us, and anxious to settle in.

Ivry dashes out to where I'm standing and looks up at me. "Mommy, can we go to the sea?"

My six-year-old is brimming with excitement, but before I can answer, he's scooped up by his aunts, nieces, and nephews who smother him with kisses and hugs as they gush in English, with strong Israeli accents, "We miss you so much. We love you."

"*Motek*, sweetie," I say. "We just arrived after a very long trip. Let's just get settled in and unpack. We'll go first thing tomorrow. I promise. Let's catch up with family first."

Ivry squeals in delight at all the attention he's receiving, while Haim shouts to his sisters from the tiny bathroom's window through the adjoining wall, "It's me. I'm here. Give me a minute to finish up."

As I watch my husband and son interact with our family, I can't help but consider what we've sacrificed in moving to the US. It feels at times lonely as if we're groping for light in the wilderness. In the last four years, I've made the crossover from being a cultural Jew in Israel to a more spiritual one in America. If I can't live in Israel, the next best thing is to learn the stories in the Torah about what makes the Jewish people a nation. In Israel, I took my Jewish identity for granted and didn't care much for these things, but we are on our own in the Diaspora, with no statehood to back up our identity, and this has motivated me to gain a greater spiritual understanding of what it means to be Jewish.

We don't waste any time; we get busy chatting. For the next four hours, we talk about a wide range of topics—some politics and economics, but mainly news about various family members. The concerns here are the same as they've always been: The astronomically high prices of gas and food. The hopeless political division of the country. The extreme poverty of Holocaust survivors (unheard of in the States). The political coalition.

Then Haim's mom changes the subject, asking us, "So, how is life in America?" She has never been. Neither have his sisters or brother. I can't imagine the degree to which Haim's absence has affected his mother, especially since her health has been failing lately due to the onset of Parkinson's disease.

Haim's family keeps speaking to us in English.

"Ivry understands Hebrew," Haim reminds them. "*Tidabroo

b'ivrit. Speak in Hebrew. We've been speaking to him in Hebrew."

"*Haim totach b'anglit,* no?"—"Haim's English is probably amazing, right?" Their eyes rest on me as they wait for an answer. I sense a need for validation as if this will justify their not having seen him for the last four years.

Look, see? I want to tell them. *He didn't desert you. He is not a traitor. An Israeli always comes home. We came home.*

Longing nestles in their eyes. When Ivry asks for another container of chocolate milk, they leap to get it for him. They are only too happy to spoil him. How I want to cry at the sight of their tenderness. How I've waited for this moment.

Hours later, I pop another spinach and cheese *bureka* into my mouth and settle in for our first night with a disgruntled Ivry, who didn't get to go to the beach. Drunks take over the street as he struggles to fall asleep against the effects of jetlag with the television still blasting. A bottle smashes nearby. Then another one. I'm thinking the worst.

"Man, since when has this neighborhood gotten so violent?" Haim asks his sisters.

They tell us that violence of all forms has escalated throughout the entire country.

This is the sad part of Israel I remember. And forgot about.

Haim peers through the moonlit shutters as I stroke Ivry's head. We're sitting on a mattress in the living room that's been set up for our stay. Eventually, we move to the other end of the mattress, closer to the kitchen, hoping to escape the noise, but it's no use.

Ivry tosses and turns. "Why can't I fall asleep?" he asks us.

An hour later, at one o'clock in the morning, shouts and smashing bottles can still be heard in the distance. I approach Haim, who's sprawled on the couch, tempted to ask him to go down and ask the drunks to be quiet, but stop myself. *He won't want to get into an altercation with drunk people, especially after such a long journey.*

Memory is selective. It fleshes out the good moments and ignores the bad ones. But when you return to that familiar place, you have to take in the whole image—the raw, unfiltered part of it.

As I finally surrender to the noises of the night, I think of how long I've felt pulled toward this place, longed to cross the empty, vast, Atlantic Ocean, to return to what I still think of as home— and yet, now that I'm here, my longing is not fully satisfied. I feel neither here nor there. How did things change here so fast? Or did I change? Or both?

Now that we're on the familiar side of the Atlantic Ocean, my transatlantic longing is taking on a totally different meaning.

On our third day in Haifa, Ivry has the chance to dig mud caves against the waves of Dado beach with my brother-in-law. A wave of bleached white apartments rears up a few hundred yards away under a cobalt blue sky. The landscape here has been taken over by a bustling array of hotels, hi-tech companies, and endless rows of upscale apartments and housing built to accommodate the growing population. Faint outlines of the majestic garden terraces of the Bahai Faith—a UNESCO World Heritage site, also known as the "Hanging Gardens of Haifa"—are perceptible in the hazy distance. Endless palm trees dot the beaches; this, at least, is just as I remember it.

Is this is truly my country? I wonder. *Other than the Bahai temple and the promenade at the beach, I don't recognize any of this.* I feel like an outsider.

Our eight-hour stay at the beach culminates in a social gathering of family and some friends. The setting sun oozes blood red on our towels as Ivry happily builds sandcastles in the middle of it all. Safely nestled in this circle together, we pass around heaps of watermelon, baklava, and zesty Israeli salad.

A cool and unexpected breeze coming from the ocean tousles my hair. At some point, his sisters nudge me in the arm on either side and ask me, "Is Haim really happy in the States?"

I look straight at one of Haim's sisters; her face lights up with curiosity. They are particularly close. She knows she can get more precise information from me than him about how he's faring.

"*Betach* Haim's English is so good now because he speaks English all the time. No? His customers probably love him a lot," she says with a huge grin on her face. I know she's proud of him.

"Yeah, they do," I assure her.

They fire off more questions—what are our work shifts and time off like, how do we celebrate the American and Jewish holidays? I breeze through my answers, painting the prettiest picture I can, needing to convince both myself and them that we made the right choice leaving Israel.

Haim's sister wants to be reassured that he's not being taken advantage of like he was in our kibbutz days.

"Is he appreciated?" she asks me.

I share the nitty-gritty details about his most recent employee of the month award and various other accolades he's been given with her to satisfy her curiosity. I glance at him to see if he might be looking in our direction, but he's busy catching up with a half-dozen family members.

"Is he happy?" his sister asks again.

My other sister-in-law stops talking and listens to my answer.

"Yes," I say, "I think he's happy. He doesn't have to stress over finding a job like he had to here."

What I know today about longing is that family may not always understand you and the decisions you've had to make. The pain that results from certain things you've had to do may not be easily accepted.

As I've experienced it, Israelis are always looking for an argument, to shut the other side down, but I don't want to engage that way. I don't want a family confrontation. I just want our family members to accept our decision graciously, despite the *ga'agua* of longing. I decide I have nothing to lose by speaking the truth. I figure this might be an opportunity to educate my Israeli family about what it's really like to live in America.

"You know," I say to Haim's sisters, "when I ask him that question, he tells me the same thing I'm telling you. He tells me he misses the old version of the kibbutz, but not the privatized monster it's become." I turn over past conversations in my head: "No way will I ever consider living in Israel again," he once told me.

At the same time, I don't tell them of the Thanksgivings we've spent by ourselves. Or the various American holidays when Haim's had to work, and I've stayed at home by myself with Ivry. I don't want them to feel pity for me. For us. But I do want them to understand that leaving this socially connected country was a deep sacrifice.

"I won't lie," I continue. "Life is America is tough. But Haim and I envisioned a better future together. I left for a promised future that Israel couldn't give us."

In the end, I tell them some of the particulars about the kibbutz's privatization—about how we felt abandoned by the kibbutz, how its members turned their backs on Haim. These are things that Haim has not told them; all this information is new to them. I'm telling them now because I don't want to feel like a traitor. I want to belong. And that moment of belonging begins now.

In the days we've been here, I've realized something unexpected: in many ways, it's harder to come home than it is to go away.

﹌

Kibbutz Sde Nehemiya, June 2007. We slowly approach the twenty -foot, yellow-painted gate that leads into our kibbutz. It remains bolted shut; no one steps out from the *butkeh* to inquire what our business on entering the kibbutz is. Automation—a sign of changing times.

It's probably just a matter of moments before another car will arrive and open the gate for us, but rather than wait it out, I step out from our rented vehicle and look for the small activating sensor in the shape of a circle. I remember it's at the far end of the gate, closest to the raised pedestrian door entrance. The sun beats down on my shoulders. I take advantage of this "locked out" moment to see up close what I thought I'd forgotten: the lush oasis that is our kibbutz, a place that feels like neither the countryside nor city. A forklift driver in the distance wears typical work clothes. I eye the fragrant lemon and tangerine orchards on the other side of the fence; together, they comprise a quiet bubble that protects the kibbutz from outside realities.

This is the same gate Haim and I passed through as a married couple after a grand celebration with close family and friends four years ago at the Thai restaurant nestled up the road. Had I not learned to stay flexible and adaptable, I might never have gotten over my insecurities in those early years; I might never have learned to make this picturesque place my home. And now, those lessons of staying adaptable continue to serve me. It takes courage to go back to a place you felt compelled to leave not so long ago, a place to which you still attach lingering feelings of rejection. Since returning to the States, there have been many moments when I've doubted our decision to leave—and as I stand here at the gate, waves of nostalgia run over me, but they're all for what was, not for what's here now.

As I suspect, a trail of cars arrives within minutes. One of the drivers has the *chupchick*— the key. He recognizes Haim right away and they give each other huge *chapchas* on the back. The gate opens. We're in.

I thought we would see some of our old kibbutz friends right away, but no one is around. Midday quiet feels unusual for a kibbutz that for years operated around a schedule of three meals a day in the dining hall. With privatization, however, foot traffic has significantly decreased. Members now have to seek out opportunities for social interaction. These are facts I know well, but my heart wants to forget them.

We park our rented car across from the secretarial offices. I take in all the details. Dark-tinted windows. Stone-lined walkway. Spanish stucco roofs. Brown wooden bench. A green bike rack without bikes in it. Wildflowers languidly blowing in the 115-degree weather. The language of longing emerges deeply here and now.

As we sit in the car with the AC blasting, the door slightly ajar, the offices before me seem like an ancient relic of the kibbutz past. Our past. *Just because I don't live here doesn't mean I have to deprive myself of feeling at home.* I let this thought sink in and look at this short visit as an opportunity to test out my feelings of longing. How much have I really missed these people? How important is it for me to remember the things I've missed?

Haim unbuckles Ivry. They get out in the blazing heat and walk toward the dining room that was once the nucleus of our life here.

A voice echoes against the windows. "Haim? Haim Sasson? *Ahalan!*"

My heart flutters. I crane my neck around and see a semi-gray-haired woman on a bike with Erik Estrada–type shades on. It's Hannah, a kibbutz member who helped take care of Ivry when he first arrived home from the hospital. She was a lifesaver in those early days, as I adjusted to life as a new mother.

"*Gingi!*" she shouts, smiling at Ivry. *Gingi* is Hebrew for a red-head. "How he's grown!" This is one word Ivry understands well. He smirks back.

"*Eize hamood,*"—what a cutie—Hannah says with adoring eyes. Her face lights up like a menorah.

"*Nu.*" She turns to me. "How's life in America?" Although she doesn't initiate a hug, I feel compelled to give her a huge hug—of gratitude, for greeting us so warmly.

And yet. America. It's the last topic I want to discuss, and yet it's the one that will inevitably draw the most curiosity from the kibbutz members we see. I wish it wasn't the only place that was an option for us; I wish we could be back in Israel on our terms. But clearly, we can't.

I glance at Haim, hoping he'll divulge details; if I talk, I might get too worked up. His nonchalance always seems to work in my favor. But he's already taken up in conversation with another kibbutz member. More shouts of *"gingi"* fire up in the background.

I smile weakly.

What can I say that's positive about life in America? I'm overwhelmed by the loneliness of raising a family there. The loose connections. The fact that you can stay alone for an entire day in the library or in your house and no one will ever know you exist unless you make an effort to connect—so unlike Israel, where you interact with others from the moment the day starts, whether you want to or not.

I want to tell Hannah these things, but venting won't help me here. My heart will always be in Israel, and yet I'm still committed to the choice we made—to the security that Haim's job brings us.

"Life is good in America, Hannah," I say, "but you know, an Israeli always remembers his roots with fondness."

Hannah smiles in deep understanding. As a parent with post-army children who have traveled the world, she knows what it's like to witness this deep longing for Israel. She tells me how her youngest has recently returned home after a long travel stint abroad, and how relieved she is to have him home.

All the unspoken edges of time float in and around the corners of our conversation. Once you make the decision to leave a place for good, you cannot predict how that decision will play out over time. Your heart will ache for clarity; you'll yearn to know that the choice you had to make was for the best. But how to explain those feelings to someone else?

And in my case, there's also that unspoken wall of separation that demarcates the borders between "haves" and "have nots" on the kibbutz.

"*Tov*," Hannah says after I've spilled more details than I meant to share.

Mine is the language of longing. Now verbalized. We're here. But only for a visit. Come back. *Lachzor*. The entire country seems to beckon to me. I contemplate that possibility—but only for a moment. My heart can't face the unemployment and social degradation we experienced here before our move a second time. Plus, Haim's made it clear he doesn't intend to come back. So it's me, the outsider, left with these feelings of longing.

We chat for another fifteen minutes or so, and I feel the Hebrew that has fallen from my lips isn't the language of the Diaspora. It's the language of home.

9

IN THE WILDERNESS

Haim calls me over and hands me the iPad. "Here. Read this." It's a message from his brother, sent via Facebook Messenger. It's July 2011, only ten days after our return from our trip to Israel.

I scan the Hebrew for the essence of the message. It's not good. A funeral in less than twenty-four hours. Haim's mother has just passed away.

Haim stares into the screen, rays of digital light soaking his face. I take a step back. Better if I keep my distance. It's easier to manage my emotions if I don't have to read what he can tell me. This news is just too much.

The weather has been nothing but humid and sticky since we've been back, even in the early-morning hours, and this news adds to the oppression I already feel. My mouth goes dry and I feel nauseous. There's a pit in my stomach and fear in my heart. I'm not so much a believer, and yet still I pray silently, *Dear God.*

I break the prolonged silence and muster the courage to ask, "Haim, what was the cause? Was it related to her Parkinson's?"

"I don't know," he says, his face blank.

His trembling voice reels me closer to his side. My Israeli-born husband is rarely so vulnerable. He's been the solid, unshakable one in our marriage, but this is the exact thing that's kept us at times from finding a deeper connection with each other.

I used to think that *sabras*, like the fruit they're named for, don't need comfort. Since serving in the Israel Defense Forces, I've equated being a *sabra* with being a Hebrew superman of sorts. In Israel, our marriage was defined by the values inherent in Haim's being a *sabra*—his general assertiveness. As a member of our kibbutz, he dedicated his life to the collective. He ignored his personal life for the needs of the majority.

We've survived as a couple because I've always known that he has my back. But emotional intimacy has not always come easily for us. Now, in the midst of this tragedy, I see an opening—a rare opportunity for us to connect more deeply. It's just the two of us bracing against the tide of the news and what feels like another crash of waves pelting us, one after another.

"Haim," I whisper. "I'm so sorry."

He sits at the edge of the bed, staring down at the iPad. I imagine his sisters catching their mother just as her eyes closed, followed by shouts of "*Elohim!*" Paramedics would have loaded her into an ambulance.

"This is going to be really hard," I say gently.

He stands and heads to the living room.

Like a puppy, I trail behind him. "What will we do? We can't make it in time for the funeral."

He makes his way to the living room window. I know him well enough to understand that he needs space to think. To breathe. To feel.

"I don't know, Dorit," he says softly.

Shards of stubborn sun pass through the slits of the Venetian blinds. In this dark bedroom, with limited access to sunlight, I sense a hard day looming before us.

We both know it's pointless to even discuss the possibility of arriving in less than twenty-four hours for the funeral. Even if we could afford the ticket, logistically, we can't do it. I consider whether Haim might go to sit Shiva. Ivry and I could manage without him for about a week, of course, but it strikes me that Haim and I have never been apart for that long since we started dating.

If anything were to happen with Haim away, I wouldn't feel comfortable turning to the neighbors in our apartment building, many of whom are students who come and go at odd hours of the night. The thought of calling on an acquaintance for help highlights my vulnerability, my isolation, here. My need for emotional security in our new surroundings is an ongoing deficit, never satisfied, that exacerbates my longing for what we left behind in Israel. These feelings distance me from the States—which needles me since we're well past the point where I need to buckle down and commit to staying here.

In Pittsburgh, my basic needs are met, but my emotional needs are not. I fear I will never make the kind of ties with people here that we had with our community in Israel, which keeps me anxious and constantly second-guessing our decision to come here. Years from now, I will accept this cultural dissonance. But for now, I'm struggling.

None of what I'm experiencing seems to be an issue for Haim. He's far more pragmatic than me. I look at his solemn expression, intensified by his bushy grey eyebrows, in the early-morning light and wonder, *Does he want to go?*

If we could have stayed in Israel, of course, these push-pull feelings would be moot.

I lean over Haim just as a strong and welcome gust of wind breezes through the open window, rattling the panes. It reminds me of the *hamsin*—a hot, dry wind that we get in Israel.

It's just a matter of time before Ivry wakes up and lumbers in from the adjoining room to nestle his head in my lap, cheeks flushed from sleep.

In less than twenty-four hours, my mother-in-law will be buried, and Haim's family will shuffle to her small two-bedroom apartment in the rundown neighborhood of Shprintzak, sea waves lapping behind them, grief bobbing in their throats.

The giving up of one's country is a "heart choice," never easy. For me it's now clear that Israel, while not the country of my birth, is the country of my heart. But in order to thrive here in the States, I will need to find ways to let go. Ann Landers says it well: "Some people believe holding on and hanging in there are signs of great strength. However, there are times when it takes much more strength to know when to let go and then do it."

Do I have what it takes to let go?

After setting Haim up on a Skype call with his sisters, I retreat to the bedroom, leaving the door slightly ajar. I need space to think. Time to breathe. A decision is pending, but only Haim can make it. And I will need to be okay with whatever he chooses to do.

In most cases, a Jewish burial takes place within twenty-four hours of death because the Torah says, "You shall bury him the same day . . . His body should not remain all night." In modern-day practice, it's rare for burials to happen this quickly outside of Israel, except in Orthodox communities. If Haim's sisters want him to be there for their mother's funeral, they'll need to give him more time. He'll have to buy a plane ticket, get to an airport, and fly across the world. I feel like we're being set up for failure.

I peek out of the bedroom and try to read Haim's thoughts from the subtle cues he gives—the way the fringes of his mustache are pulled together to form an upside-down V. *Open up to me*, I will him silently. *Tell me what I need to know.*

Voices cut in and out on the Skype call. I remain still long enough to hear the precise telling of details. How she fell and couldn't get up. How they shouted to her as she remained motionless. How she finally passed away.

The contours of Haim's face shift like tectonic plates. The Earth spins revolutions around our building. The front entrance door bangs, and from underneath the carpeted closet, the floor quakes; the entire building feels as if it's about to collapse. I hear sirens in the distance.

Pressure mounts.

The vast Atlantic Ocean is a divide between us and them, America and Israel. In my mind's eye, I am staring at Haim's mother's open grave, and it is like a wound that will never fully heal.

"So . . . are you coming to the funeral?" both sisters now ask in unison.

Haim pauses a moment and I reenter the living room.

He explains how logistically, it's not even possible. "We live in Pittsburgh. Not New York City. It takes five to seven hours just to get to the airport in New York City, and another ten to fourteen hours to cross the Atlantic Ocean." America, he explains, is just so vast, you can't even begin to imagine.

Haim knows his sisters can't possibly fathom the distances here. It's not the same to look at a map as it is to be here in person, to experience the everlasting expanses that separate rather than connect people.

Just as I suspected they would, they plead with him to at least come for the Shiva. *Even for three days, Haim, just come. Come.*

His face tightens. "No," he says solemnly. "There's no point. I won't make it in time."

His voice spells out finality. He seems set on his decision.

Ivry makes his way over to Haim while I step back into our bedroom, shutting the door behind me, guilt hovering over me. I'm wary of being the subject of blame for Haim not coming home for this momentous event in his family's life. For being the one to whisk him halfway across the world.

I cup my face in my hands and lean into the belief that Haim and I will navigate this together and find our way to the other side without too much damage being done to his relationship with his family.

"Why come if I can't make it for the funeral?" I hear him ask. "The funeral is the important part."

"But Haim!" They're shouting now. "Come sit Shiva, then."

"The funeral is the important part," he repeats firmly.

I completely get why my sisters-in-law would insist that Haim make every effort to get on that plane. He has always been the rock of their family, just like he has always been mine. Logical. Rational. Direct. Thoughtful. He is their fabric, their storyteller, their emotional equilibrium—and they need him right now.

I am trying to hold it together, trying to tap into my inner strength so I can navigate these feelings I'm experiencing. I feel responsible for his not being able to go. I feel like we should be there out of loyalty, and yet the reality is, we can't just pick up and go. These feelings again put me in a bind I hate—of choosing America over Israel. It's a choice I've had to confront time and time again.

Sitting here alone in our dimly lit bedroom, I feel myself building a case, like a lawyer getting ready to go to court. I prepare my arguments, taking one feeling and building a three-hundred-pound document around it, so I'm prepared for battle with Haim's sisters, should the need arise to defend his decision to stay here.

Even knowing what I want—for Haim to stay here with us—a familiar question arises: *Why do we have to be so far away?*

July 21, 2007, the day before we left Israel, my father, who still lives in Israel, remarked, "You act as if you aren't coming back." I felt like I'd been caught red-handed. We'd framed leaving as a temporary thing, but deep down I knew we were leaving for good. I couldn't see a way out of our circumstances in Israel, and America was our land of opportunity.

My father may have known what I didn't—that what I was

about to give up wasn't so simple. He'd stood in my shoes before. He'd given up his American life for Israel, and now I was making the move back. But I didn't imagine my father knew how I felt. He hadn't left America for Israel because he couldn't survive in the States. He'd chosen Israel for a better life for us, and to put some distance between us and my mother. Haim and I, on the other hand, were leaving Israel because life there was no longer tenable. We weren't making ends meet, and the opportunities were too few. But since our decision to leave felt forced, I could not foresee the tradeoff I was making. I could not anticipate the guilt and ambivalence I would later feel.

I'm pulled back to our present predicament when I hear Haim's voice escalate on the Skype call.

"Is money the reason you can't come?" one of his sisters asks.

I know Haim sees the issue of money as irrelevant. None of these things matter when it comes to the question of whether he should be there to honor his mother. No Israeli expat I know would use money as an excuse not to be with family.

"No, no," Haim says, confirming what I already know. "Money is not an issue."

"Nu, so what's the problem?" his sister asks.

"No problem. Everything is okay."

In trying moments like these, I admire Haim's clarity and take comfort in the fact that he can speak for himself.

"I give up," one of them says. She's the sister who's particularly close with Haim. "You've become too American. What's wrong with you?"

These words pierce my heart. *Too American.*

The torment is too much. My throat is tightening up now. I can barely speak. My eyes brim with tears. "Haim, just go if you need to!" I finally exclaim.

I want Haim to do what's right for himself and his family. But as the American in our partnership, I worry about being the subject of blame. In their minds, America wins. I'm the reason Haim is here in the first place. And yet, from the bedroom doorway, he appears as firm as ever in his decision to stay.

Just when I'm wondering if it's even possible to convince him, to my surprise, he responds to my outburst.

"Should I go, Dorit?"

I quickly scan his face; all I see is the rigid, impassive expression I have known for years. Still, he clearly feels torn.

"It's up to you, Haim. You already know what I think. I can't make this decision for you." I am surprised by this new feeling of inner strength. As much as I want him to stay with us, I have to suppress my feelings of guilt.

Trust in Haim. Trust in his decision-making abilities.

⎯⎯⎯※⎯⎯⎯

Two days later, we're together at home and I'm still reconciling with the fact that we've chosen to sit Shiva and say Kaddish in the Diaspora. It's our only way of showing solidarity with his family. It feels strange, and guilt still hovers. I'm still flooded by feelings of longing. But, ironically, the decision has solidified an unanticipated spiritual connection.

There's nowhere to go. Nothing to do. We are forbidden to work, clean, cook, or shop. Our obligation as mourners is to be alone to express grief.

Neighbors trickle in to share condolences. It's the moral duty of the Jewish community to come to our home to draw us out of our loneliness. People bring prepared food. It's of some comfort to me to discover that we're supported. We are building a sense of community after all. Our home becomes our sanctuary and the living room becomes a makeshift grieving center. Someone brings extra chairs, but we follow the ancient Jewish tradition and sit on pillows, lowering our bodies to the level of our feelings, a symbolic enactment of desolation due to the departure from normalcy during the early stages of bereavement.

As somewhat familiar faces float in and out of our apartment, I'm haunted by the feeling that we made a wrong decision, not just in staying in the States to grieve, but in returning to the States in the first place. Is it my fault that Haim didn't go? Was it because of me that he was so resolute in his decision to stay?

When someone passes away in Israel, the local burial authority puts a black-and-white notice on the building of the deceased that attracts people from across various neighborhoods to come to pay their respects. When I first saw Shiva unfold as a new immigrant and IDF soldier, I was struck by the public display of mourning. Strangers and mere acquaintances aren't seen as disruptors to the grieving process, for in Israel, no matter how diverse or big the community is, there's a strong sense of *yachad*, or togetherness that brings people together under the most tragic and difficult of circumstances.

What I notice about opening our home is that here in Pittsburgh, cultural differences are articulated by levels of Jewishness. Israelis make up only 12 percent of the Jewish population in the North American Jewish landscape, and yet something—I attribute it to language differences, a sabra mentality, and a particular sense of humor—makes them seek out the company of their fellow expats.

Haim and I began our decade-long journey with Chabad—one of the world's best-known Chassidic movements—in 2007, four years earlier, the minute we took note of the fact they were running the *shul* across the street from our home. One thing led to another and soon we found ourselves attending social and family events organized through Chabad of Pittsburgh. Chabad is especially known for its outreach. At its core, what attracted me to the philosophy was their personal approach, for I too wanted to feel a sense of belonging.

But when the Chabadniks enter our home on the first day of Shiva, I feel invaded, even though I've met a few of them at *shul* before. I know that Chabad of Pittsburgh sent out an online notification to the community, but I can't help but ask myself, *Do these people know Haim well enough to warrant their coming to pay their respects to his late mother?*

It will later strike me as odd that I put these qualifications out there. Wasn't I longing for community? Wasn't I missing the close-knit ties of Israel? It took something as earth-shattering as the death of a family member to feel connected and yet I resisted these well-intentioned Shiva visitors. I knew nobody could understand us and where our hearts needed to be, and yet I had to accept our decision, which frustrated me even more.

But these thoughts will come later. Today, I watch as one approaches Haim and lays his hand first on his shoulder, then on his head, and says, "May God comfort you among the other mourners of Zion and Jerusalem." I watch how Haim sustains eye contact with this stranger who goes on to tell me how impressed he is by Haim's spiritual knowledge. Who tells me that on various mornings he has had the privilege to *daven* (pray) with Haim for Shacharit, the morning prayer.

And now he supports Haim as he says Kaddish for the dead, a special prayer they will say at the synagogue for twelve long months to cement the ascension of his mother's spirit.

This Shiva caller looks in my direction, pats Haim gently but firmly on the back, and says, "*Hu Bachoor Tov*, he's a good man. You're lucky."

This moment is meaningful to me.

In Israel, I would never interact with a Chassidic person, let alone a man, because of the constant clashes and frictions between the religious Jews and non-religious Jews. So why here?

Just when I think he's about to head out, leaving us alone to deal with our personal bereavement, the Shiva caller says, "*B'tokh sh'ar avalay Tzion v'Y'rushalayim*"—Among the other mourners of Zion and Jerusalem.

This man has come to remind Haim that the divine powers of the universe will enable him to heal and go on with a meaningful life. That no matter the geographical distance or where we choose to sit Shiva, the ultimate consolation comes from the omnipresent God. I am touched by his message—"we are not alone"—and welcome the reminder that for Israelis, personal bereavement is not personal, it's a community experience. In its own way, this experience is bringing me closer to Israel.

Even here, thousands of miles from home.

I feel a little less alone and a little less guilty knowing we have a community backing us up.

We're on our way.

10

YOU'RE SPEAKING
MY LANGUAGE

It's already been five months since we sat Shiva for Haim's mom, and Thanksgiving looms. I'll soon be cooking dishes from childhood—turkey, sweet potato pie with marshmallows, fragrant cranberry sauce, pumpkin pie topped with whipped cream. Our streets have been taken over by leaf blowers. I follow the change in colors from submarine yellow to the cranberry red that nearly takes my breath away—a distraction from thinking about the "musts" of this holiday.

Each year, this holiday triggers my yearnings for what I don't have much of in Pittsburgh: family. And this, by the way, is a very family-oriented town. For most of the year, our community serves as our family, but on this one day, the major differences between the "haves" and the "have nots" is apparent. How do I make peace with our lack?

I distract myself with the humdrum of food shopping. I pretend

I'm cooking for an army, just like in Israel. I imagine I'm preparing three-course dinners for our Israeli families.

The day before the holiday, I take off for my husband's place of work with Ivry, just a ten-minute bus ride away. It's not often I shop at my Haim's store, but the place has lots of options, including discounted store-brand items. Each time I walk in, I am struck by the diversity there, not only in size and shape of the produce but of the shoppers—the kind of diversity that brings me back to my American roots.

As I load packages of cranberries into my cart with a happy Ivry sitting squarely in front of me, I try to reconnect with the inherent meaning of Thanksgiving, beyond the images of packaged cranberries and the frenzied shoppers squawking behind me.

Haim takes his work break for the initial shopping run to make sure we're not missing anything.

The closest holiday to Thanksgiving in Israel is *Shavuot*, a pilgrimage festival, one of the three holidays when Jews are required to come to the land of Israel and offer our *bikkurim*, first fruits, in gratitude to God. But gratitude doesn't always come easily.

On this Thanksgiving, I look to life-supporting themes to guide my story: How can I feel good every day despite the choices I've made? And when I feel disconnected, how can I open up to new possibilities and still feel optimistic?

There's much to be said for changing the narrative we tell ourselves in order to overcome obstacles and limitations and give way to even more resilience. The Pilgrims' arrival to the New World signified the unification of their faith. In the years that ensued, they would have to overcome years of religious persecution to nurture their own resilience. They would have to learn to tell themselves a different story about their own ability to survive.

I too can change the narrative I tell myself each time I feel disconnected. I too can choose resilience over seeing myself as victim of my own circumstances. When I left New York City in

1990, I took with me the 1971 vintage classic of *If You Sailed the Mayflower* not only to remember my American childhood but also as a reminder to stay resilient.

I pick up a can of pureed pumpkin and remind Ivry of the Hebrew word for squash—*dla'at*—as I hand it to him. He listens and takes in the texture of the word before he plops the can in our cart. A head turns. I'm guessing it's my foreign accent that comes alive when I speak Hebrew. Others think I'm standing out, but I'm just trying to bring Israel closer to me. To us.

I remember during the period of my army service known as *ulpan*—an intense Hebrew language course specifically for newly inducted immigrants—our army ingrained in us that we were not to speak a foreign language, or we would be punished. As a young, determined soldier, I wanted so badly to be fully acculturated into Israeli society that I would have given up my ties to home altogether. My new Israeli identity mattered more to me than my history as an American. How ironic to find ourselves here, then, emigrating back to raise our family and to re-embrace these American traditions I had let go of so long ago.

And yet, while I speak English as any native American would, my preference for Hebrew is clear. I worked hard to build my life there, and I had to earn my fluency and place in Israeli culture. In many ways, this has made me feel more loyal to Israel than I can or will ever feel to America. As a soldier, I identified strongly with Hebrew, speaking it exclusively on the base, and I continued to do so in our life in the kibbutz. In Israel, Hebrew offered cultural and emotional independence from my mother. Here, conversely, it symbolizes a cultural and emotional connection to family.

I pull a few more cans of pumpkin puree off the shelf; language barrier or not, I decide against alienation and isolation and reassess our options for family. This is the first year I won't be able to invite Candace, the lonely senior in the apartment below ours, to join us; they carried her body down the leaf-strewn stairwell almost a year ago.

Candace satisfied my longings for community and connection, by accepting all our dinner and holiday invitations for almost five years. A Bread Loaf scholar and master poet, a giver of words and gifts to my young son, she was important to me. I look down at our groceries and wonder who might replace her at our table. Will this be another Thanksgiving filled with longings?

Ivry wildly kicks up his six-year-old legs and then lets them go with a thud, making the entire metal bench rattle. Moments later, there's a clap of thunder, followed by booming streaks of lightning. I worry that he will be scared, but he peacefully chews on the banana I've given him as a snack. The first droplets of rain manage to seep into our blue shopping bags, which are crammed with items I never bought in Israel—cans of pumpkin, fresh cranberries, a huge frozen kosher turkey.

I remember the hot marshmallows settling on the sweet potato pie at my uncle and aunt's home in a secluded and strict Orthodox community in Far Rockaway, Queens. Women's voices in the kitchen—one big cackle. The tone was conversational, then it quickly moved to a high-pitched, bossy tone that alerted everyone to stay out of trouble, announcing that the kitchen was a space reserved for women who knew what they were doing.

I didn't dare enter the kitchen; better to stay out of trouble than to get too close to the action. "Carmen, Carmen," one cousin would boss my mother. Moments later, Mom would emerge with a platter, her face plastered with an East-West-type grin as if she was the one who had made that chicken. Mom liked taking directions at events like those, especially since she wasn't fond of cooking in general and especially on major holidays.

Our bus has been delayed for almost thirty minutes, and there was still no such thing as Uber or Lyft yet. Rain continues in torrents and there's no point taking turns to look for the bus anymore. It's clearly delayed. I shoot Haim a look. He scans a semi-wet and torn bus schedule with his free hand.

We could be here a while.

"I'm hungry," Ivry complains.

"Give him another tangerine," I tell Haim in Hebrew.

When we first came to Pittsburgh, I was self-conscious about making heads turn with our language, but the motive to communicate in Hebrew as a family—especially as a way to maintain Ivry's legacy, his identity—fueled me.

I want Ivry to feel comfortable engaging with Israel and his Israeli family in his native tongue, and I also want Haim to have this connection to home through his immediate family. As a family, we speak Hebrew, but we sometimes code-switch to English to emphasize important things for Ivry.

Signs of cross-cultural connections: I have general lists, journals and shopping lists in English tacked to the refrigerator and small lists on Post-its that curl up and eventually fall to the floor. *Doctor's appointment at 9 am. Fill out medical forms. Talk to Ivry's Kindergarten teacher.* English is the language of my childhood, my young adulthood. I use English to communicate with the outside world. It seems that the more I speak English in Pittsburgh, the easier my transition has been. As my mother tongue, English is a testament to all the variations of English I grew up with: my Yiddish-speaking grandmother, who spoke English with a Polish accent. My Israeli father's unmistakably foreign accent. The way maintenance workers in our building used Spanish and English as a brother-sister pair—Spanish first to my Spanish-speaking mother and English to my brother and me.

"The bus is coming," Haim says in Hebrew, and he gives me a look of hope. The same look of hope he shared when he took his oath of American citizenship on September 17, 2010, and the officiator announced to a crowd of forty-six newly inducted American citizens, "You are now American, but always remember who you are and where you come from."

The bus draws closer. Again, it's not ours.

I turn those words over in my mind. *Who you are. Where you come from.*

I had not anticipated such words from the officiant—not in Pittsburgh, where often I felt like an outsider myself, beyond the community of our Jewish *shtetl*. They were encouraging.

Only when we filled out the paperwork together and I accompanied Haim to the various citizenship appointments that culminated in a final citizenship test did I realize how trying and even intimidating the process to become an American can be. There were many times when I witnessed Haim becoming bewildered by the paperwork and the tests. I sensed his intimidation, and there were times when I questioned whether such bureaucracy meant we'd end up choosing our loyalties—to which side of the Atlantic Ocean were we most faithful?

As we listened to the speeches of the newly minted citizens and Haim raised his right hand to make the Pledge of Allegiance and the oath of citizenship before the officiator and a judge, I sensed the true meaning of a "mosaic identity": since each identity is integral to the mosaic, our collective experiences, cultures, traditions, histories, religions, and languages all mattered. This feeling of Haim being culturally validated in America was something I'd never experienced, and it filled my heart with hope.

After the ceremony, we all shouted for joy, including dual citizen Ivry, who practically pounced on his father, caught up in the excitement of the day. Perhaps America had become that place where dreams come true.

Before we headed outside, I took another glance at Haim and asked, "Nu, how do you feel? Do you feel at home? Was it worth getting married to me? You're now a real American!"

"Now I got to start paying my taxes!" He laughed. "Kidding."

All together, we stepped hand in hand outside the county building in downtown Pittsburgh. I looked up. The clouds were beautiful and billowy, and somehow I no longer felt alone.

※

A little over six years from now, in January 2018, I will find myself clicking on the file titled "Haim's American Citizenship." Memories of that happy day will flood me: an image of Ivry drawing a picture of the courtroom in the waiting room. Another memory of all of us smiling alongside a bunch of Boy Scouts. In another, Haim is in a room of forty-five soon-to-be sworn in American citizens, awaiting that important moment.

But in January 2018, these memories will also trigger a landslide of emotions based on the recent barrage of news: families who've contributed to their communities for decades are being ripped from their homes. American citizens and green card holders are being detained and deported; parents are being forced to leave children behind to fend for themselves. I imagine what these families might be saying to their loved ones at the airport, at home, the tears streaming down their faces. I am heartbroken.

How could this be happening? In a country I've fought so hard to claim as our home?

Among the stories is one that hits too close to home. An Israeli marijuana scientist and expert cannabis agronomist is fighting to be reunited with his new wife. He was sent by his Israeli employer to consult with American companies in the States, where medical marijuana is legal, only to be deported and accused of drug trafficking.

The decision-makers are sending a horrific message: This isn't your home. This isn't your country. Go back to where you came from. You aren't wanted here.

In Hebrew, the word for compassion is *hemla*, and the word for other is *zoolat*. These ideas were concretized for me in 2006 at the local school where I taught English. I had heard on the Israeli radio station how out of the 200,000 Holocaust survivors living in Israel, nearly a third lived below the poverty line. How could the State of Israel allow such a thing? That same year, I had taught Elie Weisel's *Night*, during which half of us in the class, myself included, cried at one of the most poignant scenes where Elie cannot continue working in the concentration camp, let alone continue on the infamous "Death March," but his dying father pleads that he must. This teaching experience solidified the idea of *hemla lazoolat*, or compassion for the other—in this case for the most vulnerable of all populations in Israel—in my mind.

Compassion, the emotion of caring concern. In post-biblical Hebrew it's *rahmanut*, from the word *rehem*, or "womb," originating in the idea of either motherly love or sibling love. The Talmudic rabbis considered compassion to be one of the three distinguishing marks of Jews. As a Diaspora Jew straddling two cultures, never quite finding a home in either country, I mostly yearn to be back in Israel. America, seemingly, is not my country, reiterated now by its rejection of the other. How is it possible for the American government to lay down the law over the very places that many of us struggle to call home?

Finally, the bus arrives, but it's full and we must wait for the next one.

While we're waiting, a man from behind suddenly asks, "Hey, what language are you speaking?"

"Hebrew," we both announce.

"*Shalom*," he says with a grin.

"*Shalom*," we answer back, and I find myself glancing up at his face. He wears a wide, sincere grin, and his dancing brown eyes effuse warmth. Secretly awed by how one stranger can emanate such emotions, I immediately feel a sense of connection with him.

It's comforting to hear this man say this word to us. In Hebrew, the word *shalom* means hello, good-bye, and peace. "*Shalom*" is taken from the root word *shalam*, which means "to be safe in mind, body, or estate." It reminds me of my efforts to practice compassion and to change my narrative.

"*Mah zeh?*"—What's this?—he says jokingly. "*Mah zeh!*" He laughs. "The Israelis I used to work with in New York City always used this word."

"*Mah zeh?*" is a rhetorical question that a person can use to refer not just to tangible things but also to conceptual issues. Like many words, its intended meaning is inferred from context. In Israeli society, where things tend to be unstructured and ambiguous, asking, "*Mah zeh?*" is a sure way to get attention and help. In my service with the Israel Defense Forces, I would constantly ask, "*Mah zeh?*" when struggling to understand army lingo from guns to radio code words and everything in between.

At first I smile politely, then I laugh out loud. Who is this man? He's clearly not Israeli, and yet he's joking with us in Hebrew.

"You're laughing," the man says, grinning.

"Yep." I laugh louder. "Good old *mah zeh*. I know it very well."

He tells us that he worked in retail in Manhattan, as a security guy.

"Oh man," says Haim.

"I was making four dollars and twenty cents an hour living out in Queens," he says.

"Queens? And you traveled two hours by train each way?" I ask.

"Yep. Something like that." He looks at me thoughtfully, still smiling.

The Tri-State area has long teemed with Israeli life and culture. Speaking to this man makes me consider, not for the first time, the degree to which we're isolated here in Pittsburgh.

"I was paying eighty-five dollars a week for renting a room," he shares.

"Wow, eighty-five bucks to rent a room?" I ask incredulously and look at Haim. "Can you imagine?"

"At the time, it was a lot, but a room was all I needed," the man says.

"How old were you, eighteen?" Ivry asks.

"Smart boy," he says. "Give me five."

My son high-fives this person who suddenly doesn't feel like a stranger to us.

"Close. I was nineteen at the time. A room was all I needed."

"You're a good man," Haim says. "I can tell."

"Thank you. *Toda.*"

Our bus finally arrives, and Haim and I sit not too far away from our new acquaintance. We chat in Hebrew until his stop. Before he exits the bus, he turns to us again and says, "*Shalom,*" with a smile.

This is only the second time—the first being at Haim's citizenship ceremony in 2010—that our Hebrew language has been recognized and validated by an outsider here in the States. Though it was just a small exchange, it feels meaningful. Hopefully, this road I'm traversing—which feels so long—is getting me somewhere.

11

UNSATISFIED LONGINGS

The desire to return to Israel waxes and wanes. At times I want to go back, but Haim has said flat-out that he doesn't. I periodically suggest to him that we look for jobs in Israel, but he shuts the idea down every time. The thought keeps flickering off and on in my mind all throughout Chanukah and Christmas—but by the time the first of the New Year rolls around in 2012, it has been completely extinguished.

That doesn't stop the intense longing I feel to return to Israel.

I grieve over what I don't have here: a tribe. The movie script of these feelings unravels the same way each day against the wintry Pittsburgh landscape, and I'm filled with regret. Why am I here? In the morning, I brace myself against the cold as my son and I walk the icy sidewalks to the library for a Saturday storytime. During the weekdays, I take a bus across the Robert Clemente Bridge to teach ESL students. My eyes drift to faraway corners of the various bridges as wind lashes around the bus, and I'm tickled by how, as I pass the vast Monongahela River each day, I still care enough to compare it to the Jordan River. As much as I feel in awe of the Monongahela's size, it has the impact of distancing me. Back on our kibbutz, "our river" is just one meter away from the bridge. The diamonds that shimmer and glint off the river in the evening sun create immediate accessibility, something I long for here in Pittsburgh. I have kayaked the Jordan River, jumped into it, thrown pebbles at it, and even written about it. I cannot do any of these things on this giant river; it's too intimidating. So all I can do is compare the two and consider the country I've loved and lost.

After putting Ivry to sleep one night, I lean into the computer, so close to the images of our kibbutz that I almost feel like I'm there. The images on my Facebook feed are like apparitions, like a far-distant star. I close my eyes and imagine myself in my favorite getaway "happy places" in Israel, the ones that connect me spiritually and emotionally: praying at the Kotel, the Western Wall in Jerusalem, and places I haven't ventured to since my army days, like particular nature trails around Mount Hermon. The blood-red *kalayinot*, the well-known anemone flowers of Israel that bloom as early as March, sometimes coinciding with the Passover holiday, appear in my mind's eye. There's that familiar feeling of longing again. I can feel myself choking again, so deep and intense is longing. The word *ga'agooah* arises faster than its English equivalent. That I still reach for words in Hebrew is evidence to me of how powerfully rooted the country and culture are in my heart, spirit, and mind.

I click on an image taken in the spring of 2007 and zoom in on the wooden bridge that connects the swimming pool to the kibbutz and examine the patches of mint or *nana* leaves on each side of the bridge. In the seven years I've lived in Pittsburgh, I've toggled back and forth between feeling like a self-imposed exile and the American citizen that I am by virtue of my birth. Lofty bridges, towering buildings, and distance between people are the norm here, and the most logical way to come to terms with my own personal yearning to return to Israel is to remember that within the vast diversity of the United States, I can still connect with my tribe: the Jewish tribe in my Squirrel Hill neighborhood. I can find my own space and claim my people and a connection to God here in the States, but it's on me to make an effort and find my way.

I click on another image on Facebook, which takes me to someone's album of Jerusalem and the Wailing Wall. Almost instantly, I am transported. The emotions I feel threaten to knock me to the ground. Each time I entered a spiritual place in Israel, I wondered about God and his presence. I wanted to know why the Torah, the Jewish bible, instructs us not only to believe in God but also to know and love God. Growing up in New York City, I understood Judaism to be mostly a set of rules. I went to Hebrew school as a kid, and I learned the Torah, but when I arrived in Israel I didn't feel religious or Jewish enough. The "you versus us" mentality between the religious and the secular in Israel upended my relationship with Judaism.

Here in Pittsburgh, during these High Holy days of 2012, I finally attempt to reconcile this upending by asking myself the question, "How is this fear of Judaism and getting closer to God actually serving me?" If I continued to fear members of my community, like our rabbi, then surely I cannot love another Jew, for love and fear cannot coexist. I have to bring myself to reach some answers—start to accept myself as a beginner and start at zero with learning the Torah and God's divine presence.

If I can't go back to my homeland, then the next best thing is to bring my homeland to me.

"The soul knows only one way to fulfill itself, and that is to take in what is true," writes the poet Mark Nepo, and so I give spirituality another stab; to get to the root of my own spiritual understanding, I need to break through stereotypes. If the Jewish value of *tikkun olam*, fixing the world, is the highest level of spiritual and personal growth, then I'll have to start at the very beginning: with myself.

As I stare at the Facebook page, taking in various well-known images of Jerusalem from the Tower of David to the Western Wall, I remind myself that I have to reframe how I see my own personal exile from Israel. Like Shamil, a leader of assorted tribes who were attacked and imprisoned by the Russian army with the intention of depriving them of their freedom, I need redemption. His wordless spiritual melody, typically sung on the Jewish holiday of Simchat Torah, brings me to tears when I remember how I managed to convince myself for so many years in Israel that I could only gain the spiritual access allowed by the Torah's infinite words of wisdom if I culturally identified with a religious group.

Each time I look at the computer screen, I think how distant I've become from Israel, my former life, my family. I watch their festivities unfold from my desk chair, and my heart aches. Their smiles and laughter only serve to highlight my loneliness and lack. Then I remember: My life is here in America. My family is here in America. Our lives are here in America. Staying in the here and now is one of the antidotes to longing, and so I have to forgive myself for depriving myself of spiritual nourishment in the past and focus on what I can do now.

During Chanukah in 2011, "what I can do now" is to find a cultural connection to Israel and bring a "mini Israel" connection to Pittsburgh. And so, on the second day of Chanukah, I decide to reconnect with an Israeli women's group after a nearly five-year hiatus. Time to bridge the gaps of longing and avoid isolation and alienation.

In this festive room, in the dancing light of the Chanukah menorah, my own inner light becomes subdued. These Israeli women already have well-established connections—some work together, while others work out together at our local Jewish Community Center. I'm trying to find a common thread with my own people, but my feelings of social inadequacy become even more exacerbated when I remind myself that here, too, I'm an outsider.

I sit in a corner of the room, trying to strike up a conversation with a soft-spoken Israeli woman who passes me a Chanukah donut with jelly oozing from the center. Powdered sugar falls off my hands like snow onto the floor.

This supersized American donut, pulsating with jelly, is like my heart—you squeeze it too much, it spills over with heavy drops of longing. Luckily, I manage to avoid a mishap and bite from the side.

Our last Chanukah in Israel in 2006 was a turning point. It brought us in touch once again with the true value of kibbutz: community and connection. By then, the kibbutz had been taken over by greed and materialism. Members avoided each other publicly and were more concerned with building second and third floors, renovating their homes, renting out space, purchasing second and third vehicles, buying up property, and going on trips. And yet on that festive Chanukah night, with the dining room glowing like a giant menorah. everyone forgot about money. It was as if we had forgiven each other for our shortcomings.

Going to this event feels like it might be a way to manifest Israel here.

I want to groan when the woman who just passed me the donut tells me she is returning to Israel at the end of the school year, once her husband's post-doc study is up. It's a familiar story I know well from the many Israelis who come and those who get to go back. This is not us. I press my nose against the fragrant cup of herbal tea I'm holding and there I am again, smack in the middle of our kibbutz living room.

By the time I get home after this three-hour event, my boots are filled with snow. I'm tempted to just crawl into bed and hand over my troubles to God and sleep, but I know that in the end, sleep won't take care of my feelings of longing. Just because I've managed to hold in those feelings so far today doesn't mean I can't break.

I hop onto Facebook and immediately I'm overtaken by a battalion of holiday family selfies that trigger, once again, my desire to be known and loved, seen and valued, connected, and made to feel like I belong. How easy it is for social media to make me a jealous observer of someone else's life—wishing, hoping, yearning for what we don't yet have in the States: a sense of a real, profound connection with our community.

For the Israeli expat in me, submerged in a vast sea of lost connections that can't be distilled and now exist only in memories, one way to connect is through a heightened spiritual awareness. At synagogue or during spiritually heightened days of the Jewish calendar like Rosh Hashana and Yom Kippur, longing is discussed as the desire of the *neshama*, or soul, to connect with its beloved. I've always experienced Jewish holidays as holy moments, rarefied phases that have helped me to achieve levels of connectedness. But these moments are extremely short-lived. The minute the holiday ends and the prayer crowd dissipates, it feels like a spiritual letdown, and I'm back in that cycle of longing.

This is why I turn from the computer and spill out the details to Haim of what that gathering tonight felt like, seeking comfort for my grief. I tell him about the Israeli woman I met, a stay-at-home mom who's in Pittsburgh only until June. Before Haim can ask whether we've made plans to meet again, my heart cracks open like a festering wound. Unlike other times, when I've asked whether we can return to Israel, this time I blurt, "This country has become too hard. It's hard to be in the *golah*. I miss Israel too much."

To come to terms with where I am right now means learning to accept responsibility for the choices I've made. That includes dealing with the voices of my in-laws, who, on our last visit to Israel—earlier this year—nudged me several times to get Haim to reconsider the possibility of returning to Israel. "Work on Haim," they whispered fiercely, nudging me in the arm. "Get him to come back."

If only, if only.

"You know there's no job waiting for me in Israel, Dorit," he says once again.

Leaving Israel for good in the name of *parnassa*, making a living, is justified. This is what one of our neighbors told me one day before we left. If only she and the rest of the kibbutz understood the ambivalence I felt then and continue to feel now, years later, about leaving.

Snow pelts our living room windows.

"We've got bills to pay," Haim reminds me. "We're not dreamers in our twenties. We can't afford to take the risk."

What is riskier, though? To listen to these feelings of longing or go through another winter in Pittsburgh, where feelings of longing get tested? Another winter in Pittsburgh means staring at that unfulfilled longing in the face and wrestling with my hopes and fears about staying in America for the long term.

My way of wrestling with the grief and loss is to take a step back and feel my way through the concept of divine providence—or in Hebrew, *Hashgacha Pratit*, meaning that God is orchestrating every detail of creation—for the sake of positive thinking. Could it be, perhaps, that we are meant to deepen our relationships to ourselves in Pittsburgh—something we couldn't do so easily in Israel? Is it my calling to emotionally guide those adult ESL learners? Is it Haim's to give his customers a feeling of respect and care as a cheesemonger?

Every day gives me the opportunity to embrace a choice: I can either feel my way to hope or give in to feelings of uncertainty and despair. For this, I look to Haim, who, though he has lived here for so short a time, knows how to reach people's hearts with his words. Since we came to America for him, I comfort myself with the fact that he is valued at work, despite my own seasonal cycles of longing and grief.

At what point does love for one's country become so powerful that nothing else matters? Even the price of returning? There are days when I wonder if there's any room left to dream or fantasize about returning to what still feels like our "heart home." Apparently, love for my country of choice is not enough to return.

From our living room window I see still-life images of a winter wonderland. I press my face sideways, hard against the glass and I catch a slice of myself biking back to my full-time teaching job at the regional high school alongside the Jordan River. The well-known stanza of Rachel Bluwstein's poem rings in my head:

Oh my Kinneret.
Did you exist?
Or did I dream a dream?

In the months since I attended that first women's meeting, the snow has piled so high on the back entranceway that it has created huge slides whose iridescent specks flicker in the sun. Ivry shouts with glee as he plays on them. It will take a few hours for a worker to shovel it all.

On the front entranceway, I make pathways in the snow with my boots, possessed of a newfound determination not to stay content with this boxed-in feeling any longer. There are more school delays and cancellations than I can count. Locals say this is the most brutal winter they've experienced in years, maybe ever.

Images I find online of the River Jordan keep me emotionally afloat. The water looks like diamonds flickering in the sun—like sequins on a broad slip of black velvet. I imagine myself there and it evokes feelings of freedom—the freedom to take *tiulim*, or hikes, where people are themselves, where together as a culture there's an exhilaration collectively experienced around the coming of spring. It's a time when families go out and find a shady spot for picnics, and I recall with fondness the *pomelos*, which I loved once I finally learned how to pull apart their coarse yellow exterior. I loved the luxuriousness of those afternoons, spending time with family members, speaking in Hebrew, and staying sometimes until the sun set. For me, this was a true feeling of being connected, of *bichayad*. But as long as my family stays in the States, I can only visit these memories in my mind.

When I look at the tapestry of my Israel memories through the lens of Carol S. Dweck's book *Mindset*, I see years of effort, persistence, and learning—all in the name of what Dweck refers to as the mindset of growth. In the name of growth, I look forward to the five-day writing retreat I'll be attending in March, the culmination of an author masterheart program that started in September of last year. Freeing myself from my to-do list and the relentless pressure of the "undone," freeing myself to focus on my heart's desire, and going to meet these forty authors from around the world with whom I got published in the anthology *Pebbles in the Pond: Transforming the World One Person at a Time*, requires a mindset of courage and clarity. So does persistently putting my ego aside and feeling comfortable with the deeper place of creativity where truest writing comes from. To be truly successful, I need to see my creative process not limited by my own intelligence, talents, and abilities, or controlled by my own ego. Trust in the creative process is essential for speaking my truth, my story.

March is around the corner, and I'm excited, practically crawling out of my skin, to get away. My soul deeply craves creative nourishment. Best-selling author Mel Robbins once famously said, "The key to getting yourself unstuck is to start saying yes to those unexpected impulses that want to take you somewhere new."

Somewhere new.

Being drawn to my inner artist and creative self was not entirely new for me; my drive to be creative has always been present. But I'll have to relearn how to trust the voice that wants to be in the spotlight.

In past years, I'd explored smaller-scale creative opportunities, but they never led to much. In 2001, I wanted to experience the sensation of publishing my truth in the form of poems without my Ego getting in my way, but I was on ungrounded, uncharted territory. I was also crippled at times by the voice of the inner critic who would constantly admonish me against pursuing creative endeavors. Luckily, I picked up Pat Schneider's *Writing Alone and with Others* during that time, and it inspired me to initiate my own "mini-sabbatical." I retreated to a dusty room in the archives on our kibbutz and immersed myself in a creative world, surrounded by books, writing and exploring what I had always thought of as a "hobby" in silence, without the support of others.

Within the pages of Pat's book, I'd discovered a friend. One day, I picked up a pen and wrote a letter to Pat disclosing my fears and insecurities and mailed it. When I found a letter of response waiting for me one day in my mailbox, I jumped with glee. A spark of connection from afar, almost like that from another world, had leaped out to touch me. Although I had a tribe among my fellow teachers, with this letter I was connecting to something more profound to my identity: my creative self. I was connecting with the tribe I'd been longing to find.

In his book *Tribes: We Need You to Lead Us*, Seth Godin writes, "A tribe is a group of people connected to one another, connected to a leader, and connected to an idea. For millions of years, human beings have been part of one tribe or another. A group needs only two things to be a tribe: a shared interest and a way to communicate." So much of what Godin points out relates to the tribe mentality in Israel. I'd experienced this firsthand after my move there, and yet my longing for a tribe of my own still felt unsatisfied. I now realized that this longing was connected to my longing for my mother—the mother I'd always wanted but who could never be there for me in the way I needed.

But in that dark and dank room, I discovered that there was another tribe that belonged to me: the tribe of creative people and of writers. After weeks of peeling away the layers I'd piled onto myself over time, I finally got in touch with the voice of twenty-two-year-old, insecure me, the girl who had listened to my mother say for years, "Don't go into the arts. Be a teacher so you can fall back on something."

My inner artist had been starved for years. Writing poems helped me cope. I wrote in my journal and started writing personal essays, too. I sat for hours, pen in hand, determined to break through all the "committees" that Pat Schneider says are made up of "parents, teachers, friends, acquaintances—all of whom have ideas about my writing." I was determined to find a connection.

Now it's 2012, and knowing that Christine, the creator of *Pebbles in the Pond* and the woman who will be leading our retreat, is holding space for me as a writer in her anthology, makes it possible for me to see myself, finally, as a creative artist in my own right. "You never know where your ripple will take you," Christine has said in various meditations and workshops.

I feel the urge to set my history aside and start fresh. In my new writing community, my story and journey matter. This circle represents growth and transformation. Do I dare to hold out after years of holding back?

The test of discovering my tribe begins now.

～⚡～

On this unusually warm day in late March, in a rural area of Maryland, at a retreat center known as Pearlstone, my feelings of longing finally start to subside.

The weather helps, as I'm finally free to be outside without feeling like I will freeze to death. This morning, I find myself walking alongside an Australian author named Nadine, chatting with her about her farm and business back home.

I am reeling after months of hibernating, as if I've just emerged from a deep sleep that has left me feeling unsettled. Shards of early-morning light flicker through the trees; shadows of nightfall lift and birds chirp in recognition of morning. I grabbed my camera before we left on the walk, and now I eagerly snap images in these unknown woods. I'm fulfilling a longing that's been with me all winter. Time to savor every moment.

I'm thrilled to be at this retreat. Already I have been producing so much more creative material than I ever do at home. And being here, I really do sense I'm among the tribe I've been pining for. At times the pull to find this has been as strong as my desire to go back to Israel.

In Israel, my goal was to acculturate to the Israel society, but once I was here in America, where it looks like we'll be staying for good, I realized that I could find my tribe in a place without borders; the Internet. It's possible to find a tribe online and then to convene with people for an occasional retreat. In just two days, I've connected with this group of transformational authors from around the world. Over the next few days, I'll be participating in a number of healing workshops with them. I can't know it yet, but these moments will encourage me to "act" my personal story. For now I'm just excited by the in-person connection, after having only connected with many of these authors online.

Coming from New York City, where writers are part of the literary landscape, I've felt something lacking in Pittsburgh. I don't know if there is a writing community, and if there is, I don't know how to find it. I've been so focused on emotionally surviving, that writing, and survival have never seemed to me as if they could go hand in hand.

This early morning I am feeling particularly hopeful. Nadine, who has some Jewish blood, surprises me when she tells me she learned Hebrew from private instruction and trips to Israel. I wonder where our conversation will lead us. We amble along a tree-lined path in this rustic countryside and the words of Henry David Thoreau's *Walden* come to mind: "We need the tonic of wildness . . . At the same time that we are earnest to explore and learn all things, we require that all things be mysterious and unexplorable, that land and sea be indefinitely wild, unsurveyed and unfathomed by us because unfathomable. We can never have enough of nature."

Thoreau was right. Connecting with nature is a process of discovery. I am learning to be willing to let go of what I think and relearn how to stay connected to an idea or a place. Being willing to let go of collective wisdom. Could this be what an enlightened life looks life? Almost instantly, these unknown brooks, rambles, and woodsy paths remind me of the times when I ventured to the far end of the Jordan River to find a new world of nature waiting for me. In Israel—then a new and different country—my words got lost. I was so busy taking in the experiences, I didn't always remember to put into words what I was processing. Now I have the space to do that.

On either side are log cabins, fields of grazing horses and cows, and meadows that take my breath away. Each time the woods open up into a clearing or a brook, we stop to take in the beauty. Nadine and I share Hebrew words we know for the various things we see along the way. She tells me she lives on a farm back home, and I imagine sprawling acres of countryside, feeling jealous and small when I think of my own urban home.

There are trees and wildflowers and people emerging onto their porches with cups of coffee and greetings of "Good morning!" coming from other hikers on the trail. I'm finally getting closer to experiencing the dream that's been gnawing at me all these months: A creative retreat in nature. A chance to rediscover myself.

Around eight thirty, we make our way back to the retreat grounds. I share with my new friend the heaviness that's been weighing on my heart, including the predicament of readjusting to life in America after living so long in Israel. She offers to talk with me in Hebrew if that will help me settle in. I feel lighter.

As the early-morning sunlight breaks through a canopy of oak trees, revealing patches of dew, I find myself even more at peace. Nadine eloquently holds her end of the conversation, Hebrew rolling off her tongue like diamonds into my palm. For a moment my two worlds combine and instead of ricocheting against one another, they create a beautiful, unified whole.

Today is the third day of what Christine calls our "masterheart" circle at the transformational author retreat. "Let's anchor our heart energy," she says against the background of flowing Zen music. "The kind that gets anchored when you share your story, wisdom, or experience. Your story has the power to transform another person." She said these same words on each of the six monthly group coaching calls leading up to this point. Now it's time to reveal our stories, in-person to the group.

Part of me feels ready for this challenge; I am compelled to share pieces of my Israeli story, encouraged by the words of a writing instructor when we first arrived in Pittsburgh—"Only you have seen things that you can tell"—but frankly, I'm scared stiff. Words are still bottled somewhere in my throat. *What will people think of me when they hear my story? Will someone here judge me for having left my mom?* I'm forty-one years old now, but I still feel the weight of this choice as if I were nineteen—even though I know better, and even though so many years have passed.

The number of authors with whom I'm expected to share my personal story in this circle is overwhelming. Nadine smiles on the other side, but she's not even looking my way. I am grateful to have found her, but not even this new friendship can take away the tension and angst I feel. Theoretically, telling my IDF story will be noteworthy in this circle, but getting past the fear that doing so might alienate someone makes me hesitate.

I've always felt like an outsider—mainly due to my upbringing, I now know. Marrying a well-respected and beloved kibbutz member in 2002 gave me some leverage in the tribe I so desperately wanted to belong to, but now I realize that I can't join a tribe by proxy, and this new tribe I want to enter is all about me. Haim will not be my ticket in.

As I get ready to step into the circle, I take every hard-earned lesson I possess with me. Still, I'm feeling like the "other." No one else here is Jewish; no one has left their country of origin to live in another one for any extended period of time. No one has served in the military and is now struggling with reverse culture shock. Will they relate? Will I be able to connect?

I toy with the idea that as long as I'm open to this group being a support to me, they'll continue to be safe and nurturing.

Christine stands up and rings a bell. "Hey everyone, we'll get started in five minutes," she says.

A cool, gentle breeze blows in. Someone has just entered from the patio that overlooks acres of woods and pond. I get up, press the side of my cheek against a window, and look down at the wide expanse of nature outside, devoid of houses or peoples for miles. I tell myself I'll explore this side of this unexplored terrain later today, now that I feel more settled. My eyes fall on the wavy green hills and a pond in the background. Like a picture postcard, there's a harmony of height and depth—evergreens, rolling hills, and fields of green. Spring has sprung. It's tempting not to feel a sense of renewed hope and optimism in the face of all this beauty.

I lift my cheek from the window and watch how the fog from my breath slowly emanates and dissipates, just like the vulnerable memories that reverberate as I return to my seat in the circle. Perhaps that is why I've self-imposed feelings of otherness upon myself.

The only story I'm meant to share is the one I've walked. Do I have the courage to share my story? Do I believe my journey matters?

I'm still nervous as hell. But adrenaline kicks in, and at the last minute, I decide to perform my story spontaneously. I get up from my seat and approach the center stage, the inner circle. In this way, I separate myself from my inner critic and give myself the benefit of the doubt. Something tells me it will be a long time before I will have another opportunity to act out the story I've been holding back.

I think of Christine's four levels of transformation for authors writing books: our own personal transformation; our readers'; our business's; and, finally, the world's. I suspect that if I'm to impact my fellow authors in some meaningful way, I need to connect to the divine source from within. Armed with these encouraging and healing messages from Christine, I tentatively surmise that I'm on the right track and that it's worth taking the chance.

My body shakes with excitement and anticipatory anxiety. As Rabbi Schneur Zalman of Liadi famously stated, "A little bit of light dispels a lot of dark." Maybe what sets me apart is sharing my light, my story. I have no script; I tell myself I'm simply going into this as a well-intentioned storyteller. This switch in mindset is huge. I sense that I'm being called to step out of my comfort zone and that this moment will make the difference between me seeing myself as just a writer and seeing myself as an artist with a social drive.

I do a quick scan of the audience. The good-girl inner critic who followed me to Israel has constantly tried to keep me small, to keep my voice silent. Now it's time to champion my own story.

I take a deep breath. I feel as if I've just dived off the deep end or been thrown into the gladiator arena. But there are no gladiators here, waiting to stab me in the gut. Christine has reassured me, along with everyone else here, that we're in an emotionally safe and nurturing circle. Still, that gap between knowing and believing remains.

I begin to speak. In twenty minutes, I cross the territories of my life, spanning eighteen years of girlhood to adulthood. I share the story of my departure to Israel, my struggles with cultural adaptation, overcoming the bullying and language barriers, meeting Haim, and coming back to the States. The adrenaline rushes to my head and I can feel the excitement bubbling in my words. There's nothing that compares to this feeling. The room is silent, and all eyes are on me.

When I return to my seat, the energy in the room has shifted. I thought I would be laughed at or that people might make snide remarks or expressions; I anticipated alienation. But of course, that never happens. The author sitting next to me says, "Wow, Dorit, that was amazing," and throughout the day I will hear other words of support from my fellow masterhearters:

"You're a vaudeville act."

"You're a storyteller."

"You owned that moment."

"Your laugh is something. Infectious."

I struggle to see what my masterhearters do, but something has opened in me, and I'm beginning to understand that before you can transform others, you need the courage to transform yourself. The question is . . . do I have that courage?

In her book *All About Love*, American author, feminist, and social activist bell hooks says, "When we choose to love, we choose to move against fear, against alienation and separation. The choice to love is a choice to connect, to find ourselves in the other." Christine has taught me that holding the space for everyone's story to be heard is what nurtures and motivates me to tell my story. Taking ownership of your story is not the same as believing in your story. Today I took one step closer to believing.

Could it be I'm on my way?

12

CASTAWAY

As Marcus Tullius Cicero told us, the life of the dead is placed in the memory of the living.

It's a sticky, early morning in July 2012. I lean out the window as far out as possible, surprised by how much of the Hudson River is visible from Mom's rent-controlled apartment—she pays a mere seven hundred dollars a month—in Greenwich Village. Now that the Superior Ink factory, a cornerstone of the neighborhood I knew as a child, has been demolished, the urban landscape has been completely transformed. I hop on Google to look for an image of the factory, but all I find are photos of the Superior Ink condominiums—the newly built, million-dollar townhouses that took the factory's place. The factory is nowhere to be found.

Mom is here, but not here. Her forty-two-year-old apartment is sandwiched by commercial change I refer to as "celebrityville."

Yvette, her determined and faithful caregiver, bellows a warmhearted greeting as she enters through the front door each morning. She asks Mom if she loves living in the city, and does she like

Yvette's homemade porridge?

"Carmelita," she says. "This is something I whipped up from Haiti."

Mom makes a faint attempt to smile, which encourages me that Alzheimer's hasn't completely taken over. Yvette is getting through to her, and I know their ten-year connection is largely responsible. I consider the two of them—Yvette from Haiti and my Spanish-speaking mom, born in Valencia, Spain, who escaped the Nazis in her youth. Mom has always been the type of person to deliberately avoid people in the building by taking the stairs and to wear shades and a baseball cap. Yvette is her opposite.

Mom has told me more than once that *Good Morning America* is too blasé for her tastes. Now, *Good Morning America* blasts through the apartment as she eats her breakfast.

"What do you think, Carmen? Should we go for a walk today?" Yvette asks in a sing-song sort of way that distracts from the sad reality of Mom's decline. She jokes how Mom repeatedly dodged her offer to join her yesterday for omelets and croissants at a café in a popular area of the Village—a spot that, Yvette assures her, is "a quiet and relaxing" place to be.

From my far corner of the room I see that Mom's eyes have sunk deeper into the folds of her face and softened completely. I'm grateful to see that she's well taken care of; it's such a relief, especially considering how difficult it has been to procure twenty-four-hour care for her through the city's agencies.

The decision to stay with Mom at the last minute to teach an intensive summer course for ESL students at New York University was a loaded one. This is a city that has always left me feeling more isolated than nurtured. And while Mom's disease has made it so that she doesn't hold hostilities anymore, I resent having to care for a woman who neglected to care for me emotionally when I was a child. Thankfully, being out of the country for more than seventeen years has matured and changed me. Taking care of Mom has been emotionally taxing, but not as overwhelming as I would have found it twenty years earlier.

Mom sits as still as can be, face composed, looking up at the wavy ceiling, not blinking or indicating that she's registering any sights or sounds. Yvette plants the homemade porridge on the sliding table, and Mom barely moves.

Since I've been back from Israel, Mom has physically deteriorated from being ambulatory—still able to walk alongside the Hudson River on her own—to needing to be strapped into a three-point harness in order to give her a bath. Each morning, Yvette pulls at the levers of that harness to get Mom's blood flow pumping and flowing.

Part of me wishes I could have Mom back. That all these contraptions could just go away. Yet, how fortunate my brother and I are to have Yvette, a woman of grace and inner beauty who, for the last eleven years, has made a connection with my mother that allows me to feel less distraught about her decline.

Things I don't want to see: Mom having to be flipped like a pancake to change her diaper as she lays practically naked and unresponsive to the blasts of *Good Morning America*. I still remember how she'd shout to me from the bathroom, "Dorit, don't you dare open the door!" as a way to protect herself from the twelve-year-old intruder, fueled by curiosity, that was me. Things I don't want to feel: the way she sometimes enters a memory that takes her to a random point in my life, or our lives. Ultimately, I have to deal with her in the present with all my memories of her intact, which complicates my coping abilities.

Things I'm grateful for: how Yvette particularly is a buffer between me and the perils of my troubling relationship with Mom. How she has completely transformed this two-floor apartment duplex from what before was an alienating space to one that is emotionally alive—one that more closely represents the way I parent today than it does my teenage angst.

As a teenager, I'd seclude myself in my loft that overlooked the inner courtyard of this massive artist complex, distancing myself from Mom's piano playing. All three of the lofts in this apartment were beautifully handcrafted by my father and his team of workers. Mine and my brother's occupied the far corners of the upstairs duplex, while my parents' loft, with its beautifully finished wood columns, was the only one raised above the couch in the living room and the stairwell. In the years since, a former roommate tore down my beloved loft, and my room has become Yvette's. The only two lofts remaining are Mom's and my brother's. Since these have always been the unique centerpieces of the home, it's unthinkable that the apartment could ever be devoid of them.

On my childhood couch, now reupholstered under that same loft my parents once claimed as their own, Ivry is transfixed by *Sid the Science Kid* (thankfully, he's inherited my love for the programs on PBS). We're lucky: Ivry got chosen by lottery to go to a cheap New York City camp for the summer, which has made this whole trip doable.

Memories I'm grateful for: Mom's breathtaking piano playing. (Later, after Mom's death, a neighbor will recount standing in the hallway and feeling as if she was witnessing a live performance at Carnegie Hall.) Even though her Steinway grand was sold long ago, her sheet music is still piled up in bunches and dangles out at visible corners of what was once her study and is now her bedroom—a reminder of how music was always her "main dish" and I, along with my younger brother, was a "side dish." To escape this reality, I'd entertain myself with the things Mom acquired over the years— garbage bags full of colorful baggy clothes from the flea market, misshapen pumps, ten-foot-high closet doors that served as a partition from her piano space and my world of make-believe. In an age when women were expected to be housewives, Mom advocated for the mastery of her creative self, a radical notion in her time. For her, otherhood and creativity were deeply intertwined. As a mother now myself, I understand the constant angst she experienced.

Contrary to my upbringing, Yvette teaches me by example that when you focus on the other, you avoid feeling like "the other," which has helped me come full-circle with my relationship to my dying Mom. I am not "seen" today because Mom literally can't see well, and now, because of our role reversal, I'm inclined more to be focused on "the other."

Things I tell Yvette: stories from my childhood, the things that once were. Tales of our carefree life at Westbeth. For this "new" American citizen from Haiti, I divulge all the stories and personal details I can about this deteriorated woman—stories that help us both get through the bad days, and sometimes even from hour to hour. Forging a bond with Yvette gives me the distance I need to escape this battleground that I've lived in my head. But ultimately, I'm opening new pathways toward my heart.

On days when I'm devoid of stories, I find myself struggling to find comfort from the wavy ceilings (built as sound barriers) from my position on my brother's loft bed. I'm stuck in a familiar world demarcated by unfamiliar emotional territory. The paint chipping from the loft windows, the single wooden block cube in the corner I bought at a garage sale for five bucks that still houses the same 1993 Yellow Pages, and the yellow plastic container containing live 1989 cassette performances of Suzanne Vega in Israel—those are all known to me. But downstairs, Mom's teeth are rotting, she pees and poops in a diaper, and her memory has long been gone. At some point, I tell myself that Mom's brain has decayed so much that I am nothing to her, just a voice she hears. But then I realize that if I choose to seclude myself in my own sadness, I will have missed out on an opportunity for an hour or two of real connection. I have no choice but to come to terms with the fact that our relationship is reversed—I'm now the mother and her caregiver—but that doesn't mean our relationship is over.

Our worlds are separated by a single flight of twenty-four uncarpeted stairs she can no longer ascend. Ivry, Yvette, and I occupy the upstairs while Mom is relegated to downstairs; she is the lone representative of an old, frail generation emotionally disconnected from the energetic, youthful, and inquisitive one upstairs. I speak to Ivry in hushed tones, careful to tell him about his Grandma Carmen in a way that honors her dignity. She is not a victim of circumstances. She is not the other,," but a representation of our family mosaic. He will not recollect how Grandma ran her muscular fingers through his red hair while murmuring his name.

My forlorn childhood home, a ghost town. Yvette and other members of "Team Carmen" keep Mom alive. Without them, I would likely slide back into old patterns and behaviors of alienating and isolating myself, triggered by Mom's illness. She says, "The cops are coming," in the almost hypervigilant yet fragile tone I remember from childhood, and once again, I'm a teenager.

I consider how her care is unprecedented by New York State standards, and I temporarily forget those triggers. Mom's small network of Westbeth friends has done more than could ever be expected. Mom's previous caregiver, Solange, also exceeded expectations. The United States government has been generous in providing funds to enable Mom to live at home and receive medical care and other financial support that's not available in Pennsylvania and many other states, and may not be sustainable in the future, as Westbeth's geriatric and New York's larger elderly population continues to age. The social workers at Westbeth and The Caring Community are not masters of the system, but they've provided emotional support that has given us much-needed peace of mind. Even the bureaucrats have given personal service. My accountant, who manages Mom's finances, personally knows Domingo Soto, the person who has the power to either approve or maintain Mom's caregiving hours.

In Mom's healthier years, she kept to herself, averted her eyes from others, and immersed herself in her piano playing. There were fights that filled me with angst, and the more frustrated I felt by the lack of love I felt from her, the more I'd take to the streets, feeling even more prominently the gaps between emotional security and safety, trying to find another way to feel nurtured.

Yvette sticks another tape of Andrea Bocelli into the VCR, which buys Mom another few minutes of peace as she settles into her pillow. She is having a good day.

On my way to teach an intensive multicultural literature elective with just six ESL students on the first day of this summer, everything is strangely calm. I walk to catch the Number 1 subway downtown to the Woolworth building on Barclay Street, near City Hall. The sun is shining. Soon enough, wisps of paper fly in the early morning breeze. A procession of cabs appear in the early morning rush. I am swimming back in time.

When I surface, it's thirty years later, and I discover there is a raging tsunami whipping me around with wind and waves. At first I am not sure how long I'll have to take cover, and then I realize that I'm not meant to take cover. Grieving over a loss—whether it's for a relationship, job, or home—anchors us in deep longing for what no longer is, and I have come to realize the loss might be an opportunity for me to get in touch with my courage and view my longings differently. The act of letting go opens a possibility to develop deeper connections within ourselves and with others.

Relationships crumble and disintegrate. We try to make sense of the past through the memories as an attempt to come to terms with their painful existence. And then, one day, we realize we don't want to live that kind of life anymore.

When I came back to the States, I was full of hope that I'd find deeper connections in my mother country, but that hasn't happened yet. I imagine I will never stop grieving the realization that my long-held wish for a closer relationship with Mom will never come to pass. I am not sure that her Alzheimer's has changed much in our relationship dynamic; it's more that the disease has forced me to confront the fact that my ideal was an unattainable illusion.

By the time I reach the Woolworth building, which stands not far from the office on Fulton Street that once employed me as a foot messenger back in 1989, I am sweaty and consumed by the urbanity and rough edge New York City is known for. I find myself slipping back into the New York state of mind of pushiness and arrogance, which reminds me so much of Israel. I forge my way through crowds during the rush hour, dodge closing subway doors, and race across platforms.

Once in the classroom, I stare at the roster over and over again wondering if the sixth and last student is Israeli; all the others are Chinese and Latino. I can't believe the name I'm reading: Liron. Most peculiar. I have a strong sense of déjà vu, a feeling that I've met him somewhere before in Israel. I try time-stamping his sea-green eyes and manly face, and I locate hints of boyishness that tells me he's post–Israel Defense Force. I consider what the chances are that I would run into one of my fellow IDF soldiers here. I am tickled.

I wonder how this Israeli student will respond to multicultural voices of the texts we'll read together, and to our conversations about the impact of language on identity formation and self-esteem. I wonder what he'll think about Sandra Cisneros and Jhumpa Lahiri. I am swept up by past and present voices and remember how teaching Israelis was always a struggle for me in the past. My experience with my students was often difficult. But I wonder if I've been given a fresh start here. In this case, we are both fish out of water, searching for our way home.

When the feeling of home starts settling in this colossal city, the barrier between time and space melts away for me. This is what I had originally feared the most—that my mind would be abducted by angry and sad memories from childhood and I wouldn't be able to see past them to create meaningful connections, particularly with my students, who still feel like outsiders, just like me. But I'm relieved to have discovered that I no longer feel an immense need to escape Mom—the pain of her disease—and "attack" the streets of the city, like I've done on previous visits.

After class each day, I pick Ivry up from camp and bring him to the park. It is so easy for him to make friends with other kids. I, by contrast, stayed put in my childhood playground, watching how nannies from various countries would congregate and speak their mother tongues while watching over the neighborhood children— many of them kids of celebrities.

A voice tells me to stay engaged with my son. Here, in my old stomping grounds, Abingdon Square Park, the past and the present fuse under the half-moon monkey bars. I'm in two times at once. Being at the center of the universe, like a child, means I, too, could still be in the here and now, regardless of what I lost. This ever-changing city has a push-pull relationship between the past and the present that deeply affects me. Who knows how much time Mom has left to live? For now, her stable care situation has allowed her to thrive at home, but her disease lashes and whips. I fear that my home will be swept right out from under my feet.

Ivry whizzes by me on a tricycle. His sweaty red face and blowing red hair are the epitome of living for the moment against the throb of this pulsating city. His desire to be free comes so naturally. I wonder if I can capture this by being home this summer, or if I'll be pulled under by the weight of what's happening to my mother.

I cannot afford to get too comfortable. In a few moments, Ivry and I will go back to Mom's duplex, where I'll be forced, as I have been all summer, to be with my memories—the good and the bad. And despite all my mixed feelings, I am deeply afraid of letting go of Mom and her apartment—the last string connecting me to my memories and longing. I am afraid that one day, like an umbilical cord, it'll be cut forever, and I'll be lost completely in the dark, unable to find my way home.

There's never enough you can do to prepare for losing a parent, but I am finding that being home this summer is a gift. It's offering me the opportunity to integrate the girl I was with the woman I now am. I am recognizing that the home I knew is a symbol. It's an anchor; it allows me to stay attached to my past. And this is comforting to me; since it's an idea, perhaps it's something I can learn to carry inside of me. The key lies in this expansive awareness.

Halfway into the six-week intensive course at the American Language Institute, I ask Liron to tell me where in Israel he's from and he writes his address on a piece of paper and gives it to me. On the first day of class, as the students file out, I spoke Hebrew to him and he shared that he'd finished his military service just a few months earlier, as I'd suspected.

Since then, it's been as if the walls of this windowless classroom have broken down and it's just us two. As he presses hard on the pen and looks up at me, I try quantifying his Israeli features: his sea-green eyes and cream-colored hair could be anyone's. When I expect him to be vociferous, he takes his time. He stops to ask, "Did I say that right?" or, "Does that make sense?" The focus is never on me and my background but on our communication—verbal and non-verbal. He comes across as both laid-back and reserved, making it possible for me to speak more freely with him, without getting bombarded by memories of being attacked with questions when I was a soldier in the Israel Defense Forces. My Israeli peers couldn't understand why a New Yorker would volunteer for the IDF, as they all were secretly clamoring to leave the country and get out of their obligatory military service. They didn't feel the love for their home country in the way I did, perhaps, as an outsider.

After I try to prompt him in conversation, Liron says, "I'm not so sure I'm going to study for my undergraduate degree in New York City." Every syllable is clearly enunciated. I sense a great deal of earnestness, and I wonder if he feels a pull, as many Israelis do, to stay in the United States for the pursuit of an American dream, or if he misses home way too much to even consider staying.

The paper upon which he has just written his address in his foreign-looking penmanship says "Savion," but I know he means Savyon, one of the wealthiest municipalities in the central section of Israel.

"How long do you plan on staying in New York?" I ask him.

"For a while," he says, his voice trailing off.

I see that I'm seeking validation from this connection that I know this place where he lives, that I am connected to this Homeland we both share, that I am seen for my experiences. I wonder whether he, too, struggles with his longings for home in this vast city. Does he feel displaced, as I do?

In the Diaspora, I've discovered how displacement makes me more vulnerable but also gives me the freedom to be more experimental with my habits and long-held views. There is something very uplifting about this idea of freedom. As Jhumpa Lahiri, one of the writers I'm relying on most heavily this summer, so eloquently writes, "In the way that so many writers have found freedom: by stepping away from the place, the people, the language, the culture that they knew, in search of something different, of their own making. Without the weight, and yet, you carry sort of the best of it with you."

〜☀〜

Instead of taking the subway the next morning, I walk the forty minutes alongside the West Side highway to work. A blue sky hangs above. Just a few ships and barges make their way lazily down the industrial Hudson River. Pedestrians congregate in walkways and jog along pathways.

This was the free, madly joyful river of my youth that gave me distance and clarity during turbulent months when Mom and I didn't see eye to eye about my leaving for Israel. Just a few weeks before that one-way ticket from the Jewish agency, I came here and contemplated the possibility of reinventing myself as an Israel Defense Forces soldier and cried when I realized, finally, that Mom could never give me what I needed.

Time will tell if I have what it takes to reinvent myself now in a way that will create long-lasting relationships without being addicted to my own emotional suffering. Urban and human land-scapes collapse into one and everything is always on the go in this city. I catch my thoughts: *She's not invincible.* My brother and I both know our mother won't outlive her Alzheimer's, but somehow I've secretly been harboring the idea that I have the power to bring her back to life. Each time I climb into her hospital bed, she gives me the impression she's listening to me, and in those short-lived moments, I sense she is still my mom.

I stop long enough to watch a boat floating lazily along the outskirts of the bay, festooned by the glittering diamonds of the midday sun. I walk even farther—toward Ground Zero, the site of the soon-to-be erected Freedom Towers—until Westbeth becomes just a haze of a building behind me. George Elliot says, "It's never too late to be who you might have been," and I will add that if we become more accustomed to leaning into the soundtracks of our memories, even if they don't seem to offer much happiness, we can use them to reinvent ourselves. I want to figure out how to nurture a more meaningful relationship with myself in a city that has always been the subject of distance between myself and Mom. That starts here. Literally at Ground Zero.

I am crying by the time I get to campus. Never in my life have I witnessed either of my parents breaking down, but in my youth, my mother sometimes became so consumed by feelings—mainly when she played the piano—that she was willing to give up everything to be in that spotlight of a moment.

Freedom.

If we can't be truly free, who are we?

Three weeks before the end of the six-week intensive course, Liron stops showing up. He's missing in action and no one knows his whereabouts. It's like a piece of me is gone from the classroom. A piece of home.

I plop down sheets with Lahiri's essay "My Two Lives" on my students' desks, feeling like a castaway. In the essay, Lahiri talks about how she was embarrassed by her Indian roots as a child. To cope with this pressure, she hid her family's customs from her American friends, afraid to let them know she was different from them. "I felt intense pressure to be two things," she writes, "loyal to the old world and fluent in the new."

I pop the question: "Can you recall a time in your life when you felt immense pressure to be two things—a student learning English and sticking with your own nationality?"

One student thoughtfully brings up the example of choosing to speak Chinese over English. "When and how is the right time in such a big city?" he asks. "And with whom?"

I know what he's talking about—the immense pressure of trying to straddle two different worlds and stay loyal to yourself.

He continues, "You use Chinese with friends. Informally. You use English with the others. You use more formal speech with instructors and professors."

I see the hesitation on his face. He's wondering if he said the right thing.

"Yes," I say. "This is exactly the kind of example of pressure Lahiri shows us. You are exactly right. It's hard to feel a connection to one thing when you are feeling such pressure to be in two places."

We all want to feel a deeper connection with the outside world.

13

TAKING THE GOOD

Mom died today—April 30, 2013. Yvette has just called to let me know.

When I tell Haim, who has just finished twelve months of mourning and saying kaddish for his own mother, he grasps my shoulders and whispers in my ear, "Be strong."

Over Yvette's voice, I can hear the garbage truck screeching as it unloads dumpsters in the early-morning hour. She tells me Mom died peacefully in her sleep, but her voice doesn't stay level for long. In a barrage of tears, she recounts how she turned Mom from side to side in vain before finally realizing that she was no longer with us. I hear the pain and fear in her voice as she recounts how she pleaded, "Carmelia, wake up. Carmelia, wake up!" Like me, she'd come to believe that Mom might be invincible.

Yvette hands the phone to a kind neighbor I haven't spoken to in years and the next thing I know, I'm replaying moments I thought I'd long forgotten—moments before Alzheimer's took the mother I once knew, before the responsibility of caregiving became all-consuming. A memory surfaces of me hanging out with one of this woman's sons at their duplex apartment, biking with him and a bunch of other friends along the Hudson.

Instantly, I'm back at Westbeth, surrounded by neighbors Mom tried hard to avoid because she never wanted to engage, and I feel I've activated an unwitting memory quest. Who was my mother? A woman of contrasts. A woman who showed determination and fury in the face of chaos. A woman whose family escaped the atrocities of the Holocaust but who lived in the shadow of fear forever afterward. A woman whose father collapsed in a New York City subway from a heart attack when she was a teenager, leaving her to seek out her own support system. A woman who assisted her Polish mother with a dry goods store in the Bronx when they first came to America. A woman who, despite all the obstacles, pushed through with her music, her career, with perseverance.

I often tried to understand what prompted Mom to seek people out only when she needed them, and why didn't she care more about preserving relationships and building community. Maybe she knew how difficult it was to sustain a relationship in a building riddled with suicides and self-obsessed artists trying to eke out a living. Maybe it was all in the name of emotional self-protection.

I haven't yet fully mastered how to forgive Mom her shortcomings. I spent my entire youth holding out for a real home-baked birthday cake or a genuinely warm hug, but her reality was one of trying, often unsuccessfully, to straddle the two worlds of motherhood and artistry. Still, she tried her best. She did buy birthday cakes and let us paint Easter eggs, even though doing so wasn't exactly Jewish. And always, when I returned home after eight long weeks away at summer camp, she'd flag me down at Grand Central Station, her hands waving wildly. These were some of the few times I didn't feel the piano had gotten the better of our relationship—times when, for a brief moment, I felt hopeful that maybe my dreams of becoming her beloved daughter had come true.

Now our time has run out. With Mom gone, my New York City home is no longer. But these few moments of talking with an old friend console me and open up a new reality—that Mom will live on in spirit, beyond the body that stole her mind so many years ago. I am already beginning to make my peace with this loss.

⁂

Five days have passed since Mom's death, and Haim, Ivry, and I are taking the eight-hour bus ride to New York City to bury her. I wonder if I'm showing yet. I'm five months pregnant with my second child. This action of welcoming new life just days after burying my own mom is turning the concept of home on its axis.

After my brother arrives in New York City from the West Coast, I stand tearless at Mom's fresh grave in Staten Island, New York, buffeted by the early warm May air. Her body has just been removed from the coffin, and like the Jewish tradition dictates, it's now being returned to the earth.

From behind me, across a stone white fence, a jackhammer rips through the silence. Prayers for the deceased are uttered in Hebrew at this Jewish Orthodox cemetery. Mom's voice cuts through the sad notes: *Honey bunny.* The few notes of a maternal connection. I was once her cherished little girl.

During the eulogy, my cousin, an Orthodox rabbi, compares Mom's life to a symphony. He describes her early days touring the world for the love of classical piano; the challenges of combining motherhood with a career; and, finally, the descent into the unknown disease that would slowly take her away.

Please stay, I plead silently. *Protect me from what I don't want to see.*

"But no one can truly speak about Carmen like her children," my cousin concludes, and he looks intently at me and my brother.

I step forward. Particles of light hover in the air as I tell anecdotes of how she chose to live a passionate life through music. Speaking of her, my enthusiasm rises like the bubbly notes of her mazurkas and concertos. I know I am sharing from the heart, and yet I'm surprised when the crowd starts crying.

Mom's family wasn't keen on her reclusive behavior, but we all learned to accept it. This is a forgiving moment. In recent years, her disease has been a barrier to this, but now pain and suffering have taken a backseat and we are here to celebrate the entirety of her life.

I speak of Mom in the present tense and allow the effects of that to wash over me like a wave. I nose-dive toward my memories of her—my last attempt to solidify our connection.

In the backdrop, the shadows of death linger. But I remember who she was before, how her fingers flew across the piano keys and brought the works of Piazolla, Chopin, and Beethoven to life to the beat of the metronome. After her Alzheimer's took over, Yvette sometimes played more contemporary versions of these greats from an album and Mom, in her reclined hospital bed, would fix her gaze on the ceiling with an open mouth, as if the notes were rising like colorful balloons. Once, I saw her stretch out her hands in an attempt to play.

Dirt mounds over her now. I lost the fight. We lost the fight. But at least I have this little girl growing inside me now. She keeps me grounded when memories threaten to pull me away from this world.

The day after we bury Mom, I sit with my sister-in-law's family in the East Village, waiting for the right moment to get into Mom's apartment. I'm not quite ready to go back there yet. There is the emptiness of it, yes, the heart-wrenching sadness that Mom won't be there when I walk through the door. But there is more to it than that.

Best-selling author Neale Donald Walsh says that "life begins at the end of your comfort zone." I'm slowly realizing that true letting go redefines boundaries—physical, emotional and spiritual. And in this case, my comfort zone begins with letting go of a home within a home.

⁜

I wait another three days before venturing to Mom's. I need to get distance from the memories, though I don't want to feel like a stranger to them, either. To buy myself time, I take Ivry, now nine years old and an avid chess player, for short walks to various parks. He runs from slide to swing like a free spirit, madly joyful, before turning serious and playing chess against strangers at various parks around the city.

At some point, I slow down enough to accept what I've been avoiding: the fear that I no longer have a New York City home. Gradually, I lower the volume of the fears I inherited from Mom about the unknown. I determine that I will do my best not to pass these fears on to my daughter. I look at Ivry, note how he is so much happier than I was as a child.

I can take the good of what my mother gave me and let the rest go.

⁜

Finally, on our last day, all of us—my brother, his wife, Haim, Ivry, and I—go to Westbeth. The first thing I notice upon entering Mom's apartment is the sun cascading over her brown table, where her plastic pillboxes and breakfast bowl still sit. I flutter past the pills that seem to be waiting there for her to come to take them. *The pills that kept her going.*

Against the wall stands her unmade bed. Here's where Yvette tried in vain to wake her up. I replay our last conversations in my mind. The morning Yvette phoned with the terrible news. And all the times that led to that moment.

I'm here. Home. And I don't want to leave.

Upstairs, I go through her drawers one by one. I hold her clothes to my face, trying to smell her, long distance. *It's no use*, I think, entangling myself in a web of excuses. I say I am just cleaning things out, but I'm really trying to get Mom back.

Behind the façade of a caregiving bond is a stressed, lonely, overwhelmed, exhausted daughter. It requires hope, effort, and teamwork to emotionally support someone with Alzheimer's. Above all else, it is an act of immense sacrifice to be a caregiver to a mother who can no longer recognize you. But the new life I carry—my little girl—empowers me. I intuit that I can heal the mother-daughter line with my daughter. I can parent her without feeling the constrictions of the heart that separated my mother from me.

I also understand something about my mother after her death that I couldn't grasp while she was alive: She tried to overcome the world of patriarchy by letting go of the expectations of what it meant to be a mother. She never allowed herself to be defeated by the societal story. Her pride, happiness, ambivalence, and rage allowed her to write her own story by moving away from the expected maternal role so she could fulfill her artistic endeavors.

For years, my brother and I were the "side dishes" to the main course—her music—and that's hard to forget. But perhaps I can begin to forgive it.

We cross the border to Pennsylvania. Cows and green patches dot the landscape. I want to hold a memory, any memory, but Mom's New York City ghost has no place among these trailers, these nameless gas stations, this sprawling farmland. Slowly, I begin the process of letting her go, convincing myself of what I felt in New York City—that it's possible to reinvent the concept of home inside of me, that geography is irrelevant.

I'm still wearing the black garment, shirt cut across the neck area, I wore to Mom's burial.

"Erect her tombstone on the eleventh month to ensure her soul will climb up to the chambers of heaven," my cousin said when we parted ways at the graveyard.

I try to imagine Mom's soul climbing stairs like octaves and scales.

The company sends us a blueprint of her headstone. What I imagined would be a giant rock will actually be just a small slab with just enough room for her name and the inscription: "Beloved grandmother, mother, friend, musician."

Mom's tombstone will cement her in another state, but her presence floats everywhere. Her concert tapes and brochures, and the numerous letters she typed to solicit gigs around the world haunt me. In an attempt to bring her closer, I've listened to a few tapes and read through hundreds of letters. Having her belongings in my apartment still feels too surreal and trippy, as if I am floating in some kind of time capsule.

The thing I've resented my whole life—Mom's dedication to her art—is the very thing I've now come to respect. How she claimed the room of our New York City loft apartment that faced the inner courtyard as her study, tuning out the needs of the outside world. As a mother and artist, I have come to understand the concept of space over time. Growing up, our spaces were far apart.

Spaces. Hers versus mine.

My heart flutters. How is it possible to move on despite the pain?

And then, before I know it, my water breaks and I'm in the hospital. My daughter is coming.

~⟋⎮⟍~

"This is new territory," the doctor shouts in Hebrew in the birthing room in Pittsburgh. "This is exactly where you stopped with Ivry. You can do it!"

For months, he has pored over the hospital records written in Hebrew detailing Ivry's birth and the circumstances that led to an emergency C-section in 2004 at a hospital in Tzefat, Israel. We have discussed the labor and its complications in-depth each visit. With Ivry, I was drugged with a poorly timed epidural that robbed my body's ability to feel and push through the contractions, only to be wheeled downstairs to a frigid room where I was operated on by a pair of male doctors who only spoke Russian. They worked mechanically, unable to sense how frigid and cold my body had become.

Tonight, though, is different. After carefully monitoring the contractions from his home for hours, my trusted doctor is here in his scrubs, coaching me along.

On the last valiant push, our baby girl emerges, with a mound of brown hair and inquisitive black eyes that are open and ready to take on the world.

We call her *Ayala*, Hebrew for female deer, to remind us that her kick into this world is what we need to emotionally sustain us.

I gloat over her for hours, refusing to give in to the calling of sleep.

She's mine. All mine.

14

SURRENDER

Once my brother and I had emptied Mom's apartment for good just a few weeks following her death, there seemed to be no reason at all to go to New York City unless I wanted to visit her tombstone. Of course, I stayed in close contact with Yvette during those early weeks, wondering how she'd spend her next chapter after sixteen years of caregiving for Mom. In the months since she has called every now and then from her cell phone to ask about Ivry and Ayala. Time will tell if she and I will stay in touch now that we don't have the glue that was my mother holding us together.

For months, I could still hear Yvette's voice telling me how she tried to move Mom's limp body the morning she died. I could sense her deep sadness over losing the person she'd learned to care for so deeply. *I take care of your mother like she's my mother*. We supported each other in our efforts to care for Mom, and together we accomplished more than we could have on our own. This was in keeping with a wise saying culled from the Talmud and adapted into English: "If you lift the load with me, I will be able to lift it; and if you will not, I won't lift it."

I want my mourning to be lifted. I want the loss of my mother to transcend time and place. "Your Mom is everywhere. She lives in you and through your children," Shiva visitors say. But having her everywhere isn't the same as having her alive.

I still feel unmoored all these months after her death, rounding the corner of our apartment building. Why was I still here? We chose Pittsburgh for its proximity to New York City. Squirrel Hill was meant to be a bridge to New York City, a temporary stepping stone; New York is home. Could letting go of that home give me a reason to believe that Squirrel Hill can become what I long for it to be? How I want to trust that inner voice that yes, it is possible; but the loss seems just too great.

As I turn my key to the apartment, I wish to undo all the times I told myself that Mom's musical mind was one big disease, to wrap my arms around my eight-year-old self and tell her how loved and treasured she really was. That the "Love Mom" on aerograms and letters really meant she loved me.

I never had the space to forgive Mom while she was alive. Now that she's gone, I recognize the importance of moving on with my life to avoid staying stuck. Martin Luther King Jr. said, "Forgiveness is not an occasional act, it is a constant attitude." To truly forgive Mom, I need to embrace the present.

My only attempt to forgive Mom while she was still alive happened on a ten-day visit from Israel in 2001, at the very beginning of her descent into Alzheimer's. Wanting to avoid a lifetime of regrets, I contemplated the idea of telling her how sorry I was for leaving her for eleven years.

Already, Mom's identity had been stripped to almost nothing. She giggled her way through our conversation.

"Oh, Dorit. It's okay."

I was surprised, both by her quick response and because I'd been hoping for a different response.

"Do you love me, Mom? I never wanted to hurt you."

She giggled again. "You're okay, Dorit."

"You mean Honey Bunny?" My way of reassuring myself that Mom was still intact was by prompting her.

"Oh yes," she said with a nervous sort of laugh. "Honey Bunny. Don't worry about it. It's okay."

Even though I was already losing her that day, I understood more deeply than ever in that moment, perhaps because of her vulnerability, that she loved me. It was that love that had brought me to bare myself like the few lonely trees outside our window, now stripped to nothing, leaves incessantly flying in the wind, allowing both her and myself to be seen. Loving Mom in a way that would affirm love for myself. I didn't want shame and blame, didn't want to further damage our connection.

As mesmerizing as Mom's music always was to others, I never fully appreciated it. I was too angry with her for loving something else so deeply. I could only focus on her shortcomings.

I have come to understand that it was never a lack of love that pushed me away from my mother. It was our personality differences. She needed to isolate herself, while I was always quite the opposite—always seeking out connections to avoid feelings of isolation. I've always had an underlying fear that I will turn out to be like my mother, inward and introverted, despite evidence to the contrary, but I understand now this will never happen. Connection matters too much to me.

☀

We moved to Squirrel Hill in 2007, not exactly knowing what we were getting into. Over time, our Pittsburgh *shtetl*—our town—has become our new spiritual and cultural zip code. I've tested this shtetl for its community closeness, and time after time, I've been reassured by its strength; and yet still I wonder if I will one day outgrow these connections and give in to my longings for Israel.

Any self-doubt I had about my mothering abilities vanished when Ayala was born. Still, I worry about raising our daughter in Pittsburgh; even though we're supported by the Jewish community here, I wonder if I can do better by my daughter. Pittsburgh is not Israel.

Ever since the day I schlepped Ayala home from our local hospital in her twenty-pound car seat, I've been convinced that the answer to my doubts is resilience and determination. I must embrace and accept the consequences of our choice to stay in the States with a "can-do" attitude: Yes, I can leave her alone in her crib while I go down three flights of stairs to put clothes in the basement dryer. Yes, I can find a way to get us to the pediatrician in the frigid temperatures or take Ivry to school on the public bus when there's a school delay and Haim has already left for work.

The contrasts between our lifestyle here and the one we had in Israel still overwhelm me, however. My days are filled with thoughts of whether I am resilient enough to make it in this still-newish world I'm trying to figure out.

I decide that perhaps I can close the spaces caused by distance by making a more deliberate effort to be seen. So, even though it's freezing outside, I get into the routine of paying rent in person: on the first of the month, I bundle Ayala up and we take a short bus ride to the management company.

It's February 2014, and we're in the middle of Snowmagaddon. I contemplate the best way to strap Ayala to my body in these freezing temperatures. I surrender to mountains of layers: snowsuit, sweaters, blanket, hat. Wind lashes and whips around us as I trudge, cow-bellied, to the bus stop for the fifteen-minute bus ride to the rental office. The whole way, I wonder if all this extra effort is worth it.

We trudge five blocks in the snow against howling winds and all I can think about is how we can bring in income enough to buy a car so I won't have to brave the bus in this wintery mess. Since Ayala's birth, I've been thinking about laying down roots, buying a home. It's a mental game I haven't wished to play before now, always harboring the idea that we might go back to Israel if things didn't work out here. But now, investing in a place suddenly feels more important than the freedom to leave on a whim.

Ayala whimpers. I couldn't have planned this any worse. I feel helpless in this whiteout. Vehicles are buried in snow, and once again I feel stuck. Cars inch forward toward the traffic light. Tucked in the back of my mind are images of Israel—a ray of sunshine, a blue sky, blood-red anemones sprinkled all over the hills of the Golan Heights. I force myself to focus on the snow-covered sidewalk in front of me. If I dare open this file of images, I'll lose my resolve. The last eight Pittsburgh winters have exacerbated my feelings of longing to the point that I can't afford to go there anymore in my mind. I can't even go there on Facebook.

I must surrender.

Surrender to snow.

Surrender to cold.

Finally, we're on the bus. Up and down the hill we zip. On these short bus rides to the management company, I always romanticize the porches, the colonial brick, arched entryways of the sprawling, turn-of-the-century residences that line these streets. Away from the unadorned beige kibbutz homes with red roofs, I still think of as home, I wonder if we'll ever own a place we can call home here.

While the agency runs our credit card, the plump management employee takes one look at Ayala's angelic face, still bunched up in her sleep sack, and says, "Oh, she's gotten so big already. Poor thing, she looks so cold."

Why did I drag her out of the house on such a snowy day?

Coming to the management office at the beginning of each month to pay rent has been an exercise in nurturing connections despite the many changes we've witnessed as tenants over the years. The apartment we've outgrown. The renovations of other units in our building. The ongoing construction. The rent increases each July. Even with all that change, there's something comforting about coming here to pay rent every month. This was the first and only place in Pittsburgh that handed us the key to our home without interrogating us or running us through a security check, scrutinizing us for the credit we didn't have after years of kibbutz living. All we had to do was sign the contract and provide an up-front payment, which we obtained by selling our car in Israel. Easy enough.

Now we are in desperate need of extra space. I am tempted to ask this veteran employee about upgrading to a three-bedroom rental. Then I remember the maintenance man who replaced our bedroom ceiling fan three years ago and shame immediately rises.

While he was working, I asked him if the management company rented out three-bedroom houses.

"Yes," he said. "But those are really expensive. You wouldn't be able to afford it."

This odd response was a projection of his own reality, of course, and had nothing to do with me. But I said nothing. Within five minutes, he gathered his tools and left me feeling incredulous and stupefied.

Why say such a thing to a stranger? I tried stomaching his response and ended up bottling up his words. Ultimately, "you can't afford it" has become a part of not only my world but also Ivry's. He's had no choice but to come to terms with being the only one in his class who still lives in an apartment. Every time my near-tween complains to us about what he lacks compared to his friends, I nearly reach a breaking point. Why can't he play in a backyard like other kids? Why do we still live in a place surrounded by so much noise?

I tried to evade the questions at first, but finally had to say the words that have been haunting me for years: "We can't afford it."

I'm teaching my son lessons in self-worth and he is watching. Will money be a sticky point for him as he grows older, as it has been for me all these years? Clearly, I've allowed this stranger's words to determine our family's reality in a place I'm still struggling to call home.

In front of this employee, I dare to ask the question despite my misgivings.

"Do you rent out three-bedroom houses? The kind with an extra bathroom and perhaps even a yard?"

I hold my breath for a minute.

"Yes, we do. Where in Pittsburgh were you considering?"

A simple answer. No emotional complications.

I tell her Squirrel Hill and she spells out our options and time-lines. As she does, I thaw without the need for protection.

I trudge back to the bus stop with a sense of relief, and again the snow whips around us. Ayala whimpers and cries, but now I bounce her steadily, confident that we can move ahead with these next steps toward figuring out if moving to a bigger, better space is an option for us.

If you can't go to Israel, you must bring Israel to your home.
Onward.

In December 2014, just a few months after receiving our rental con-tract renewal, Haim and I head for a nearby coffee shop in Squirrel Hill. There is talk of a major rent increase in our current apartment, though we haven't received official word. We're at a crossroads. Should we renew, buy a home, or leave Pittsburgh altogether?

I'm drawn to the longing while Haim is fueled by practicality. Rather than be at the mercy of an unsettling economy, we start by detailing the pros and cons for buying a home in Pittsburgh versus going to New York City, a city that is beyond our means but still lives in me. I tell Haim there's no one right answer. So we brainstorm everything.

Snow drifts and glides from one side of the window to the next, like a horizontal hourglass. It's the start of our eighth holiday season in Pittsburgh and the familiar scene looms: holiday well-wishers are waiting in line. Familiar holiday tunes from my youth playing on loop.

The dream is a signature away. Freedom in possibilities. Freedom in choices. But too much freedom might be overwhelming, maybe even impractical.

I remember how Haim looked as he stood in front of the guard's quarters at the kibbutz. Tired. Haggard from the war. I wanted to prove everyone on our kibbutz wrong—show them that Haim was deserving of a better life. Now that we're already in Pittsburgh, and all we've been through, does it make sense to trade community for the unknown?

My heart races against the clock. The price of dreaming. The risk of building anew. After thirty minutes of talk over bland-tasting coffee, we put down our pens and look at each other.

"The price of commitment is never easy," I hear myself say. For months, I've been trying to reach a decision. Haim will follow my lead. My heart spells out what my mind doesn't want to hear: the distance, the cost of resettling, the time it would take to rebuild ourselves professionally somewhere else—especially in New York City, where the cost of living is higher.

"The children," I say. "Do we want to uproot them?"

How important is it to return to Israel?

We both know how being in a community from such early ages will allow them to feel a connection to their surroundings. We don't want them to lose their Jewish identity as we try to eke out a living in New York City. We both know how much harder it would be to nurture and sustain that identity there; New York is a high-energy city that values materialism over community.

Returning to Israel, on the other hand, would be challenging for us both. Pittsburgh has been good to our family in many ways, including financially.

What I need is a blank slate. To find our own voice. To find space. Our "pros" and "cons" columns get longer by the minute. Customers come and go. At some point, I look at Haim and point to the Israel column.

Time to negotiate. Maybe there's still a chance. It's been almost eight years since Haim and I have had such a deep "soul" conversation.

"What about Israel?" I ask. "The kids are still young. There isn't a war in the Upper Galilee anymore."

Haim shoots me a look. *Been there, done that.*

The art of negotiation. We buy another round of coffees as the lists continue to grow longer. We go back and forth between the columns. Israel. New York City. Pittsburgh. They are three well-worn travel routes.

Can our hearts steer us closer to the right decision?

That evening, as we head toward home under a starlit sky, I tap into a space that I keep reserved for Israel. We cross the street past multiple cars blaring their horns. I want to do right by my husband at this point in our sojourn in the States. One day, I'll learn that wrestling with longing requires a practical approach.

At the next traffic light, I look at the rock-solid expression on Haim's face. I can tell he's holding in his reservations as well. If he follows my lead and we end up deciding in favor of Israel, then I know this move wasn't in vain. But I am highly doubtful.

"I can always come back," I said to family a few weeks before we officially left the kibbutz. "I can always come back," I said to friends at the kibbutz pool with an edge of bravado as kids a few years older than Ivry hurled themselves into the water like cannonballs. But can I?

The pros list we made for Pittsburgh outweighs New York and Israel by far when it comes to practicality—mainly because Haim is gainfully employed here, with benefits. To come to terms with longing for a place means acceptance and reconciliation, and perhaps from this place, a pathway to something new that might even open up. The next chapter. But saying yes to Pittsburgh means Israel isn't in the cards for us. And I still feel that Israel, our heart home, is where we need to be.

Time will tell if I will outgrow these feelings.

We turn the door key and noises from the upstairs fill the hallway, as if an entire army is up there. The entire apartment shakes like a mini earthquake is taking place. Where am I? What is happening?

Haim still wears that same stoic expression, but he looks at me and asks, "Where's that noise coming from?" Usually, he's nonchalant about these things and moves on. But right now he looks concerned. "What was that noise?" he asks again.

The babysitter who's about to take her leave, looks up and shakes her head with a shrug. The noise has stopped.

The kids are sleeping. Once the babysitter leaves and we have the quiet to ourselves, Haim surprises me. He doesn't retreat to himself. He doesn't open the *siddur*, as he usually does to *daven* the evening prayers. He's quiet and pensive, almost lost in thought.

"So what do you think?" I ask quietly. "Do we stay here?"

I start looping my way to my next thought, but Haim is already mouthing the word: *Pittsburgh.*

15

LINGERING

For the next year, Pittsburgh is like a fog passing through the U.S. Steel Tower. Each time the clouds disperse, and the stately steel dominates the landscape, I gather strength, reminding myself how far I've come and what being in this city means to me and my family. Seasons inch by, linger, then disappear. The letters on that tower—U-P-M-C—are always visible, no matter the angle. I remind myself that sometimes you have to wait to evaluate the results of a choice you've made. Like the fog, you just have to pass through it; and in some cases, there is no turning back.

Once again I'm on a bus with my husband, son, and bubbly ten-month-old daughter, heading back to New York City—this time to visit Mom's grave—despite the fact that thirteen months after her death, her headstone isn't ready.

In the early-morning hours, as we wheel our suitcases to our hotel, I notice how dirty everything is compared to Pittsburgh. From one street to the next avenue. The sheer number of voices, of bodies. The bustle. Each direction spells out a memory. Mom's presence is everywhere: I see a little girl slipping one hand into her mother's warm palm and the other clutching her shopping bag. This kind of unsatisfied yearning is not unique to people who long for a place; it exists after death or divorce or separation from loved ones, too. It's about a desire to be connected to someplace or something when you cannot. It's about deep loss.

I remember at age twelve, in Gimbles, the long-closed department store that is now H & M, I shared with Mom my excitement over buying a shirt that had puffed leaves with neon rainbow stripes. That purchase marked my entry into the fashion world. Mom loved shopping and she loved to see me happy. If she saw me wanting something long enough, she'd ask, "Do you want it, honey? We can buy it, no problem," upon which she'd pull out a Macy's charge card and put the clothes on layaway. I never knew how many layaways she accumulated over the years. There always seemed an endless supply, and I was never concerned enough to ask.

Our time together and outings in the city were always short-lived, scheduled around her intense rehearsal schedules. How comforting it was, though, to feel that for at least a brief moment in time, I mattered.

We wait on a jam-packed street corner to cross the street to our hotel and I can barely see past the person in front of me. A parade of New York City buses heads downtown, their familiar route numbers lighting the way in the dark. Waiting, along with countless others, to board the M-10 bus to her Greenwich Village loft apartment is a nine-year-old holding Macy's bags stuffed with her prized goods. She turns for her mother's hand, but the image of her mother evaporates in the congested air. The crowd dissipates and once again, I'm a stranger in my hometown—a daughter still in mourning, trying to figure out which side of the crowd I belong on. Am I a shopper?

No, I'm a motherless daughter.

When we no longer have access to the person at the center of our formative experiences, memories beckon us to rediscover a new emotional equilibrium. I'm traversing those fine lines, trying to figure out how to ride alongside the pain. The closer I get to my physical home, the harder I have to work at coming to terms with the loss of my mother.

We journey toward ourselves and within ourselves. As painful as it is, this experience allows me to develop a greater perspective on who I've come to be as my mother's daughter, and as a mother-less daughter. In this way, I realize, I am gaining deeper access to my mother—but only if I can let go.

This experience happens in stages. It doesn't flood in all at once. There are logistics and life to attend to, after all, and mourning ebbs and flows. I lug our suitcases into the lobby and finally into the elevator, feeling like a tourist in my hometown. Clearly, I don't belong here, and yet I'm here. I brace myself for what threatens to be a very awkward twenty-four-hour emotional journey.

I drag out time in the room as much as possible. Our day has been planned out, starting with a trip to the Israeli consulate to renew Ivry's passport, which I regard as a welcomed distraction to take the bite out of the pain. Our ninth-floor, bolted-shut window offer views of another building just two feet away. Feeling time-trapped, time-starved, I take in all the nondescript cement, pigeon poop, blackened windows. Where am I? Who am I? Where is my home? I am everywhere and yet nowhere. I am a mother and yet I'm still a daughter, missing my own mother. I feel an urgency to stay put in midtown Manhattan, to create invisible borders, boundaries. The future seems so hazy, like an unlit cavern. My north star has been extinguished. My fortitude is gone. My confidence is meagre. My family has been uprooted. All because of a disease.

We ride down the elevator and once again push through the crowds. *Ninth Avenue to Hudson Street*, Mom would always tell the taxi driver. Which meant heading south. But I cannot afford to let myself go there in my mind. We push through the crowds, and I hold Ayala tightly in my arms. Eighth Avenue is behind us and completely out of view. *Push forward. Go to the East Side. Second Avenue, the location of the Israeli consulate. You have to write a new story if you want to emotionally survive.* These are the words I tell myself.

Being anonymous in this city is familiar enough but being disconnected is not. "You're the New Yorker," Haim often says when we're visiting, and I get momentarily thrown off by the slew of new buildings under construction.

From Eighth to Seventh and finally to Sixth Avenue and we then give in and board a crosstown bus. We leave the familiar—Conway Big Lots and even the big sneaker place run by Israelis where Mom often hunted for bargains— behind us. Names become less familiar, but the attraction of the city is still there; I take in everything, from the shopkeepers hosing down the sidewalks to the hot dog stand on the corner.

From the other side of the glass window, I become a spectator, disoriented by a change in fare rules, by all the new stores. It's almost as if I'm learning a new language of home.

There are no rules for becoming a stranger in your own town; you have to just go with the flow. But each time I do, I find myself spent, exhausted.

Ayala laughs at a stranger, looks at us, and then looks out the window at the life speeding by. As I weave images of Mom through these endless street corners, I realize that in life, not everything is spelled out for us. It is our job to heal the pain within ourselves. I've unwittingly been on a memory quest since the minute we arrived in New York, and now I see how this journey has been piecing together for me things that I couldn't see while my mom was still alive.

This afternoon, we meet up with my brother at the dollar pizza joint back in Midtown Manhattan. He, too, has made the trek here for what he thought would be a visit to Mom's headstone. We find a place where we can comfortably sit in the back and hear our own voices. He tells me Mom's home is now occupied by a new tenant and the monthly rent has been jacked up to two thousand bucks. Still a bargain for New York City, I say. He agrees.

The table next to us was left strewn with paper cups and plates by the group that just vacated it and is now being cleaned by a worker. The nonstop hustle and bustle of this city is overwhelming. I wait for him to finish before continuing, but no sooner does he move away and a couple slides into the seats and once again, I feel my space trampled upon.

"I feel bad we had to leave Mom and go to Israel," my brother says. I feel some of that guilt too. When we first emigrated to Israel—he as a minor and I as an eighteen-year-old—we did so because we needed to establish emotional independence, to get away from Mom's fears and phobias. Over time, however, our personal and geographical loyalties complicated our ability to provide care for her.

"Nothing we can do about that now," I say. "The past is in the past. I just wish we didn't have to lose the apartment."

Removing both our names from the lease was yet another sacrifice in the name of Mom's care. Westbeth first opened its doors in 1969. Mom was its second tenant. She was a resident there for forty-four years. We both know how sought-after the neighborhood is, how people wait twenty years for an apartment to open up in that building. We both also know that the price of staying on the lease would have meant staying in that apartment with Mom, watching her suffer at the end.

My brother and I agree that there won't ever be another opportunity to be on the list for a rent-subsidized apartment anywhere in the city; thus, our geographical link to Mom ends here. *Keep it in the family*, Mom advised us years before she got sick at the age of fifty-nine. Our apartment was more than a family heirloom; it was a cache of family memories, sweet discoveries, and nourishing art. Relinquishing our ties to Westbeth is another act of letting go, and we both know there will never be another place like it. Our home.

We go back to Seventh Avenue on the crosstown bus; still, I don't dare to turn my head to look south. Temptation is everywhere. Distraction, too. Too many childhood ghosts. Too much sadness.

We'll meet my brother again tomorrow, this time at Penn Station to go to Long Island for a family reunion, and then we'll go back to our respective towns and cities, where we'll try to make sense of our own collective and individual memory quests. I'm craving structure to fill this empty, gnawing hole.

Then something surprising happens on the corner of Eighth Avenue. Unconsciously, I turn my head south as a way to orient myself, and Mom's building comes into full view, the beige triangular roof looming in the distance. Traffic heading downtown is at a standstill and without thinking, I pull out my phone in the middle of the avenue and snap a picture. Haim doesn't realize I've done this and is already at the other side of the street, Ayala in his arms and Ivry by his side.

I finish crossing the street and look at the picture. To my left are the zigzag shapes of towering and rugged edifices overlooking nameless bodies and souls splashed with yellow. Headlights drip until they melt into a puddle and there's nothing left to take in. But if I look closely, I can see the faint glimmer of Westbeth's shape in the background.

I recognize the irony of this moment. I'm on Ninth Avenue, but I'm not following it all the way to Hudson Street like I have so many times before. I have no reason to anymore. There is no destination on this trip. Just the journey.

16

BEARING FRUIT

It is a bitter winter this year of 2014–15, but our communal heating system keeps us going. Sometimes too much so. One night, Ivry complains of being overheated. "This place is a boiler!" he shouts and throws open the window.

Flurries of snow land in a pile next to our mattress on the floor. My leg has become red and irritated from scratching due to the heat. We leave the window open for a few minutes.

"Can't we just turn the heat down?" Ivry wails. I encourage him to come sleep on the floor next to our bed. Aside from the fact that we have no control over the building's temperature, I want to reassure him that one day, he will have more than just his own room; he will have control over what we currently don't have any control over.

I go to bed and dream of a big backyard and a front porch just like we had on our kibbutz. The next morning, I wake up with a queasy feeling that something is wrong. Where is my son? I look around and shout his name, but he doesn't answer.

I walk into his room and there he is, squirming in his bed. Everything about this moment in this apartment feels unfamiliar: the elephant-loud thumping of the neighbors upstairs, the hissing of the radiators, the slamming of entrance doors, the foreign tongues, the fights of the couple the next building over. I take it to mean that soon we will be moving forward into another kind of life.

≈⧹⧸≈

It's March 2015, and we've finally closed on a property in our neighborhood. We take pictures of ourselves holding the new keys and post them on Facebook. Within minutes comments, "likes" and "shares" stream in. The power of social media to connect a community.

Haim points out that we closed on a day of joy in the Hebrew and Chassidic calendar: Yud Aleph Nissan, the birthday of Rabbi Menachem Mendel Schneerson, the leader of the Chabad dynasty of Hasidism, which is celebrated by his followers as a festival.

The following month—just a few weeks after Passover, the holiday that celebrates freedom from slavery in Egypt under Pharaoh's rule—we move into our new three-bedroom row home built in 1921 on a quiet, narrow street sandwiched between two bigger thoroughfares in our neighborhood. Daffodils still quake under blanketed sheets of snow as we are officially welcomed to the Burgh. We have liquidated our modest savings to afford the down payment in order to make our monthly mortgage manageable.

The place comes complete with a porch and a backyard similar to the one in my dream. For months, I will wake up unconvinced that this place is truly ours. I no longer think of our kibbutz home. That image has subsided now that we have a bathtub that fits my full body, a rose and lilac bush in front of the porch that is the size of our galley kitchen, a deck, a backyard with a raspberry bush and garden, room for a possible office or study, a huge basement with our own washer and dryer, a room twice the size for Ivry, and a room for Ayala. Room to grow. I don't have to spend my days in perpetual longing for our kibbutz home anymore. We are finally going to be settled here.

Having this kind of home is hard and humbling, profound and uplifting. At first, I feel undeserving of the space. Of the freedom for creativity and peace and quiet from that bustling, small corner apartment building immersed in sirens and constant street noise and neighbors pounding on our heads at all hours of the night.

Now, instead of feeling victimized by longing, I share the insights of homeownership on the other side of the Atlantic Ocean. There's a saying in Hebrew: "Change your place, change your luck." I become more vivacious almost overnight. Maybe this newfound inner strength will give me the impetus to do what I need to do next: truly build roots in Squirrel Hill.

A friend at the synagogue tells me we are deserving of being homebuyers. That we are deserving of the good life. No one in New York City or in Israel would tell me that. Another opportunity to let go of the longing. Starting over by building roots here in Pittsburgh is the moment of moments: Mom is gone, my childhood home no longer exists, and now we're working on committing ourselves to one side of the Atlantic.

We will not move backward.

This is the clean slate I've been looking for. This must be what it feels like to live the American Dream.

To the right of our new backyard is what I think is a fruit-bearing tree. Come fall 2015, I am convinced we will start harvesting apples in time for our first Thanksgiving. This U-shaped, ten-foot tree with snow-lined branches appeals to my restless transatlantic heart. I recall the almond-budding *shkaydim* and the tender avocado and apricot trees on our kibbutz, from which Haim made jams that I loved to spread on top of challah from the kibbutz *kolbo*, or supermarket. I want to reexperience eating Haim's freshly made preserves (fresh anything!) on this deck. I want to relish getting to hear birds instead of sirens and thumping noises from the students who've lived above us for the past eight years. I dare to dream that even on this side of the Atlantic, I can still keep my kibbutz home alive in my heart and mind as we start anew.

Now I understand: It has taken me nearly eight autumns of stepping on crunching leaves to realize why Israelis stick with each other in the Diaspora. They need the support of another native-born sabra to thrive here, for they know they are in the minority.

It's April 2015; winter's still in the air, but it's just a matter of time before the snow will disappear, and tiny buds will start emerging on our fruit tree. It's as if there's a secret, unwritten chapter of wintering no one has told me about. I feel like I'm waiting for a baby to be born. When will this long pregnancy end? I knew harsh winters from growing up in New York, but all those years of living in Israel made me forget. Israel, like California, is temperate, while "wintering" in Pittsburgh is a way of being.

Ayala and I buy flower seeds from the local grocery store and plant them in our tiny front yard, which is partitioned off from the neighbor's by a short wall of bricks. Now eighteenth months old, Ayala holds a red plastic ball in one hand as she pats dirt down with the other. She points to dandelions and baby blue and pastel pink perennials, and, at her command, I plant them. We sit on beach chairs, make up silly songs. The sidewalks are empty and there are still clumps of dirty snow gathered at the edge of the sidewalks. The sunshine is a teaser against the icy breezes.

All month long I hang out with Ayala on the front porch, watching the progress of our flowers and how they're blooming.

"They aren't growing enough," I tell Ayala. "What do you think we should do?" I recall with fondness the classic children's book *Chicken Soup with Rice*. Maybe we could perk these flowers up with chicken soup, which I jokingly refer to as Jewish penicillin. I am trying to stay hopeful about our choice to live here, and somehow the flowers' ability to thrive has taken on great importance.

I keep watching.

Come May 2015, our tree magically transforms our backyard. Tiny green buds emerge and soon sprout into exquisite white flowers with flashes of hot pink complemented with a tinge of green that takes my breath away.

Soon, the harvest begins. I gather basketfuls of crabapples and carry them across the deck and through the kitchen to waiting pots of steaming hot water. Ivry eagerly bites into a raw one, only to spit it out.

Hours later, Haim produces jars of homemade crabapple preserves. Our collective chapter of bearing fruit has begun, and for the first time, I feel the first glimmer of home here in Pittsburgh.

The first week of July, we discover our first real edible fruit: the raspberry garden. Ayala and I sit next to each other, digging our toes in the soil, sorting through the rotten ones, and picking out the good. We somehow manage to save more than we eat, juices running down our faces, and those we chill in the fridge. One morning we devour them with yogurt; another time we blend them into a smoothie.

I buy a fancy mixer and begin baking challah almost every Thursday for our weekly Sabbath meal. The fragrant smells of the baked bread waft through our home. We mush our raspberries into a jam-like paste and spread it on the challah for our Shabbat morning breakfast, but then decide eating them that way is like eating a bunch of seeds. Mom would have liked such a homemade breakfast, but I resist allowing her to take up residence in my mind. I need to start over again on my own terms.

Harvesting our first American fruit requires me to let go of my expectations about how I think we should build connections. I recall when we cracked open the battered and leathery pomegranates from our new backyard on Rosh Hashana and scooped out their translucent pink seeds with a spoon as our way to celebrate our newly renovated kibbutz home. In my final weeks of pregnancy with Ivry, we said a blessing over the "new fruit."

During our first fall feasts in Israel, our kibbutz orchards were in full bloom. Each morning, I'd throw open the windows and look past our pomegranate trees and the rooftops to the orchards, a blooming sea with billows of blossoms. I would see to it that the bedroom window that opened onto the orchard was ajar before leaving for work each morning, so that sweet fragrance of apricots, almonds, and avocados could fill the house.

Ayala squeals with delight each time we go out to our tree to pick more crabapples. We follow the arc of a red-tailed hawk. She waves at the sky and I have no idea who or what she is waving to—it's a language all her own. In Hebrew, I tell her to listen to the sounds of the breeze and feel its gentle touches. She listens attentively and squeals. There, beyond the canopy, there's a blur of the familiar, a rustle of leaves each time squirrels scamper to and fro. All this becomes my American movie. I remember how my Iraqi grandmother would, at twilight, appear on her well-lit porch in Givatayim, a suburb of Tel-Aviv, to welcome me when I came for visits. No matter where I came from, whether an army base or from our kibbutz up north, she was the beacon, the light, that would inevitably guide me home.

Our backyard is in between sandwiched rowhouses facing other backyards. During our first few weeks, our new neighbors, one by one, politely introduce themselves. Our roots are sprouting.

~∿~

A friend calls our new home our "forever home." What will it take for Squirrel Hill to feel like our "heart home?" I wonder. Each morning, Ayala and I walk out into the dewy yard. This morning, as we do, it starts pouring. It's somehow shocking to me as if my body is unwilling to accept the seasons after so many years of desert living. I marvel at my own resistance, even as I force myself to adapt; I draw Ayala close.

Seasonality forces Pittsburghers, of which I am now one, to tote an umbrella even on sunny days, to appreciate the short spurts of sun that come unexpectedly in between storms. It's a local joke that the weather here is "the pits," and it's easy to feel isolated by its temperamental conditions.

Crows circle overhead. When I look up, there are swarms of birds unperturbed by the rain. I stand practically knee high in our untended bushes of horseradish roots and imagine our kibbutz backyard in full bloom. Being a homeowner challenges me to think about the seasons in a new way. As I transition, cold to warm and dark to light, I think about how I can accept with forgiveness and love what I have been through. Putting down roots, for me, means closing the door to the dream of returning to Israel, but it also means opening doors to new opportunities and new ways of thinking.

From a sea of birds, a red-tailed hawk swoops down and hops from one branch of our crabapple tree to another under a purple-tinged sky.

I cry, "Look up there!"

Ayala squeals.

"It's a bird," I say excitedly in Hebrew. "Up in the sky!"

I remember the words of the American-Israeli blogger I knew back in 2008 when I blogged about missing Israel during Rosh Hashanah: "We're celebrating the same holiday and looking up at the same sky."

Those birds could easily be us.

Under that same sky.

※

The anticipation of summer comes early in 2015 when I zip up and down our street on my shiny new purple bike. It's snazzy; it speaks a new hip language. It is so light that when the wind is behind me, I easily push my way past the build-up of cars on one of Squirrel Hill's main streets and do our errands in no time at all.

That bike is the best thing that has happened to me in a long while. I ride it fast, pretending I'm cycling along the Hudson. More than twenty years have passed since I was that biking teenager, but in this way, I come full circle. I cycle with heavy bags of groceries balancing on the handlebars. I cycle with a backpack. When I first test rode it, I wondered if I still remembered how, but I was determined to break free of limiting beliefs—my brain needed a release. I couldn't be holed up again this winter season.

Since we still don't have a car, this bike has become my freedom. Thanks to these two wheels, I'm starting to feel as if I am on a mini-vacation from all these years of self-imposed darkness.

I buy an expensive bike seat for eighteen-month-old Ayala, who looks out on the world through curious eyes, and a new bike for Ivry. Riding bikes together feels like an adventure. The minute crocuses start emerging, we will take off for Frick Park, where we'll zip along unknown nature trails, meandering paths that stretch on forever. Day by day, the process of finding space within myself and alongside others is becoming a little bit easier.

⁂

On a rather cool, breezy Sunday afternoon in July, Ivry, Ayala and I bike to the entrance of a park I've passed by countless times. Frick Park is a sprawling 150-acre space that crosses four neighborhoods, including our enclave of Squirrel Hill, making it one of the biggest parks in Pittsburgh.

The map one gets to know when adjusting to a new home is not just physical; we also chart our feelings onto the landscape. Being here is an opportunity to let go and start fresh. Cars on an elevated road sound like muffled water running through a drainpipe. The sun illuminates the trail from behind the trees and immediately Debussy's *Prelude a L' Apres midi d'un Faune*—"Prelude to the Afternoon of a Faun"—starts playing in the background of my mind.

Steadying the bike over stones and fallen branches as Ayala takes it all in, I hear the woodwinds in my mind —flute at first with subtle muted horns behind it, as the midday sun blazes over the path, then the strings as we observe a grand canopy of trees from a wooden deck that juts from nowhere, and finally the harp, playing out the harmony between heaven and earth, as I glimpse blue sky. I'm discovering independence. I don't have to rely on buses or rides anymore. I've become one of those graceful bikers that I've observed all those years from a bus.

By the time we reach a bubbling brook at the bottom of what feels like a mountain and we cool ourselves off, I can see how Debussy's inspiration led him to create the imagery of a lush forest with a faun—a mythical half-human, half-beast—depicting its desires and dreams in the heat of the afternoon. The famous piece introduced the world to the first modern composition based on tritone or whole-tone scales, a musical interval of three adjacent whole tones—releasing music from the constraints of conventional harmony and theory. Similarly, I am breaking self-imposed conventions of how I think I'm supposed to build roots in this small town. I've realized that all this time, I've been relying on the idea that others will feel sorry for me or check in on me. It's a habit I'm determined to break.

Perhaps I haven't yet learned how to let down my guard in a way that will make me feel more approachable. Perhaps I have been holding out for people to approach me, just like I used to wait for Mom to change and take pity on me, recognize my loneliness. Perhaps it's time to do things differently.

⁓⁕⁓

It's a cool summer evening in late July. I park my bike sensibly, meters away from the young neighbor who seems to be obsessed with washing his car and who, along with his parents, just moved into the newly built house next door. His Asian-born parents are almost never to be seen and he is only too happy to chat. As he watches me lift heavy bags of groceries, he chirps, "Great summer day, isn't it?"

"You're right," I say. "It's a great summer evening. Perfect for sitting outside."

We talk about cars, a subject about which I know very little, his studies, and how he feels in his new neighborhood. As we continue our conversation, he tells me he is a first-generation American and about his parents' decision to leave communist China for America. I ask questions that get him talking, and soon it's as if we're old friends.

When I tell Haim what I learned about our new neighbor in such a short time, he says, "He's really fascinated by cars, isn't he?"

I, on the other hand, am more interested in the cultural differences between the older and younger generations: the tight-lipped Chinese parents who code-switch between Chinese and English and their American-born son, John, who speaks only English.

John, like me, knows what it is to be pulled between two very different worlds.

Ruth and I start talking at synagogue. I learn that she is a devout Jewish single parent in her fifties, a transplant from Eastern Europe. One unusually warm fall afternoon in 2015, we walk home from synagogue together from Shabbat services and talk about her life in "the old country." The sun slices through the single ruby-leaved tree on the nearest corner, making it possible to see where the stems begin and end. The appeal of remembering, as I understand it from Ruth, is an invitation to go beneath the surface of the here and now and discover in every moment the connection to language and identity.

The moment I recognize that Ruth sees—and understands—my loneliness is a moment of true awakening. Knowing that someone in Squirrel Hill like her "gets" me affirms how emotionally safe I've begun to feel here. I suppose it's taken me these eight years of living in Pittsburgh to discover that, different origins or not, we are all inextricably linked. What matters now is how I pave the way forward in this "new country."

Ruth escorts me to the front steps of my home, and we talk some more. Thanksgiving is on the horizon; I get spontaneous and invite her to come, and she accepts with a smile.

Ruth's only son is grown and gone, so she comes alone on Thanksgiving, bearing small, sweet gifts. "In old country, we don't have a Thanksgiving, and I am just so fortunate that I can celebrate with you," she tells us. She has never celebrated Thanksgiving; in these last five years since she arrived in Pittsburgh, no one has invited her. She points to the toy she has brought Ayala and laughs exuberantly, exclaiming, "Oh, she is so cute."

We crowd around Mom's oak leaf table, which takes up far less space in our new home than it once did in our apartment. A friend said our new dining room looked rather empty with such a small table, but I enjoy the spaciousness.

Ruth is the first person we've welcomed into our home. Within three seconds of her arrival, I know this is exactly what has been missing from our lives: guests.

Our loneliness binds us in a humorous sort of way. As she tells me, "You're a new kid on the block," so we raise a toast of *"le-chayim"* over grape juice and the wine she has a liking for, which she prefers to mix with seltzer.

While piling up her plate, her twinkling eyes tell me how relieved she feels not be spending Thanksgiving alone. The walls don't feel so lonely. The corners don't make me feel so caved in. We drink a bit too much wine and she laughs at my children's shenanigans.

After the meal, my daughter gives her a good-bye hug.

"Oh, my goodness, just look at that, she doesn't want me to leave!" Ruth says playfully. By the time she does, however, the birds have begun their call and the intense longing that usually fills me up has been pushed aside. In its place is hope.

17

FINDING SPACE, FINDING GRACE

The last warm days of November 2015 slowly come to a stand-still, and winter finally swoops in. Leaf blowers take over our quiet street. I compare the vibrancy of foliage to that of years past while Ayala jumps from one leaf pile to the next. Is it just that she's grow-ing bigger, or are the leaf piles getting smaller?

No longer am I overwhelmed by the giant size of our neighbor-ing streets; rather, I take my time on the ten-minute walk to the main street. Family routines. Moments of peace and quiet. These are the elements that make up the infrastructure of home. In our new house, I trace the cracks on the walls with my fingers, won-dering when they formed. Who lived here before us? What stories can this home tell us?

Nothing in this home is familiar, and yet this is home. The lives we live here will define our future memories.

I start feeling more settled one late afternoon as I watch how the light bounces off Ayala's face while she naps in one of the sunniest rooms upstairs. *Angel baby*, I think. *Angel baby*, I write in my journal. The room grows dark with the shifting of the sun, but she remains unperturbed. Her face soaks up every ounce of remaining light. I want to hold her close, but I don't want to wake her, so I just observe her.

My children are already at home here, already starting to shape it and make it their own. Bouncing laughter off the beds. Chasing fireflies in the summer and crunching in and over leaves. Light and sky—the right things.

The notion of endurance is the core idea J.R.R. Tolkien expressed in a poem that appears twice in the *Fellowship of the Ring*: "Deep roots are not reached by the frost." As long as we live here, I want to continue emphasizing the endurance of our multicultural roots. That we will survive. That we will thrive. That we are transplants who are free to plant again.

The last leaves of 2015 crumble and whirl until the soundtrack of my longings seems to melt into the snow. Faraway images of our kibbutz magically melt under small pools of hot chocolate held in mugs by tiny hands.

I grab Haim one cold evening in December—a random, spontaneous act—and for the first time, we have time together, uninterrupted, to watch an entire two-hour run of the Israeli version of *The Voice* on YouTube.

For the past eleven years I have watched Haim consume news and media from Israel. Up until this point, I've never fully thought through all the options I have to be connected to Israel, including through *The Voice*, and what they might do to ease my longings. It's like I've discovered an entirely new world that Haim has always somehow innately known exists.

By early January 2016, we've started binge-watching *The Voice* together regularly. I listen to dreamy tenors and sopranos singing in French and English and Hebrew. A young woman comes to audition and sings a popular Israeli song in her airy, light voice. She will go on to land a major record deal and become an Israeli music icon.

The Voice carries me through our first winter in our new home. Doing so sends memories spinning around my mind like a carousel: one minute I'm walking through the Ben Yehuda marketplace on Friday morning to prepare for the Shabbat, the next I'm driving with windows down past the Sea of Galilee on my way up to the Golan Heights. How easy it is to transport myself to these places in my mind. But for the first time since coming back to the US, I am not intimidated or overwhelmed by the longings these memories stir.

During a peaceful, languid evening under a glorious full moon, I eye our finished basement. For the first six months, it felt so surreal to wake up each morning and know there was an entire extra floor in our house that we weren't even utilizing. It took months for that to sink in and to figure out what to do with the extra space.

Though I imagined from the beginning that this might be a writing space, I haven't had the time and resources to invest in transforming it into that dream. Working from a simple white table, which is what I could initially afford, felt less than inspiring, so I began overthinking everything and then ignoring the basement altogether. During those first few months of homeownership, I wasn't ready. But now I am. I need to claim my space at the table, like all the writers I adored in college and beyond. Enough is enough. I will figure out, one way or another, how to make this basement a creative refuge without breaking the bank.

I hop online and look for do-it-yourself ways to transform a cold, dark basement into a writing office. Build a desk and shelves. Unpack boxes. Live with color.

Virginia Woolf's *A Room of One's Own* argues for both a literal and figurative space for women writers within a literary tradition dominated by patriarchy. Woolf writes, "So long as you write what you wish to write, that is all that matters; and whether it matters for ages or only for hours, nobody can say."

The first time I attempted to claim a writing space was in 2001, when I worked alongside the Jordan River. Then, there was no space between the landscape and the roles I was living. Here, that space is vast. This dark and cold Pittsburgh basement cannot compare to the beauty of the Jordan River, but it is a space I can claim, and I am determined to make it mine.

In mid-February 2016, I borrow a radiator, purchase a cheap plastic table, and head to the basement. Armed with images of J.K. Rowling and her rags-to-riches writing career, I am determined to change my trajectory. *Don't pursue a career in the arts*, Mom would argue. *Pursue a career you can fall back on.*

I think back to 1982, when I was twelve and Dad moved out of our Westbeth apartment and Mom rushed to remove any trace of him. Up went replicas of Monet and Van Gogh to replace his paintings. Down went the strong wood with see-through holes the size of Lite-Brite pegs and up went a thick, L-shaped, white-painted wall that partitioned the loft from our living room. For her music study, she ripped down the fifteen-foot, cream-colored starchy curtains Dad had hung and had brown cork panels put up to drown out sounds from the hallway.

But when Alzheimer's took over, none of these newly configured spaces mattered. There was nothing left to tear down. Her music, her identity—both were lost, gone forever. Did she ever realize how much I loved those curtained closets Dad had put together? Did she remember how I'd loved to play in them as a child?

In this dismal-looking basement beneath the frozen Pittsburgh tundra, pelted by the sound of the boiler, the hum of the washing machine, the unfamiliar space almost feels like a threat. *Get anchored, lean into the familiar.* Slowly, I reach into a huge blue milk crate perched on the windowsill and pull out a carefully wrapped piece of homemade dollhouse furniture Dad once crafted for me from a kit, some of which hasn't been opened since we came to the States. Each package is the size of a baseball.

Once again, I'm that little girl who created objects with simple materials. I unwrap each piece and rearrange the items on the dirty and grimy windowsill, and I'm refueled, overcome with a sense of wonder. There are myriad decals on the toy chest: a teddy bear, a train, a drum, a top, a ball, a horn boat, and a panda bear. They're all still perfectly intact. Time has not weathered the playfulness of their colors. A red-colored lid complements the white chest perfectly. I lift the lid, remembering how it felt to plop all the "toys" inside the chest, including a baby rattle and a green and yellow plastic toy truck—both the size of thumbnails.

The next treasure is a white-ridged wall dollhouse with crooked window and door decals. I turn it around to rediscover four equally partitioned rooms. What was I thinking by trying to squeeze a plastic, miniature-size baby into a room that was just half the size of her leg?

One of the packages contains a hand-crafted crib reflecting Dad's labor. I am relieved to see that each of the ten toothpick railings on either side of the alligator- and panda bear–themed crib mattress are still intact.

"Your dad has hands of gold," Mom said back then, peering into my seven-year-old hands. She had emerged from the kitchen, the spoon she held dripping the hot chicken soup she was making from a mix. We oohed and aahed over the pieces before I skipped back to Dad's visual arts studio, which had a street view of the printing factory across the street and the Hudson to the far right.

Understanding where you come from informs the knowing of who you are. I am the daughter of artist parents, and yet I have always struggled to claim this writing identity for myself.

I unwrap the rest of the furniture and create a fitting display on the chipped windowsill. Then I Google the route from here to Westbeth to reinforce that this thought-route in my mind, I've been mentally traveling still exists.

Reassured, I am grounded in space and time, I hunker down to work, ready to practice taking on new habits—to show up every day in a space where I can sit with the memories and write.

⁓⁄⁄⁄⁄~

In the basement, she comes into view.

Mom's fully contoured, back -- in a long, flower-print dress with black pumps. She slips another piece of paper into the Smith Corona typewriter at the makeshift L-shaped work area in the downstairs of our duplex, ready to solicit another piano-playing gig in the name of spreading love of classical piano around the world. She works furiously through the night, alternating between piano playing and promoting herself.

I paint even more details onto the woman attached to those fast hands in my mind's eye; the camera zooms in from behind onto her lovely, modest features, the early wrinkles on her forehead. She's always silent. No words come out.

It's weird that each time I thought of pursuing a writing career, I'd remember Mom. *You need a profession you can fall back on—like teaching.* Arguing with her was futile. And those words made it so I couldn't feel at peace each time I tried journaling or creative writing. Only writing academic papers seemed justifiable.

Visualizing Mom at work without hearing her "practical advice" allows me to find reconciliation. Internalizing her words meant not entertaining the thought of writing, and for too long I listened to that voice. Now, though, I can claim that writing identity I lost. And writing about Mom will allow me to re-experience her, to understand our closeness, and also to process all I've learned about her determination and passion.

In one of the boxes, I come across a tremendous find: An old cassette marked with the words, in her penmanship, "For Dorit." This cassette has traveled around the world with us; I first unpacked it in our newly renovated kibbutz home. I played it then, thinking it was a music cassette, and instead discovered a recording of Mom arguing with me. Hearing my belligerent, youthful voice instigating a fight with Mom over trivial issues made me feel awkward and stupid, especially because that was the only audio I had of her voice. But then the taped-over part ended, and I heard her playing a Chopin mazurka, and I wanted to cry. Two time periods. Two personas.

I crave a different story about Mom—not the voice of the inept parent who I kept squashed into boxes, but her story of redemption. All those hours slaving over the piano, practicing for her next gig, meant proving her life against the worst kind of evil humanity has ever experienced: the atrocities of the Holocaust that befell her family and forced her family to escape while they still had a chance.

I remove the handwritten label from the cassette and tape it to the wall, a visual anchor of our relationship. She and her family escaped the Nazis and I am now in Pittsburgh, free to pursue my passions. "For Dorit." I am her legacy. All the things she wanted— love, happiness, and success—came through her art. And she passed that on to me. From mother to mother. Now I understand.

The winter of 2016 rages on. In the bleakest of moments, I refine my new mindset in that basement—filtering the negative from the positive, accepting the loss of my mother, and the sacrifices of my own youth while I fill the white spaces of a new document, a work-in-progress, and have new thoughts. I listen to white noise, podcasts, interviews with well-known writers—anything to help reinvent myself. In my mind's eye, I see myself channeling the energy of Evelyn Couch in the movie *Fried Green Tomatoes*. "I need light and air," Evelyn shouts to her husband as she knocks down a wall in her house—a task Mom would most definitely have approved of.

At age forty-four, the thought of knocking down our cedar closets and walls is empowering. The space between imagining and doing is the difference between a real and an imagined self—so, on this brutally cold winter night, I do it. I'm craving air, light, and space, freedom from these foreboding cedar closets, and this dark décor. I channel my inner Evelyn and take a hatchet to the wall. "Towanda!" I shout, until there is nothing left but space to breathe, feel, and imagine.

But in reality, it's too cold to work in the basement. So, at five o'clock on cold winter mornings, I write from my bed, huddled in a bathrobe warmed by a heating pad. I write about Israel, the country I've given up, the country I will most likely not return to—at least not for a very long time. I write about my kibbutz and the Jordan River. These images help me articulate my longing.

The basement project will have to wait until winter's over, but at least I'm writing.

⁂

The dreaded snow finally stops in mid-April and I emerge once again, this time on the deck with my laptop. I have written from my bed all winter long. I'm clamoring for spring. I keep looking at the crabapple tree for a sign that I can start planting, dreaming, imagining again, but the buds haven't emerged yet.

Ayala is only too happy to play with the toys on the deck that have been sequestered in their snow-crusted bins for the past few months. To bolster my spirits, I take down the gate that has kept her enclosed in the porch area since we first moved in. She's big enough now that she doesn't need its protection. I trust my motherly instincts that she won't wander off.

As soon as the gate comes off, space instantly opens up. The formerly enclosed porch opens up to a new world of freedom. Israel is calling again.

One rather warmish night in March, as the pinkish glow of sunset silhouettes the trees outside, Haim and I watch, once again, the Israeli version of *The Voice*.

In the middle of the episode, I grab his hand. "Can we go to Israel this summer?"

I don't need to spell out the reasons. He knows exactly what I'm feeling. In fact, from the wistfulness of his greyish features, I can tell he feels those emotions too.

Two days later, we purchase our tickets. Departure date: July 2016.

The countdown begins.

18

LONGING TRANSFORMED

Haim chucks his walking shoes into our dusty coat closet, opting to bring only flip-flops. In the dead heat of the summer, it's probably going to be something like 110 degrees in the shade in Israel. But I urge him to reconsider. "Think about your feet on the plane and in the airport, where air temperature is not regulated. Won't you be cold?"

Into the suitcase go my socks and multiple pairs of sneakers.

I realize how preposterous this all sounds to him. Cold isn't an issue for Haim. He's fine with much less clothing. I, meanwhile, am dependent on sneakers and socks even in the heat of Israel's summer, afraid to feel too naked and exposed in its desert climate. (After all, I wore army boots, long sleeves, and pants when serving on a desert base as an IDF soldier.)

"It's okay," he says. "I'll be fine." He looks at me as if I've gone mad.

This deeply rooted routine of worrying about every; it's something that's always been with me. Worry has always been a false way of making me feel I have control. It's a blend of inherited phobias from Mom, but it's also seeped its way into my identity. I pile up more shoes in the suitcase.

"Why do you need so many pairs of sneakers?" Haim asks.

I look at him and I look at the already weighty suitcase, and I laugh.

Time to shed some layers.

⁂

On Tzefat's main street, my brother, who has joined us for this trip, helps push Ayala in her stroller along the cobblestone *midrahov*, a pedestrian mall. Haim walks alongside me in his ratty flip-flops. Holes are starting to emerge in them, but he doesn't seem the least bit affected by them.

In the background, Judaica stores emanate holiness. This beautiful town is known for its distinctive Kabbalistic roots. It's a town that shuts down on Shabbat. My eyes fall on the vast open pages of *siddurim*, prayer books, in the shop windows to my right.

The push-pull I've been feeling ever since our move between the US and Israel was exacerbated by Mom's death. Maybe that's because I felt robbed of the communal experience of grieving and mourning that is so very much a part of Israel.

Burying Mom led me to start attending Shabbat services regularly in Pittsburgh. I hoped to find a link to something bigger, something that would either catapult or quiet my soul. I attended a service at a nearby conservative synagogue during that first month after mourning, and I felt like I was on a spaceship to Mars. I was knackered from breastfeeding but spent the little energy I had looking to connect on a higher level of faith. At night, I'd listen to Hans Zimmer and other new-age type music videos on YouTube, trying to connect to the ethereal. *V'hu 'Eli v'hay go'ali, v'tsur evli b'eit tsarah. He is my God, my living redeemer, Rock of my affliction in time of trouble.* I couldn't figure out how to allow the wisdom of those Shabbat prayers, which felt to me like the vintage pieces at my grandmother's Queens apartment, to sink in. Words that an expat like myself might cling to from afar: connection, strength, hope.

I was trying to devour what felt like God's personal diaries, the blueprint of creation—sometimes feeling I was more Jewish than Israeli or more Israeli than Jewish. What I really wanted was to feel at home in both modes, but I felt constantly compelled to choose between them. And attending the Pittsburgh synagogue wasn't enough; I didn't feel at home there. The experience was thin, like the soles of my husband's worn flip-flops, and I felt the distance could only be repaired by coming to Israel. Prayer was not enough to bridge the gaps.

Haim lingers in front of one Judaica store and points to a chal-lah cutting board, silver plated, "Shabbat Shalom" etched into it in Hebrew, that's catching the sunlight. We've been talking for a while about replacing the one my mother-in-law gave us for our wedding because the words "Shabbat Shalom" are starting to disappear, but I haven't the heart to let it go.

Longing and exile. Exile is a common theme in Judaism—from Jacob's stay with Laban to the Israelites working for the Pharaoh as slaves. I have accepted our Pittsburgh zip code as our new home, but in the back of my mind, there is still a zip code yet to come and I'm not sure what that will look like.

"Let's see if we can find some other challah boards," I say. "I'm not so crazy about that one."

Haim agrees.

Prayer books. Challah boards. Silver-plated candlesticks. *Hassids* and religious families pass us by as if they are separate parts of my histories, and again I remember how when we lived in Israel, I never ventured into a synagogue, turned off as I was by the reli-gious fanaticism around me. In Pittsburgh, we still haven't taken on Jewish traditions and customs relating to Shabbat and Jewish holidays, but I have opened my heart and mind to the words of our rabbi, hoping for a deeper connection with Judaism. During one Sukkot, a biblical Jewish holiday that celebrates the festival of the harvest, he said, "Praying to God is not something we have to do. We pray to God as a way to tune in to God."

Tune in to God. Here was a sentiment I could relate to.

Now, as I look at the trail of religious families meandering by, I wonder if my outsider, outlier status has something to do with the peace I'm feeling. I notice some Judaica in the next shop window and motion to Haim that I'm stepping to the side for a bit.

The awning provides just enough shade to reduce the sun's glare. My eyes quickly become accustomed to the difference in light. I take in the sight of all the polished silver, hoping there might be something that might complement our Shabbat table. It takes a few good moments for me to realize I'm not really drawn to the actual objects in the shop window—but when I do, I realize that this moment is capturing me from the inside out. For the first time in ages, I'm not obsessed with categories or labels. Nor am I being tricked by longing. I see clearly that these shiny objects are a temptation, not grounded in any reality.

What is actually important is that I'm home in this mystical city. I let the cadence of those words rise and fall in my mind a few times. *Home. I am home.*

It's hard not to crack under 105-degree heat. It's almost lunchtime and I'm ravenous for Israeli food—*amba*, tangy mango sauce, dripping down crispy balls of falafel, and sesame paste *techina* slathered on home-baked pita breads. I'm amazed at how easily I'm still able to access all these words; they roll off my tongue with ease.

I eye the falafel stands. "I'm starving. We're starving. Let's stop and eat." I start pulling Haim in that direction.

I'm a wolf with an insatiable appetite. All I want to do is fill myself up with Israeli food, experiences, connections. I've been waiting for this moment for five years.

"*Rak rega*"—One minute—he says, holding up his two fingers as if to snap. We've approached the central part of the pedestrian walkway, the vantage point that overlooks the complexity of streets and alleyways surrounding the artist colony. My estranged heart takes these sights in: the alleyways, the quaint stone steps of stone-clad buildings, the raised arches of synagogues, the sky blue–painted buildings—they bring me closer to my Creator. Being here, I see that the beloved places, images, and feelings I think I've lost aren't really lost at all.

Ayala manages to unbuckle herself and walks over to Haim, who lifts her onto his shoulders.

"I'm hot, I'm hot!" she wails. Her cheeks are flushed pink. I peel off her hat and hold a water bottle to her lips. The water is hot, too, but it's the best I can do. What were we thinking of coming here in midday?

"Let's sit down to eat," I say. "Someplace where there's air-conditioning."

As we head back up the *midrahov* to an enclosed sit-down place, I consider once again the Hebrew word "*ga'agooa*"—longing for a place to call home—which appears prominently in Psalm 92. It's typically recited during Kabbalat Shabbat, welcoming the Sabbath at sundown on Friday, and describes the ideal life through the metaphor of a tree deeply rooted in a house of worship. Each time I've recited this psalm at a Pittsburgh synagogue, I've thought about Israel and the security, safety, and comfort I feel here, so elusive to me in our new home of Pittsburgh.

Can I be that tree, regardless of the push-pulls and wherever they end up taking me?

~✲~

The strange wording of *Lech Lecha* is a profound moment of Genesis (12:1) when God commands Abraham, the forefather of Judaism, "Go to yourself." A source of endless debate by countless rabbis and scholars, *Lecha* is one of many exchanges epitomized in Rabbi Dov Lipman's *Coming Home*, a book that analyzes Judaism's stress on living in Israel throughout the centuries. Making *aliyah* or ascending to Israel is one of Judaism's highest ideals, but we willingly made the choice to leave. Ever since I had been searching for words and wisdom to soothe my wounded heart and come to terms with our decision.

On this visit, I ruminate on the idea of journeying to oneself. The subtexts speak to a deeper spiritual level, of God encouraging Abraham to leave the negativity associated with his place of birth, to go on a journey "to himself," to self-actualize his *aliyah*, and what would be the first ascension of the Jewish people. For years, I've struggled with the negativity associated with *yeridah*, leaving Israel. I am on a mission. I want this visit to Israel to fix something that feels broken. I want to put an end to the way I've felt misunderstood by others. I'm not a foreigner to this place. I'm not lost. This is my home as much as it is Haim's.

As we walk up the street in search of a place with falafel and good air conditioning, I look behind me and immediately notice that Haim, who has been carrying Ayala on his shoulders, is no longer behind me. It dawns on me that Haim doesn't have a cell phone.

Tzefat is known for its maze of alleyways and side streets, and in the thirty minutes my brother, Ivry, and I spend searching for him, I start to panic. What if he wandered off the main street? Technically, he could end up anywhere. He doesn't have a particularly strong sense of direction. But, I remind myself, this is Israel. Haim will know how to find us.

My brother and I frequently turn around to see if Haim has magically appeared from one of the side streets, and each time we do, we look at each other. Maybe he just took a wrong turn?

"He'll show up in a few minutes," my brother says, knowing the right things to say to placate my natural propensity to worry.

We wait.

On a whim, we decide to be proactive and ask some shops and restaurants.

"Have you seen a tallish man with glasses and a baseball cap with a young child on his shoulders?" my brother and I ask in turn.

They all shake their heads. "No, we haven't seen such a person." Their voices are gentle, their faces express concern. Smells of smoked lamb swell around us on this heat-soaked afternoon.

If this happened in the States, my feelings of anxiety would be amplified. Here, the worry is less. I lean into the thought that this country has and always will have my back, even if I'm millions of miles away. That is the Israeli way.

I know I sometimes come across as needy or overly emotional. I have learned during my time in the States to keep my guard up, but I still tend to shoot from the hip a bit; my emotional makeup is the same as it's always been. And I know this tendency to lash out comes from Mom. When she didn't agree with something, she'd shout, have a fit, spit, curse, and sometimes even get up and leave. A few times she said she would kill herself if she was pushed too much over the edge.

Now, searching for Haim, I try to keep my tendency toward panic in check, taking my cue from the country we're in, a place where people have figured out how to stay calm and patient during difficult situations.

We go back down the length of the street, asking, wondering. By now, we're panting from the heat.

After thirty minutes—an eternity—we finally find Haim. I want to cry from relief. I pull Ayala down from his shoulders and say excitedly, "Oh my goodness, Haim. You scared us silly. Where the heck were you?"

He explains how he managed to miss a turn and ended up on side street. Ayala looks hotter than ever. There's no shade. We're like wilting flowers in a decaying field. We set off once again in search of air conditioning.

∼∕⁄∼

Minutes later, as we sit at a table loaded with home-baked falafel and warm pita bread, air-conditioning blasting from above, I hand Haim my cell phone. "Better you have this than me," I tell him. "I'm not going through *that* again."

I look at my brother. We both breathe a sigh of relief.

"How could you have missed us?" I press. "You were just behind us. I kept waving so you could see us."

"Okay, then," Haim says, his face smeared with tahini paste. "Shoot me now."

I want to laugh but restrain myself.

Like an admonished child, he promises not to get lost again. *Lech Lecha.*

∼∕⁄∼

A week later, on a late August afternoon, the Dome of the Rock in Jerusalem sits like a crown jewel overlooking the old city, including the Western Wall. Prayer-goers at the Western Wall float like stardust. By the time dusk enters, the entranceways are bathed in golden light. What has always felt like a city for the religious has now transformed into an electrifying place, almost like a fairy tale. We decided to come here and spent our final two days before flying back to the States mainly to retreat from the heat, which has been relentless.

Even in the heat of midday, Jerusalem is jumpy—more so than other cities, because of its added level of spiritual intensity—and I wonder if I'll have the patience to truly connect with it from my heart and soul in such a short time. From outside the Old City walls, people shout and wave at each other like stage directors.

Within thirty minutes of dropping off our bags at a nearby Airbnb near the embassies and other high-profile residences, we hail a taxi to the Old City. Our driver and Haim get right to business talking about local topics. Haim is so gregarious both in Israel and in Pittsburgh; he'll talk to anyone, anywhere. But it's so much easier for him to express himself in his mother tongue about local Israeli topics that even Israelis in Pittsburgh don't always have a clue what he's saying.

Entering the Old City is not only about coming full circle with home and heart, but it's also about fulfilling an expectation. Surrounding us are fifty-foot-high ramparts, larger-than-life, four, and half-thousand-year-old brick walls that lead to the City of David and the Old City. These walls have seen war, bloodshed, and yes, longing. The streets get narrower and the walls seem to cave in on us, but here I feel protected.

Everything is familiar and yet nothing is familiar. *L'shana Haba'ah b'Yerushalayim*— "Next year in Jerusalem"—is a popular phrase often sung at the end of the Passover Seder that evokes a common theme in Jewish culture and religious consciousness: the desire to return to a rebuilt Jerusalem that was destroyed by the Romans in 70 C.E., after the period of the Second Temple. For millennia, this has been the most common way religious Jews have expressed hope for a future redemption. Even though our family hasn't yet embraced a full observance of Judaism, the phrase still speaks deeply to me as an expat and cultural Jew. Jerusalem is the Jewish capital, not just of Israel but of the world.

Sidewalks completely disappear under a throng of tourists. I'm amazed at how deftly our driver handles the wheel while multitasking—chatting with Haim, answering his cell phone, and fiddling with the air conditioner to get the temperature just right. Another Israeli moment coming together.

My longing subsides the closer we get to the center of the Old City. The heart of the city is my heart's center. How can I leave a place that has become my spiritual center of the universe? A city so full of holiness, it's impossible to escape it? I whip out my phone to take a video as the road gets narrower. This is a slice of my personal history. I've traveled this route a thousand times in my head.

We arrive at the parking lot. Out comes Ayala's stroller, which, having been crushed under a taxi in Haifa, now wobbles on unsteady wheels. To me, it symbolizes endurance and how we are all pushing through our own physical limitations in this heat. Pressing on through the Old City in the late afternoon is like walking through fog or inhaling worn-out gauze, but you emerge with a deeper level of clarity.

Hours roll on, and the Old City reminds me of a cantankerous old woman. Buildings and storefronts are set in stone. Mosques from the Muslim Quarter wail their daily recorded prayers. But the heat, thankfully, fades and coolish breezes pick up as the sun drops lower.

My brother is not with us, having flown back to the States a few days earlier. Now, our only cell phone stays with me. We descend on smooth steps and make our way through security and, finally, to the courtyard square leading to the Western Wall itself. The crowds are immense. The risk of getting separated is high. But my longing is still intact.

I agree to stay with Ayala while Haim takes Ivry to the men's section. At the first shady spot, I crouch next to her stroller. She's restless, so I play shadow games with her, but I am restless too. Many years ago, as a young IDF soldier on a visit to the Old City, I was invited to enter the women's area, but I declined, watched from the outside. The prayers felt too formulaic and I didn't have a clue where to start. I didn't belong to any religious camp and was afraid I'd be out of my element.

When Haim emerges from the crowd, I tell him I'm taking

Ayala to the women's section. Perhaps it will be easier for me to take in the experience now than it was all those years ago.

We make our way through a smaller crowd of women and, together, we sit on a chair and observe the wall.

"Why are there so many people, Mommy?" Ayala asks.

"This is where people come from all over the world to pray," I explain. "They write little notes to stick in the cracks of those huge walls to connect to God."

Ayala cranes her neck out like a baby bird in the nest, taking everything in. I look at succulent plants lodged high up in the wall's cracks and at the pigeons flocking back and forth. We stand and move closer to the wall and I feel myself letting down my guard.

Moments later, Ayala has dozed off in the stroller. I fan her with her hat with one hand and grab one of the prayer books from a table set up in front of the wall with the other. I open it up, wondering if God is listening.

I tune out the voices of the women—some praying, others crying. Ayala is fast asleep, and for a moment, it's just me and these immense walls. I gaze at these big, holy stones, and emotion wells. How I want our exile in the States to come to an end. But since returning to Israel isn't in the cards any time soon, I'll have to settle for this feeling instead. Every time I light our Shabbat candles on Friday night in our Pittsburgh kitchen, I'll close my eyes and remember this holy moment. Remember that I'm not alone, that the light of our candles will connect us to Israel, no matter what our zip code is. For now, this spiritual zip code is the one I will carry in my heart.

Even so, I know leaving my heart home won't be easy.

Like zombies, we move through the security check at Ben Gurion Airport. I clutch two sets of passports for each member of my family—eight in all. It's a bittersweet moment, a coming and going routine I know well. Exchanging the American passport for the Israeli one and vice versa. One home for the other. Texts in Hebrew come blasting in at light speed: *We will miss you. Did you pass security? Have you checked in yet?*

In the grand scheme of longing, this moment will of course, be short-lived. Once we exit Israeli airspace, this in-between space will cease to exist, and all the connections and exchanges we've enjoyed will be relegated from texts on our phones to messages online. We'll become a Facebook family once again, reduced to "likes", "shares", and emojis.

I text Haim's brother-in-law back. Unlike previous visits, I want my pain to be recognized. "I don't want to go home," I write in Hebrew—meaning, "This moment is extra difficult." I look at subversive use of "home" in this context. It's as if associating home with Pittsburgh will remove some of the emotional hardship.

My brother-in-law immediately senses my heartache (God bless him) and springs into action, which I'm not prepared for. He suggests we start looking for employment for Haim back here in Israel and already he's texting a list of jobs Haim can do. I hand the phone over to Haim, my heart confused. Where do I belong?

I'm determined to rise above this feeling of emotional displacement. I'm reminded of a line in Craig Storti's *The Art of Coming Home* that sums up my predicament: "When I got back, I found I was no longer a round peg in a round hole, but a square peg trying to find a hole that didn't seem to be there at all."

I have become that square peg. I keep trying to be adaptable, to embody the qualities of sand, but instead, I feel constantly erased by the tide. First wash out, I'm an expat. Second wash out, I'm rekindling my Jewish soul. Will my heart be erased by these always-changing tides?

"Maybe we *should* give Israel, and this job, a try," I say to Haim.

"Dorit, *nu*," he says. I know he means, A *locksmith? Like, seriously?*

I already know Haim is more committed than I am to being in the States, but being here in Israel has allowed me to momentarily forget that reality. All I want to do now is hide my head under a blanket.

Whatever side of the Atlantic Ocean we're on, my husband knows to be practical, realistic: You don't show your longings or even live by them. You just keep going despite them. This is how Haim copes with expat life in America. But it will take me days, even weeks, before I can readjust to life back in America.

Haim can be the practical one; for now, I'm going to allow myself to long for the Israel I've built in my mind and let myself believe that our exile hasn't been for naught.

Reluctantly, I hand over our Israeli passports. I want to scream and shout, *No, this is my home! I am changing my ticket! I am staying here!* My heart beats out the notes of my emotions, unwilling to reconcile with the idea of having to return to its state of transatlantic longing once again. But my tears stay firmly lodged in the corner of my eyes. I know what we're up against.

Haim, meanwhile, is more practical, more emphatic than ever: *I couldn't get a job in Israel when I was forty-four, Dorit. What makes you think I'll get one now?*

So, as I always do, I restrain myself, for expat life is complicated and messy, and we are a family unit. I am the teacher, the modeler of emotions. I hold myself together.

We head to the plane waiting for us in the west wing of the airport. I am bombarded with more texts about job possibilities for Haim. My brother-in-law fills me with hope, and perhaps it's misleading, but I can't help but cling to it. I've spent many years cycling in and out of longing, mulling over our economics, and ultimately grieving over the reality that the cost of living in Israel is higher than the price of staying in Pittsburgh.

I know this moment will be short-lived. My emotional state at the airport is not a broader spiritual indicator. I've been down this road before. I must bear in mind that my real purpose, beyond these longings, is ultimately to connect to my Jewish community.

Under a canopy of stars, our plane refuels. We wait. I look at all the passengers, some talking in Hebrew and others in English. The linguistic mish-mash is almost too much to bear.

This is when I lose it and start to cry.

19

BEGINNER BOUND

In mid-fall 2016, shadows of twilight descend upon Pittsburgh, and I think that perhaps I've found the ticket out of my longings—the journey that will help me plant deeper roots in Pittsburgh's soil. We've been home from Israel for a few months already, and Ayala and I are currently engaged in what will become a weekly ritual of lighting the candlesticks, one by one, to usher in the Shabbat, which starts at sundown on Friday.

In Israel, I never took the Shabbat seriously, and our kibbutz lifestyle supported that. Nobody seemed to be interested in nurturing a Jewish identity; in fact, for years, our kibbutz was anti-religious.

This autumn of 2016, I've finally recognized that being in exile is not synonymous with assimilating. I can adapt culturally, absorbing new customs like sand, but I don't have to give up on a Jewish way of life.

Ivry looks on as we light the candles, his face swimming in golden light. I haven't paid close enough attention to how quickly my boy, my first-born, has been growing—not just physically but also in his *Yiddishkeit*. He's now just one year shy of his Bar Mitzvah and he's gravitating more toward learning his *Parashah* (his portion of the Torah that he'll chant at his Bar Mitzvah ceremony). He's almost as tall as me, and his voice seems so manly now (especially when he's angry, which seems to me to happen more and more often these days). He was the first to protest taking on the customs of Shabbat for the first time, but he's going along with it now, mainly to appease me. Ultimately, though, I know our decision will help bring our family closer together.

I light two candles that represent two commandments: *zakhor*, the Hebrew word for remembering the significance of Shabbat, both as a commemoration of creation and of our freedom from slavery in Egypt, and *shamor*, which means to observe the Shabbat by preserving and sanctifying it. Then I add more candles, one for each family member, including our latest addition, a twenty-year-old Japanese homestay named Yuki who's studying at the University of Pittsburgh. She has no idea that the feat lying ahead of me—my first Shabbat undertaking—is almost Herculean. Even after nine years, I feel deeply how the spiritual oasis I'm attempting to nurture on the other side of the Atlantic Ocean lacks the backdrop of our kibbutz. But in the absence of that community, what we do now breathes in view of a different set of eyes—those of God.

From sundown tonight to sundown tomorrow, I won't check my phone, turn lights on and off, cook, or work. I'm obsessed with calling out all the things I won't be able to do as "restrictions"—and yet the idea of giving up my scheduled Saturday activities in exchange for spirituality and God feels in some way liberating.

Haim, who already prays three times a day in observance of Jewish tradition, knows that prayer is not what distinguishes Shabbat from the rest of the week. For him, taking on the Shabbat is an opportunity for greater spiritual enrichment. I look up at his face. He has a natural spiritual affinity that I lack, and yet he accepts me where I am and never makes me feel left out.

I linger for a moment longer, taking in the warmth of the candles, and I breathe out a sigh of relief: I don't have anywhere to be. I don't have to be anything to anybody. I can just be present in this moment.

Like a football team, our family of five huddles closer around the Shabbat candles filling our kitchen with light. Flames flicker, casting shadows on my growing doubts, as I try to stay focused on the prayer: *Barukh ata Adonai Eloheinu Melekh haolam, asher kid'shanu b'mitzvotav v'tzivanu l'hadlik ner shel Shabbat*—"Blessed are You, Lord, our God, King of the universe, who has sanctified us with His commandments and commanded us to light Shabbat candles."

Shabbat has officially been ushered in.

This moment washes away the intensity of the week. Over the course of five years in Pittsburgh, I've imagined taking on the Shabbat as something bigger—the concept of repairing the world, or *tikkun olam*, as expressed by Rabbi Menachem Mendel Schneerson: "If you see what needs to be repaired and how to repair it, then you have found a piece of the world that God has left for you to complete. But if you only see what is wrong and ugly in the world, then it is you yourself who needs repair."

I have long been broken, in need of healing, still drawn to Judaism but deeply triggered by the "you versus me" mentality I experienced in Israel. Some of my earliest and most formative experiences of Judaism in my adopted country were soaked in prejudice, rooted in guilt and alienation. I witnessed observant Jews who'd embraced nativism or xenophobic nationalism and felt that I, a cultural and secular Jew, threatened their ideology by the simple fact that I didn't observe the Shabbat or attend synagogue.

In Israel, depending on one's level of observance, keeping the Shabbat is a given, a commandment from God. Now that I've become intentional about getting Shabbat off the ground, I remember I'm in the Diaspora, where life isn't organized in such a way as to make things easy to take Saturdays off—and offline. Managers don't care an iota about your Jewish identity. Haim has never expressed to his employer that his connection to Judaism is important, feeling that it was more important to be a reliable employee—especially on the weekends since that's when people usually shop. And when he became more spiritually observant, he didn't start wearing a kippah, like others might have done. But the result for me, without my even realizing it, was that I've missed opportunities to cultivate our family's spirituality. Embracing the Shabbat is giving me a new lens into how to create these connections within my own family.

"*Shabbat shalom,*" we all say to each other.

I want the light of the Shabbat to wash away these feelings that threaten to overwhelm me. I'm hoping for tenderness—anything positive, really—to offset the concerns I harbor about successfully taking on the Shabbat. I'm afraid of not wanting to be disconnected—afraid of boredom and isolation and not knowing what to do with myself on a twenty-six-hour detox from the digital world. How will I make up for all the lost time? What if I fall behind in work?

I squeeze Ayala, who smiles at me. Ivry, meanwhile, glares at me.

"It's okay," I say reassuringly. "You'll survive." This is my way of not provoking an argument. After all, Shabbat is supposed to be about peace and tranquility.

The golden light clearly transfixes Yuki, and the more I look at her, the more I notice how those subdued black eyes hold deep curiosity. I'm aware that with us, she is having a cultural experience within a cultural experience. She had never met a Jewish person before coming to the States, let alone participated in any Jewish rituals. Coming from Japan, a deferential culture, I imagined our family's arguments and outbursts must come across as abrupt to her, but she always remains calm, taking everything in stride.

We are both beginners longing for connection. However, she is too shy and self-conscious to ask questions about our Judaism and I don't want our religion or rituals to pose a cultural barrier between us. I know I'm particularly sensitive to these kinds of issues, having been ostracized by other immigrants in my cohort of IDF soldiers who'd speak other languages in front of me, intentionally leaving me out.

Now, as we stand around the Shabbat table, I make a concerted effort to include Yuki, explaining to her why Jews observe the Shabbat and why we bless two challahs along with the grape juice. I've historically allowed myself to feel behind and on the outside when it comes to Judaism; in Israel, I became somewhat invisible to myself as a Jew. But I see this as an opportunity to start anew. Here in Pittsburgh, I want to experience true holiness on my own terms.

Yuki nods politely as I talk. She waits for Haim to bless the wine and challah, but Ivry's fingers are already creeping toward the challah.

"Sublimation," we tell him. "Don't eat the challah. Wait for the blessing."

Haim places his hands over Yuki's head and blesses her. Ivry looks at me and rolls his eyes. ("Mom, she's not even Jewish," he will tell me later as he's getting ready for bed.)

There's something welcoming about a white-tableclothed Shabbat table after a long week: our faded challah cutting board from Israel, a goblet of grape juice, a prayer book, homemade Israeli salads, including matbucha and babaganoush (roasted eggplant delicately spiced with lemon and ginger), hummus, and tahini.

I glance over at Yuki and feel called to share my experience participating in a Japanese green tea ceremony at a UN base situated on the Israel–Syrian border in 1997. Her eyes light up like a Chanukah menorah at this story. I show her a picture of me at age twenty-seven, dressed in dressy burgundy polyester pants, hair cropped short, holding a teacup, and sitting back on my heels with my upper body vertical, maintaining a still expression of reverence and submission. She looks at the picture and explains to me the details of participating in this ancient ceremony in Japan, the intricacies of its rituals. Now we have bridged a divide, and there's a shared understanding—that human impulse that exists across all cultures to memorialize and honor things that matter.

After the blessings and the first bite of challah, Haim brings out a slew of items, among them a brisket and a Sephardic cholent dish whose recipe he grabbed from a YouTube channel. We go around the table, each in turn, stating one thing from the week that went well while Ayala casually interrupts us to ask to dip challah in another cup of grape juice, her latest Shabbat concoction.

At three years old, Ayala reminds us that at any time you can choose to absorb yourself in a moment of joy or happiness. This is how we reset the clock, mark, and remark moments. Change over the months and seasons of our lives is inevitable. We cannot control what happens, but we can steer our own experience through the newness. Already, I sense new beginnings and feel right in my choice to adopt the Shabbat ritual here in Pittsburgh, now and moving forward.

The day before she leaves for Japan in late January, I ask Yuki about her final plans before her flight. She's been packing all day, carefully wrapping souvenirs, throwing some things out. She keeps her smile contained as if she's about to boil over any minute. I search her eyes for the twinkle. It's still there but buried under a fluster of emotions.

She bows her head and her body gently sways. "I'm going to miss you," she finally says. "You've been so kind to me."

I'm touched. I've worried a bit that I've been too guarded, even as I've tried to include her in our family. She is quiet and reserved, and in juxtaposition to our chatty and outgoing family, I've been concerned that we might be overwhelming to her. She is peaceful and unassuming, while we have a tendency to provoke arguments.

Her small body heaves between sobs in the soft light of Ayala's room, which has been her home away from home for the past five months. Ayala has been alternating between the other two bedrooms.

"Yuki," I say softly. "We'll miss you a lot." I take in this moment, connecting to all the times I'd left behind places that I had grown fond of. In her five short months, Yuki has begun to feel that the States is her second home.

I step in and pull her close and remind her to take the frozen challahs we baked together to her family. A few days later, she will Facebook me a picture of her family eating our challah, along with a note about how happy they were to eat traditional Jewish food. I will consider how our similarities are stronger than our differences and feel grateful to Yuki for the gift of connection. She's given me an opportunity to grow and to learn, and to see my own family, heritage, and traditions through another lens—one that is fresh and accepting and inquisitive. From this place of openness, I feel secure in continuing to take on the Shabbat, validated as a beginner who is learning, still, to connect to Judaism on my own terms.

It's the last Shabbat in February, and I start experiencing intense, jabbing stomach pains while we're at dinner at a neighbor's. I manage the ten-minute walk home with Ivry leading the way, keeping focused on his gait in the snowy moonlight, hoping I won't double over into the snow. The second we arrive home, I throw open the door and vomit all over the living room floor.

Ivry keeps his cool, as he always does, and runs to get my phone. I know what this means: I have to break Shabbat. The minute my fingers begin to dial my doctor's office, I'm in a trance having a spiritual relapse. Emergency situations pertaining to life and death override the Shabbat as a basic law. The pain is relentless, and I can't see myself suffering the entire weekend. But still, breaking this covenant for the first time since I began to observe it doesn't sit well with me.

Ivry and I pile into a Lyft to take us to the nearest hospital, leaving Haim behind to watch Ayala. A few hours later, as I'm wheeled away for a CT scan, I whisper a Jewish prayer while Ivry stays in our hospital room, bundled in blankets.

The images show gallstones that are causing my gallbladder to act hyper-sensitively. Each time a doctor or nurse enters the room, I remind myself of their holy work; oddly enough, this keeps me in Shabbat mode, and I don't feel compelled to engage with my phone. I try seeing the holy in everything, but truthfully, it's strange reentering this everyday world I willingly left earlier this evening.

No one here can understand the angst of breaking the covenant of the holy Shabbat. Just a few months ago, as I lit the Shabbat candles for the first time with Yuki, I struggled to put my phone on vibrate and ignore it. I wondered how I'd manage to press on when the entire world was still spinning around without me. How would I stay focused on prayer? How could I make Shabbat holy with mundane thoughts swirling in my mind?

Now, I enjoy the freedom it provides.

※

Like a movie you don't want to rewind, I revisit that angst at three in the morning upon returning from the hospital, eyes heavy from lack of sleep, hands laden with doctor's notes and prescriptions. It's as if I've traveled a thousand moonlit nights and mountainous expanses.

I imagine a forgiving God, a contrast to the foreboding one in *Mishpatim* that I used to envision. As I settle into bed, I try initiating some kind of conversation with him as a way to console myself:

I tried minimizing my violation of the Shabbat as much as possible. I didn't check Facebook. But I still feel horrible about it. And I still trust in my covenant.

My God doesn't respond right away, but months later I will recall how, in Chapter 24 of Exodus of *Mishpatim*, after a lingering, cloudy mist descends over Mount Sinai for six days, God calls Moses on the seventh day in order to teach him the Torah's laws. He stays on the mount for forty days and forty nights.

Perhaps from this place, I can begin the process anew.

Our quiet, narrow street runs parallel to one of the main streets of Squirrel Hill that leads to Schenley Park in Pittsburgh's East End neighborhood. When we first bought our home in 2015, I couldn't believe how easy it was to get off the beaten path and enter a world of quiet. Now it's 2017 and in the two years I have lived here, I've gotten to know our street so well that I've become protective of it, almost in the way I was of the kibbutz when we lived there.

Shabbat in wintertime. When I think of the dreary grey and snowy weather in Pittsburgh we've had to endure, I try hard not to judge, attempt to maintain an open and accepting mind. And when I return from services, I get to thinking, *This is the time a person could really feel at home.*

This idea wasn't born overnight. Two weeks after Yuki's departure, on yet another grey and snowy Shabbat, I revisit a *Hayom Yom*—Day by Day Torah—lesson of what it means to transform the physical matter into spiritual (a Chassidic and Kabbalistic concept) in an attempt to ease my mind and avoid getting sucked up by emotions.

The first thing that comes to mind, of course, is our home. For months we have welcomed enough visitors to feel at home. But hosting Yuki for six months is what truly consummated this lesson and grounding us in our community.

Taking on the Shabbat each week for the last three months has been an exercise in re-sanctification—moving away from Facebook to engage more deeply in holy texts.

Today at synagogue, our rabbi stresses that Judaism is an action-based religion, and the more action you take on, the more the relationship to God changes. I wonder if I can sustain this unfolding relationship with God in Israel, where stepping into a synagogue has always felt like a threat. Where I've never felt Jewish enough.

It's precisely as I'm mulling all this over that the rabbi asks us to turn the pages of the Torah to the rather lengthy reading of *Mishpatim*, which scholars refer to as the Covenant Code and which details fifty-three acts of *mitzvot* (good deeds), twenty-three imperative commandments, and thirty prohibitions.

As the rabbi gives his commentary following the Torah reading, I try settling in with the biggest takeaway: partnering with God. There's just one thing in my way—intermittent triggers of the Hassidic nativism I've had to contend with from time to time. I need to override them if I want to reembrace my spirituality. If I don't show up and claim my place at the table, I'll stay triggered by that nativist rhetoric. And because my spiritual longing for Israel is not the same as my cultural longing, this often gets me stuck.

I follow the rabbi's words, absorbing them like a sponge.

I imagine myself entering a modern-day covenant, like Moses. I don't want to be dispossessed like the Eastern European Jews who emigrated to America in the nineteenth and twentieth centuries, who emphasized their individual prayer and brought all their cultural baggage. Instead, I want to achieve spiritual connectedness without feeling compelled to choose spirituality over culture and vice versa.

As I take in what our rabbi is saying, I reframe the idea of a covenant from a nativist ideology to a simple agreement. I'm obsessed with trying to make this connection accessible. By the end of the reading, I hear a message rise from an image I envision of Moses ascending through the mist to Mount Sinai: "You are not alone; we're in this together."

We are in this journey together, helping each other. We're not alone. And my participation must be active. Voluntary.

It seems I've been missing out on a piece of Jewish consciousness all along.

20

THIS BRAVE NEW WORLD

The same afternoon that I make the decision to seek a writing space outside our home, the torrential rains pick up again. The super bloom disappears in a flash and already the days are as hot as an oven. The hot air gusts in through cracks in our air-conditioner, and the rain beats down on brown patches. I stare at our overly weedy garden, my eyes misty yet hopeful, like a sleepaway camper waiting for a care package from home.

Gone are the days when I thought I could convert our drafty basement into a writing space. This month, April, our basement flooded from a burst boiler, and for two days straight, all I heard was the sound of new floorboards being hacked by an electric saw. Bit by bit, the workmen pulled up the wet carpet, revealing a dusty earth floor. I basked in possibilities and all at once, I fought an overpowering urge to rip out the cedar walls and antiquated bar area and renovate the entire basement.

While one of the workmen banged down the last of the new floorboards, the other invited me for a look. He stood to the side respectfully, and as I passed by him I smelled a medley of chocolate and cigarettes on his breath. His smooth-shod feet were inexplicably quiet as he disappeared out to the work station he'd set up in our backyard. His boss, a heavyset man with broad shoulders who liked to walk barefoot outside as much as indoors, was always considerate and greeted me cheerfully in jean overalls each morning.

He quoted a handsome sum for the work it would take to renovate the basement just as Haim walked down.

I blanched at the number. "You're kidding, right?"

"No, I'm not," he said. "There's a ton of work to be done here."

I furtively stole a glance at my husband. *No way, Jose.*

Now, looking out at our backyard, I realize it's time to look elsewhere for a room of my own.

In early May 2017, Kathy, a lawyer, private messages me through the neighborhood site NextDoor—a message that will change my personal trajectory when it comes to building roots in Pittsburgh. "We just really like sharing our space," she writes after I inquire about the quiet private room she's posted about on the site. The single room she's offering as a creative space—for free—is a mere ten-minute walk from my house, and since our cold, uninviting basement isn't an option, for now, it seems like a good option. Besides, the more I think about it, the struggle of writing at home would be hard to overcome.

My ability to give myself permission to write, however, has a long history of waxing and waning. Parenting requires constant nurturing—a deep focus on the other. There have been times when I've felt I had to be stealthy just to write in my own home, which means, at the very best, I'm acting as a worse mother—unfocused on my kids—in order to follow my passion.

On good days, the lens of writing intersects with mothering as I observe, watch, and learn. But on bad days, I can't let go of the writer guilt. My demands seem tenuous, unrealistic. I must have time to write in a quiet environment that does not upset the rest of the family structure. I must sometimes keep to myself and respond to my inner needs. But if I have a full day of mothering, there's no room for writing. By day's end, my arms have become flaccid and my inner voice dry and limpid, as if words have proven worthless.

Before I fully entertain the possibility of getting a room outside our house, I try one last thing: listening to white noise on YouTube loud enough to block out noise and to feel transported as if I'm hurtling through the stratosphere on a mini-jet. Behind a locked door, I listen to all kinds and gradients of the noise, including softened brown, flashy pink, ambient, thunderstorms, and fuzzy static. To me, these sound more like names for Zen mood music than white noises. I resent the fact that I've been forced to choose. *Why can't I just have quiet?* It seems the only solution is to fight my way through the noise and then ignore it, tune in to myself and my needs.

My mind is a battleground warring for my attention. One side of me demands and demeans: *Your parenting comes first.* The other claims any moment possible to write, no matter the circumstances: *Go with the flow.* But what I'm really struggling with is my inability to let go and connect with my heart and soul without agonizing over the details.

I return to Kathy's message. The generosity of her offer, a room to write in for free, is accentuated by the fact that other offers have been purely transactional, the highest going amount at $350 a month—for me, an unthinkable sum. It's as if she's saying, "Here. I give you permission. Don't worry about paying rent. Just write!"

I stare at her words, filled with generosity. They penetrate in and through me. *I imagine you want to be able to leave your files and books here, but if you don't, you could always establish yourself on the dining room table. That's where I work. Were you wanting to get started right away? How many hours a day will you be here? Would it just be during the day? We're totally flexible; I'm just curious.*

I tell her what I envision now—that I'll be there three days a week, working around my teaching schedule and kids' pickups, which will put me in her home Mondays, Wednesdays, and Fridays during the workday while she works as a lawyer.

And yes, I write. *I'd love to get started as soon as possible.*

I'm learning to let go of the fear. I've realized that the faster I can do that, the easier it is to skirt the drama. The law of attraction is real. Positive thoughts lead to positive actions.

I want to let go of the old stories I've been holding on to and to overcome my mental resistance when it comes to nurturing my creativity and self-expression. Play up the warrior in me, the inner strength. I have the ability to discern and make the right decisions. This is the steel way I'm learning to approach my life as a writer.

Today, I'm creating a new physicality. Entering a brave new world, a new frontier.

Kathy invites me for a site visit. It's official.

As I approach Kathy's house, giddiness takes over. The broad, tree-lined street, full of stately, turn-of-the-century homes has an aura of dignity that brings to mind the world of one of Edith Wharton's novels. A golden late-afternoon haze nestles around the majestic spring display of peonies, magnolias, and gardenias planted in Kathy's front lawn. There is no such thing as an unruly hedge here, unlike on my own street. I feel as if I'm walking into a fairy tale.

Often, I've had fantasies about running away, of staying on the bus past my stop, and going somewhere where I would have uninterrupted time to write. I've yearned for anything that would give me more space without having to transition from one task to another. In various iterations, I've written in my journal how overworked, overextended, and time-starved I am; I've described myself more than once as an "air traffic controller." Today, however, I'm investing in myself.

When Kathy opens the door, she seems a little aloof at first, but the muscles in her face soon loosen up and her friendly nature takes over, which puts me at ease. We pass through her living room (it holds a grand piano, which immediately reminds me of Mom), and she invites me into the dining room. Through its bay windows, I can see a portico and a luscious enclosed backyard with grand pine trees around its perimeter that give the impression we're in the countryside.

With the exception of piles of papers and books on the dining room table, the space itself is orderly, spacious, and well-tended. Kathy's husband is nowhere to be seen. Her sunny smile and blond hair are accentuated by the natural light. The fact she has opened her home to me, a perfect stranger, makes me want to earn my keep.

On the third floor is a fairly large, lived-in room that occupies half of the floor. There's just one window, located to the right of a semi-alcove taken up with an armchair covered by cat fur. It has a low ceiling and contains a small arrangement of furniture, including a bed, a small wooden desk and chair, a bed and bookshelf, and an end table, complete with a simple lamp. There's even a bathroom for added convenience. I plop myself in the armchair under a patch of soft light; it's extremely comfortable, and I look around for the cat who must complete this picture. Kathy says that the desk drawers are still filled, but she can always empty them.

Five minutes pass, perhaps more, as we chat, and soon enough her cat emerges from the quiet shadows. I'm mesmerized by this space and all the details Kathy is sharing with me: for years they hosted high school exchange students (nine in all), and between 150 and 200 people have stayed in this room for anywhere from one night to five years.

I feel honored to join this lineage of space sharers who have come from all over the world. I tell her about hosting Yuki and how transformational that experience was for me and our family. What

I really want to tell her is how Yuki's homestay also gave me the opportunity to believe in my ability to make someone else feel at home, but I feel too shy to utter the words.

The lesson of space sharing is a lesson in rediscovering one's lost self. In Margaret Clarke's novel *Healing Song*, Roberta runs away from her pleasant home, her loving children, and her good and decent husband, not quite knowing how her life will ever be the same again. Trying to explain her reasoning for leaving, Roberta pieces together her isolation and loneliness in her marriage, her growing need for space.

I see how I've been like Roberta—how I've attempted to distance myself, to find my own time and space without invoking a chorus of guilt. While Haim is totally supportive of my need to create, the notions of creating space and mothering do not fit together intuitively. I remember yesterday's mini-breakthrough. Let go of trying to perfect these two worlds. One doesn't need to fall at the expense of the other. You can have both worlds. *You can have both worlds.*

"So, what do you think?" Kathy asks. "Will this do for your needs?"

The cat has found its way to my lap; my heart melts. "It's perfect!" I beam.

"She really likes people," Kathy says as I stroke the cat's fur. "But the other one is afraid, and you probably won't ever see her."

"For years," I tell her, "it's been my fantasy to write with a cat in my lap." I look up. "If my son didn't have allergies, we would have a cat."

"Yes, felines can be wonderfully good companions. Good creatures."

For so many years I've yearned for this moment—a room of my own. I used to be able to write in the presence of my children, but then the writing began to feel forced; I couldn't relax, felt as if I had to be ready to shuttle them somewhere at a moment's notice. The secret life of a writer-mama, like that of lovers, is difficult to negotiate and yet is vibrant, complete with compromises and desires. I think about Virginia Woolf, fully aware of the histories that bind us, and all women writers, to one another.

This room is my chance to be free, or even just to strike a balance with my ongoing domestic duties. The space to write, after all, presents a solution. No more getting cut off mid-sentence or responding to small emergencies that arise at home just because I'm there.

While I'm looking around, lost in the possibility of what might be, Kathy searches my expression. What is she looking for? I wonder. A sign of dissatisfaction, uncertainty, or maybe hesitation? I look at her and feel the struggle fading away, leaving only the validation and self-respect behind.

On our way downstairs, she informs me that I'm unlikely to see her or her husband when I'm here. They work long hours outside the home during the day. I would prefer not to run into them anyway.

"You can come whenever you want, though." Kathy smiles. "You're totally welcome to write in the room while we're home, too."

"Thank you," I say, genuinely touched.

We head back downstairs. Back on the first floor, my heart lands with a thump. Kathy hands me a set of keys affixed to a keychain etched with an image of the Duquesne incline.

"Yours," she says with a smile.

A set of keys to my writer heart.

A *room of my own.*

This room away from home has become my refuge, my respite from the general chaos of my life during the entire month of May. I've been assigned a class I've never taught before at the university, and the learning curve is high.

"It's okay, Dorit. Go write," Haim says when I complain how hard I'm working.

Retreating to the room at Kathy's feels like I'm stealing time I don't actually have. I suddenly see that separating myself is a physical act, and something I have to claim. I read Julia Cameron's *The Artist's Way* and *The Right to Write*, full of personal accounts and wisdom, with the mindset of treating them as checklists for settling my fears and doubts. I am finally giving myself space to write, but now that I'm here, do I know how to let my creativity flow? Cameron writes, "We should write because it is human nature to write. Writing claims our world."

I feel a gravitational pull to Cameron. Her words reassure me that I can find my way to trust despite some of the wounds of my past, and to push boundaries and tell the truth despite the possible consequences. Even during chaotic times, when tossing around ideas and words feels like being on a grand old ship in a stormy sea, and especially on those days when I can barely see the next hour ahead, my need to reflect and express myself always guides me safely to harbor.

I stay committed to my plan this first week. I head out with my writing bag on Monday morning. I glide through side streets, my arms reaching out to touch the ferns and weeping willows, sucking in enough outside oxygen to get me through another few hours of self-imposed cocooning. Staying holed up in my room away from home until pickup time is the only way I'm able to define myself as a writer. Like a new mother who has been deprived of sleep for a long time, I thirst for the freedom and possibility to dream, create, and explore new ideas.

And yet this new routine is hard to get into. This new space triggers uncertainty and ambiguity. Spaces feel sticky and tenuous. But eventually, I settle in and start to steer a path forward. Writing about the home I've given up in Israel enters like a storm swallowing the glistening sun on a glorious spring day. One moment I'm fearless, the next I'm windswept by emotional uncertainty.

The cat comes to keep me company, and by and by, she kneads

my legs with her paws. The last time I saw her, three days ago, I fantasized about her taking to me in a way that would allow me to complete the vision I created in my head of my new writing space. But often she gets in the way, tail waving in victory, and it's as if she's trying to sabotage any attempt on my part to type on my laptop.

I try not to get in my own way, which is not particularly easy for me. But as I settle in, I wander less about the house—stroking the kitty's fur, eyeing patches of verdant green, looking wistfully out of the bay windows—and begin to feel bolstered by the fresh words and the flashing cursor on my computer screen.

On a piece of paper, I write all the ways I can create boundaries and structure for myself in this process:

I value and respect myself enough to say no to the things that suck up my time
25. *I have compassion for myself*
26. *I am vulnerable enough to ask for help when I need it*

Like a guard in a building from which everyone has dispersed, I remain on duty. I ground myself in identity and purpose. As the weeks go by, I slowly and gently strike a balance between mothering and writing. It reminds me of a dance—where one takes the lead without the other losing their sense of agency.

I can do this. I can have space for both.

For these three weeks in May, the image of writing in a room of my own is in fact many images: of enjoying the spring blossoms in the morning despite my racing heart, of trudging with my bulging laptop bag under the mid-morning sun after dropping off the children, and, hours later, leaving Kathy's house feeling as full as if I've eaten a three-course meal.

As May comes to a close, I'm getting copious amounts of writing done. I feel an unprecedented sense of accomplishment, and I find myself enjoying Pittsburgh more than I have since we arrived. Cars rumble along cobblestone streets with excitement. Children emerge from nowhere, happy for the extra bit of warmth and sunshine. People congregate in front of the mouths of ice cream shops, creating an instant bottleneck. Cars blare their music, the sound pulsing in the heat.

Is this the joyride of manifestation? I exchange smiles with passersby and for the first time since coming back to the US, the act feels genuine. It's as if fairy dust has been sprinkled on me, imparting the sense of communal peace I've been longing for. In these micro-moments of connection, I have scored an ultimate and long-elusive goal: a sense of community with my fellow citizens. I no longer feel alienated by my own isolation. As the indigo-colored evening transforms into blackness, I think back to my writing room and the internal space I've created simply by manifesting and giving myself permission. Another goal accomplished. This is the ultimate sand-and-steel breakthrough. A hard-earned moment.

I stay up late, reading into the night, far away from the main thoroughfare and crowds, and the shrill shower of car horns and lights. In this Squirrel Hill enclave, where bars close at midnight and restaurants at nine, time is something that rolls away like receding ocean waves. I watch how flashes of the setting sun glint upon our crabapple tree's blossoms. I'm still being pulled along in the current of the vast ocean of time, but not enough to forget the impact of a given moment.

An email from Kathy slithers into my inbox just before midnight on the last day of May. She's just returned from a ten-day trip to Paris, and she and her husband have decided to renovate their third floor this summer. *I'm really sorry—having you writing in our house*

seemed like such a good, easy idea. I wasn't really thinking about his being home in the summer.

Just like that, my room in the eaves is no longer mine. I seem to have plummeted through the floor to the center of the stairwell, back into my crushing heart.

For two weeks, I safeguard the key Kathy gave me in an envelope that I've tucked away in a drawer, secretly hoping that the room will somehow be mine once again. In the interim, I steal nuggets of time to write and finally settle on doing what I can in the early hours from a corner of my bed. I wait for the moment when she might ask about the key, but she never does. I try keeping my longings at bay. *Just because you lost the room doesn't mean you can't manifest that possibility again*, I tell myself. *You can do this!*

After those two agonizing weeks go by, I email her and let her know I'll stop by with the key, thinking as I type the words about how I built a home away from home and now, unexpectedly, I have to rethink what having that homey sanctuary has meant to me.

When Kathy gingerly opens the door at my knock, I steal a peek inside, wondering if anything has changed, but the house behind her is hidden in shadow. I hand her the envelope, which she accepts politely, with a smile. We exchange pleasantries. I want to tell her how writing in her home has unexpectedly connected me to this community and given me a sense of freedom, but I don't. I'm too disappointed, and I feel the acute loss of what I so recently had pressing upon me like an anvil. I feel banished, even outcast. There's nothing left to do but move on.

I bid her good-bye and set out on my return walk home. I have been shoved back out into this brave new world. What will I do now?

21

PASSING THROUGH

August 2017. Another attempt to stretch outside my physical boundaries, this time at an Airbnb in Milford. On a nearby table, propped between two bookends, are pictures of a kind-faced father of medium height with wavy brown hair and his two children. He looks the way he speaks on the phone—generous and helpful, free of pressure and time constraints.

Vacationing in this historic, family-friendly hotspot two hours away from New York City, I find myself excited by the proximity to my childhood home and yet grateful to be far enough away from the city itself to have room to breathe. The distance and newness is enchanting, but also unsettling. I want to tell myself a new narrative—that I belong everywhere, even places where I have no personal history or connections. Yet I sense resistance. I'd rather be floating in the Mediterranean or walking down the promenade of Tel-Aviv. What am I holding on to? What can I let go of?

I keep my ears and eyes open, trying to combat my feelings of resistance. Being on vacation means you're entitled to let go, relax.

But unlike last summer, we're not going to Israel, and my heart tenses. Another summer where my heart has to live with longing and without family. I try not to get too bogged down by these thoughts. I have to adapt to our decision and our realities. Israel in the summer is expensive. And hot. And I'm not happy being hot.

On our first Friday afternoon in Milford, as we walk the two blocks to the beach from our Airbnb to size up the waves, I try stepping into an Israel state of mind, but the range of images don't quite match up. An Asian mother meticulously towel dries her children before packing up. She gently places toys and containers into a colorful straw bag, one by one, as if bagging items at a check-out counter.

It doesn't take long for Ivry to conclude that we were wrong to have booked a place here (these waves are not like those of the Pacific, or Haifa beach, for that matter), and for the next two hours he tries stirring up a confrontation. I want to argue back like an Israeli, but instead I distract myself with Ayala as we hunt for seashells, crabs, seaweed, and pieces of kelp in the soft sand. The sand is one image that connects us—Israel and me, together. I remind myself to stay adaptable, to have the courage to stay open to connections here and now and be open to whatever way they show up.

In the distance are stick figures of a family bobbing up and down in the ocean like buoys. Talking the vivacious talk of a family of cross-generational Israelis speaking rapid-fire Hebrew—no silence, no gap, no private witness—they waddle from the grey-blue ocean like ducks in a row. Ayala and I scoop out sand to make cakes as I listen, taking them in like a spy. But Haim, unlike me, is in his element. He has no reservations approaching this family of Tel-Avivians. I'm afraid if I talk, I'll tense up with longing. Better to stay numb, polite yet distant, and channel my resolve of steel. That makes it easier for me to maintain a sense of connection to America, to forget my past personal history with Israel.

Keeping my distance is my safety net, a survival tactic. Always safer not to engage, not to take heart risks. But holding back longing hurts, too. For longing is a heart muscle, and the heart is stronger than the head. And when I stay silent and observe my heart, my unsatisfied longing for Israel sometimes gets so intense that it threatens to swallow me whole.

Knee-deep in the water, Ivry stands with a surfboard. "Seriously, Mom? We came all the way for this?"

"Sure, what's wrong with them?" I say. "They're just a different kind of waves."

Haim laughs and explains to the nearby family how, ever since we arrived, Ivry has been craving the ferocity of the Pacific Ocean's waves. Against the brilliant sun still high in the sky, their laughter carries out on the waves. One of them cries out affectionately, "*Gingi!*" in a loud but cavalier voice, which has the effect of distracting him.

"*Gingi,*" the man says again, and suddenly, my heart's on fire and my sun-kissed son goes from pouting to smiling. *Gingi* is more than just a word spoken by a stranger; it's a term of endearment. They are embracing my son as one of their own.

No need to respond. In just a few hours, Shabbat will enter, and my heart will already be melting. This moment plants a seed of longing even as it envelops me in a sense of belonging.

This evening, I visit the craggy section of rock down on the beach and recall the easy way those Israelis interacted with my son earlier today. It makes my heart feel warm and fuzzy. Beach houses rise like cliffs, their protruding verandahs overflowing with color and personality, and sliding glass doors refracting the frothing drifts of sunset rippling brilliantly in and out of waves. Tiny waves lap the shore.

I stare out over the sea, out at the stars, dots of longing, and immediately I'm transported to Haifa. We went just one year ago for one last dip in the ocean before heading to Jerusalem and then back to the United States. *Soak in every moment for you won't see your heart home for a very long time*, I told myself when I reached the water's edge. I turned my back to the crashing waves, met Ivry's excited gaze, and together, we flung ourselves forward, face-first, into the glistening Mediterranean Sea, arms flailing.

~☼~

New York City's Grand Central Station is opulent on a Sunday morning in mid-August. Surprisingly, the people around us aren't in a hurry. Still, my first instinct is to walk far and fast. Haim, Ivry, and Ayala follow my lead. I remind them I'm a New Yorker and urge them to keep up, but still they linger behind me.

We're here on a day trip from our Connecticut guesthouse and on our way to the well-known Ohel, the gravesite of the seventh Lubavitcher Rebbe, in Queens. The Rebbe's resting place is a source of blessing, spiritual guidance, and inspiration for Jews and non-Jews alike.

For now, though, I'm leading the way in hopes of finding a bathroom, everywhere noting the familiarity of home—the sign indicating the Number 1 train that would take me downtown to Mom's apartment building, the shuttle I took as a foot messenger for months. All at once, I'm filled with adrenaline. Muscle memory tells me to move even faster, but I don't want to lose sight of Ayala, whose little legs can barely keep up.

So much time has passed since our last quick visit that I feel like I've lost my roots here entirely. When we finally reach the grand hall, I can't help but look up, mesmerized by the celestial ceilings, the world's largest Tiffany clock, the lights spilling horizontally from each side of the main hall as if they're stage lights on the set of a glamorous movie. I stand in the hallway, looking toward the subway signs—the grunge, the fast-paced world that was so deeply a part of who I was for so many years. Now that I've lost Mom and her West Village home, New York in some ways feels like just another huge cosmopolitan city with nameless faces, except that I still feel the pull to my West Village home.

There is so much potential for frustration in trying to bypass the awkwardness of being a tourist in your hometown. You have to adapt and go with the flow, embody the qualities of sand. You need to be adaptable, even when the change feels constrictive or intimidating.

For some reason, the closer we physically get to Mom, the farther away from her I feel. In just a few moments, we'll be on the Number 6 heading uptown to 51st Street and Lexington, where we'll get on the E Train to Jamaica. But for now we just need a bathroom, and I've just realized that one is not going to material-ize out of nowhere. I have to overcome my pride and ask someone, who directs us.

You're a New Yorker, huh? I think to myself. *You can't even find the stupid bathroom.*

As soon as we're done, back through the pell-mell we go, passing stalls of fresh fruit, baked goods, and heaps of sandwiches. For a moment, I'm once again that foot messenger of 1989, just passing through Grand Central, hopping from one subway to the next. But then I return to the present, where I am a stranger in my own city.

I turn to Haim. "Okay, now how do we get to the E Train uptown?"

"You're the New Yorker," he retorts.

Right. I'm the New Yorker.

His response makes me want to scream in frustration. How inept I feel as, unable to reorient myself, I'm forced to ask for direc-tions again—this time to the upper level and the uptown subways. My palms get sweaty, and my teeth clench. I feel triggered; all my old fears come flooding back. The fears of a tween-aged girl who worried she wouldn't get enough letters from Mom while she was away at camp or find her tribe among the rich Jewish kids she'd be surrounded by there. The fears of a girl who catastrophized that she'd get bitten by something, that her mother would get kidnapped while her precious daughter was gone. Mom was an accomplice to that girl's fear—she fed all her worries like an IV drip .

I look at Haim, who's carrying our sweaty daughter. He seems to have no capacity to empathize with the emotional struggle I'm experiencing, and I feel torn between finding the words to explain it and finding the way to our destination.

We walk up and down numerous flights of stairs before finally getting to the E Train and sitting down on its cool seats. Ayala's sweaty hair stays matted to her forehead, but within minutes the air-conditioning brings her beet-red face back to a normal complexion. My jittery heartbeat tapers down and my thoughts stop racing, and I'm able to breathe again. Less adrenaline, more space. We're both getting cooler, returning to our baseline state. Satisfying longings is like building something with Legos: you have to do it one brick at a time, and there's no shortcut.

Our Lyft from the Jamaica subway station drops us off in front of the Ohel and we make our way to the well-lit gathering room before heading to the Rebbe's resting place. Ayala writes a prayer note to the Rebbe that looks like a love letter, with lots of hearts. When Ivry joins in to help her, I snap a picture of them and post it to Facebook with the caption, "They love and learn from each other." Social media—here a photo of freshly baked challah, there an invitation to a Shabbat meal—has become my primary tool of connection.

Here in Queens, sporadic Hebrew zooms in from all directions until the sounds become a fountain swirl of colors, images, sights, sounds, and memories. I post again to Facebook, "At Ohel now. Send your prayers, wishes. Even the little one has her requests. May all our prayers be answered." I post this with another photo of my kids.

A few minutes later, my message box starts pinging. Prayer requests come through. *I see you. We're connected. You're here.* I'm encouraged; people see my value. We share the same goal.

The Rebbe's mission was to reach every single Jew, no matter where, with love and kindness. Haim has brought cookies for the kids, and he drinks another coffee, code-switching from English to Hebrew and back again with passersby while I hover, taking everything in silently, as has become my modus operandi. Israelis come and go, yet Hebrew lingers. I want to break from lurker mode but can't seem to let my guard down.

I want to write a new narrative for myself, one that allows for connection without letting in the suffering that comes with longing. On a piece of paper, I write the names of those seeking a blessing along with their mothers' names and requests, as is customary.

Letters in hand, I walk along a narrow path that diverges into separate entrances for women and men at the gravesite. Haim and I have decided, as we often do in such situations, that it's best to take turns so we can each take in the experience without having to run after our kids. All around are tombstones of Jewish souls I will never know. In the blue, hazy distance is the New York City skyline, the high points separated by waves of houses and smaller buildings that seem to bow in reverence to the newly erected Freedom Tower.

Holiness is everywhere—in the form of words, written and spoken; in the form of the pixels that form images on my screen. In this moment, I feel close to the Western Wall in Jerusalem, where I left my prayer note in the cracks.

I veer to the left and enter the gravesite, where memorial candles and prayers books of well-known *siddurim* greet me. Behind me, a woman is immersed in a book of psalms. I quickly nestle in the back and let others step forward to observe. Up front is a tombstone surrounded by masses of prayer notes. A man sways with his eyes closed, rocking like a boat on the sea after a storm. I want to pray with that kind of *kavannah*, intention.

The Rebbe, whose vision was ahead of his time, saw the perils and dangers of modern life as far as Jewish identity was concerned. I'm praying to return, that somehow we'll find a way to do so one day, but so long as we're here, I've willed myself to believe that perhaps we'll get close to *aliyah* in the States through spiritual ascension—that through prayer we can create a mini-Israel for ourselves here.

I look around at the vast numbers of people entering and exiting this holy site. Those who come looking for connection and who leave filled with godly communion. *Here goes nothing.* I toss my letters like coins into the sea of prayer notes from people all around the world while the lady behind me murmurs her way to the exit.

It's late summer 2017 and we're five months away from Ivry's official Bar Mitzvah date: January 4, 2018. Pressure's on to finalize the location. Pittsburgh or Jerusalem? Like a pendulum, I've been swinging between the two for the past few weeks.

Today, finally, Haim and I talk through our options. There's no way we can do two major celebrations. Haim's family wants it to be in Israel, understandably, but I balk at the price of flights during December's winter break.

A friend suggests looking into January flights, which means Ivry will have to. skip a week of school, but it will lower the price significantly. Back and forth we go until Haim and I agree, lock in dates, and buy round-trip tickets. Israel it is. One mentality, one family. I feel relieved to declare this fidelity out loud.

We decide to do a smaller version in Pittsburgh so Ivry can celebrate with his friends. The caterer writes our preferences: Israeli salads, bourekas, salmon, little kebabs, and falafel balls with tangy tahini and hummus.

The sun's setting, fireflies are dancing and for the first time, I'm dancing with the tune of home in our heart. *This is how you celebrate a Bar Mitzvah*, I want to shout to Ivry. *At your heart home*. The land of your ancestors. Your family. Your country beyond your birth certificate. This is our spiritual pilgrimage coming together.

"How many people do you anticipate?" the caterer asks.

I say one hundred as a starting point, but it's nowhere near the number I've imagined in my head, which is significantly lower, for I know we are not that well-connected here. Although the price she quotes is higher than I expected, it's a small price to pay so my son can celebrate with his American friends.

The caterer zips off and Ivry wails, "Nobody in my class is doing a Bar Mitzvah in Israel. Why we do have to go all the way to Israel? Why can't we go to Hawaii instead? We've never been to Hawaii."

I fight the urge to engage with him in an argument. Instead, I lean against the brick wall of our patio and watch as little orange and yellow specks float in the sky. I point out the beauty of the fireflies to Ayala.

"Why do we always have to do the Israel thing?" Ivry demands.

To me, it's obvious why we'd celebrate a Bar Mitzvah in Israel, but I understand why Ivry's acting out. He's embarrassed about our differences, despite the fact that he attends a Jewish day school; he and one other boy are the only Israeli-born kids in his class, and even the other boy isn't celebrating in Israel. I want Ivry to feel like a proud Jew.

It's hard to understand how our soon-to-be thirteen-year-old can feel so jaded about Israel, considering that he's only been there a few times since our move. But I'm also keenly aware of how important it is to stay connected to family and for the kids to stay connected to their culture.

Nothing I can do or say will sway him. I have to walk through the mud and ravines and feel like the enemy. "Think good and it will be good," I remind myself, thinking of the spiritually-based therapy inspired by Viktor Frankl, world-renowned Jewish psychiatrist. I must transform these feelings of worry, so I can focus on the inherent good of this situation. I must trust that my anxiety will subside.

Late this evening, after doors have been slammed and harsh words have been exchanged, I hop online and research Jerusalem "hot spots": The City of David, Hezekiah's water tunnels, the Ramparts Walk in the Old City of Jerusalem, and of course, the *Kotel*, the Western Wall, where Ivry will recite his Torah portion: *Parashah Shemot*, The Book of Names, Exodus, which starts with a list of the names of the children of Ya'acov, Jacob.

I'm not just a mom in researching mode. This Bar Mitzvah is an excuse to go home again. I hashtag our preparations through the last quarter of 2017 on Facebook—#BarMitzvah2018 #IvryBarMitzvah2018—and my longings evaporate like fog on a sunny morning.

We're going home.

22

COMING HOME

"Move back," a ground crew member growls. New Year's Day 2018. We're waiting in a small, roped-off area in Newark for our flight to Tel-Aviv. A huge group is closing in on us. People are immersed in their phones, but I have too much on my mind not to be fully present—I'm afraid to lose track of time.

I warn Ivry not to disappear on us. He's hungry and wants to explore. *Teenagers.*

There's that in-between, neither-here-nor-there feeling. Haim takes out his *siddur* and the entire contents of his bag topples. Not yet time to board; so close, yet so far.

Haim is performing his evening prayers, the words flowing effortlessly. At some point, he stands up and bows. It's typical to see groups of religious and observant Jews pray on the plane, but I don't see anyone else bowing like Haim at the gated entrance and it feels out of place despite the fact that a few Hassidic men have just arrived on the scene.

Ivry looks up at his father and mouths "wow" before sinking

further in his seat. I want to tell him his father is a model of what it means to be a proud Jew, especially in the Diaspora, but clearly Ivry's embarrassed, so I just sit down next to him and pop in a pair of earbuds to listen to music, my own way of tuning out.

I'm still trying to figure out how to connect to my own godly essence. Even after years of trying to assimilate in Pittsburgh, I'm still thrown off by memories of religious Jews back in Israel—which are especially triggered right now because we're about to get on this flight to Israel. In such a small space, I anticipate a run-in with one of these religious groups. *If you aren't one of us, then you don't count.*

Still, I've held onto my book of psalms all these years. I've got to set an intention now.

Create space for a new narrative, I think, hoping my self-talk will help settle my nerves. *Tell yourself a new story about the Israel inside of you. The Israel you left. The spiritual Israel you are coming back to. The trauma may still be there, but you've made the choice to embrace this path. This moment begins now. With you. Think good and it'll be good.*

If Haim prays with words, then I pray with music. I turn up the volume on my earphones to drown out the woman next to me, who is crunching on Cheetos, and her girls, who are happily giggling over some YouTube video. I'm buoyed by the opening words of the song "Out of the Depths," which comes straight from Psalm 130: "From the depths I have called You." It's by The Idan Raichel Project, a band that mixes Hebrew and Amharic chants into their music.

The deep, soulful vocals of the song give me chills and create a new pathway in my brain, filling up the gnawing hole of deep longing I carry with me. My heart is broken, but music helps me, gives voice to my struggle—my doubts and sorrows over leaving a troubled land.

All at once, I am the Negev Desert. I am the waterfalls of our Jordan River, surrounding our kibbutz. I am longing. My son may never understand the sacrifice and the ramifications of our bittersweet decision to leave our heart home, but I can't forget it.

More people gather around the gate. That claustrophobic feeling. Haim kisses his frayed prayer shawl and then gently presses it to his eyes. My spiritually attuned husband gets lost in prayer while I struggle to stay in the moment. A study of our contrasts.

In less than two days, we'll be united with both sides of our Israeli families. They've all been waiting to celebrate this child's Bar Mitzvah in his birthplace. In less than fourteen hours, I will take out our Israeli passports and transition to an Israeli state of mind, leaving my American life behind.

The gate agent calls for boarding. Haim lifts Ayala up onto his shoulders and she giggles with excitement.

I'll see you on the other side, I think. I hand over our tickets to a smiling crew member.

"Welcome home," someone behind me says in a loud whisper.

Evening falls over Ben-Gurion airport, Lod, Israel, and its surrounding areas. I check my watch: January 2, 2018. The pilots inform us that we are descending into Israel's airspace.

I spent most of the flight watching the little plane icon making its way across the Great Atlantic and over Europe on the screen in front of me. As Ayala dozed off, I dreamt of all the things we'd soon do. High in the stratosphere, I was in a peaceful buffer zone, neither here nor there. I looked down at God's handiwork, the ethereal landscape, and felt an innate returning of my soul.

Being high above ground has always given me a greater perspective. Maybe it's the lack of control or the elevated energy that gives me the headspace, room to think and feel, breathe, be. High in this fluffy zone, I find the strength and passion for my Israel, bypassing all excuses why living in Israel is impossible. Here, there's peace.

Rectangular brown and beige shapes come into view—a vast

desert striated with ribbons of water forming a bottleneck in some places, but not others. In less than an hour, I'll be handing over our Israeli passports and shedding layers I associate with the steely mentality of the States. In Israel, I can let my guard down. In this hot climate, with its mild winters, there's no place for steel. It's even clearer to me now how all these years I've readapted to the American life as an Israeli has been a balancing act. In this moment of coming home, though, I get to decide how much of an American I want to be.

The plane completes its descent, and I clap the loudest of anyone on board when the wheels touch the ground.

Ivry, still in the same slouched position with his hoodie over his eyes, turns his head and rolls his eyes at me for clapping so loudly. I ignore him and snuggle Ayala.

Outside the airport, luggage in tow, we hail a taxi driver who leads us in the pitch blackness away from the bustle of the airport. There is no snow on the ground, but I'm still stuck in my down jacket: it's 47 degrees outside. Haim wastes no time and gets straight to local chitchat—Hapoel Tel-Aviv's latest basketball game, the upcoming elections, Prime Minister Bibi Netanyahu. These conversations bring out Haim's heartfelt connection to his home country; they're brimming, teeming with life.

I put SIM cards in our phones and call family. Then I lean back, take in a deep breath, and say aloud in Hebrew, "Ah, how good it feels to be home." I know this unwritten code of connection will cut through time and space and directly into the heart of this taxi driver. Here I can be open and vulnerable, knowing my heart is home.

Ayala complains of hunger and our driver immediately hands her a big bag of *Bamba*, a crunchy peanut butter snack.

"Say *toda*, Ayala," I prompt her.

"Thank you," she answers in English.

"You're welcome, *hamooda*, sweetie," the driver responds in Hebrew.

My heart swells at this familiarity, how people here treat all children as they would their own. My longing expands twofold. In the ghostly night, we pass signs for Tel-Aviv, and when we take the Jerusalem exit, my heart starts pounding. One step closer to our spiritual pilgrimage.

For the past eleven years, I've been more conscious than I ever was in the earlier part of my life of oceans as mighty borders; I've learned that they separate and isolate, just like bridges. And because they're so vast, each continent behaves like there's nothing owed to the other. As I make out Jaffa Gate, our official welcome to the Old City of Jerusalem, I remind myself that right now, there's no need to worry about choosing one country over another, because I'm home.

On our first full day in Israel, we stand on a hilltop overlooking a breathtaking observation point at the entrance to the City of David, the Fortress of Zion, which King David won from the Jebusite king and in which he then unified the Tribes of Israel as the official capital. Sun shines brilliantly. An olive tree gently flutters in the breeze. Ayala and Ivry, clearly jetlagged, bicker with each other.

When I was a new foreign IDF recruit, personal number 3866256, the IDF brought us to the City of David on an organized tour. I marveled then at the elegant towers, the narrow stone catwalk surrounding the city, and specifically the Jerusalem stone. To think that an ancient civilization had lived here moved me. I was and am mesmerized by these stony remnants of everyday labors of a long-vanished people.

Our American-Israeli tour guide, who picked us up at our

Airbnb on Chabad Street an hour ago, talks about the city's grand infrastructure and architecture, as church bells ring and the sound of prayers emanates from the nearby mosque.

Our Bar Mitzvah boy protects his face from the blazing sun with a baseball cap, wearing just a T-shirt in this 40-degree weather as if to say, "Bring it on. I can take it." I turn around to take in the holiness of this panoramic view. My being is becoming lighter. We are at the center of my spiritual Universe. It must be so for Ivry, too. I can see how the muscles in his still-boyish face are relaxing.

I eye the Jerusalem stone, waiting for a story to magically emerge. I feel safe in my own skin. I've never experienced a moment like this before—felt such spiritual unity with my people. Our history is one of thousands of years of hardship. We are a nation of sand; our adaptability in exile has proven our resilience—from exile to home, the Jewish state. I mentally file this moment as a takeaway to bring home with me.

To our right, Mount Zion. Perched high above, *Har-Habayit*, the Temple Mount, with its glowing gold dome, a structure that for hundreds of years has been venerated as a holy site to Judaism, Christianity, and Islam. Down below, little black dots collectively move toward the Western Wall like moving targets in a video game.

Our tour guide points out that the black stones below us date back to 70 AD and the destruction of the Second Temple. She tells us how the Muslims chiseled the stones down to make their own temple "next door"—a fascinating reminder of coexistence.

In two days, we will celebrate Ivry's Bar Mitzvah, usher him into the Commandments with his Torah reading, *Parashat Shemot*, the Book of Names. Today, however, we are one collective unit taking in the beauty, history, and culture of this place, that, despite the fact that we're expats, is still our home.

I think of the famous redheaded King David for whom the City of David is named—the namesake, too, of Haim's late father, whom Ivry never met, though he carries his middle name. King David. A transplant like me. A discoverer of lands and a visionary who left the city of Hebron over three thousand years ago for this hilltop city. What would he say to my troubles, my strife, my loneliness, my longings? More than a larger-than-life biblical hero, he was a human who faced real challenges—hiding from Saul, in constant fear of attack by his enemies. How was he still able to place his trust in God?

When, on November 30, 2017, just a month shy of this trip, I found myself laid off from my adjunct teaching position, I blamed our choice to leave Israel, even though it's been nine years. *See, I chided myself, this is what happens when you leave your country.* But I came back to myself and found strength in the opening line of Psalm 130, the same psalm that inspired the Idan Raichel song "Out of the Depths." I read the words over again as if I were King David himself, trapped in pools of adversity. *From the depths I have called You, O Lord.*

In the months since, I've marveled at King David's poetic wisdom, his deep foresight. He modeled trust, tenacity, perseverance, courage—universal lessons that I needed to hear, to integrate, and which I now carry with me as a guide as I explore my heart home.

Like a peacock, our guide stretches her arms to a 300-degree angle, drawing our eyes to the city's live panorama—a living biblical classroom in a modern-day world. She talks about the destruction of the Second Temple, of which just one large wall has remained thousands of years past King David's death.

Just one wall, separating me from that past. I close my eyes and remember the day I found out I'd been laid off. I felt totally destroyed. Defeated by ambiguity and uncertainty. I've considered whether my unemployment status might send us back to Israel, despite how impractical it would be to return, especially for Haim; we left Israel because he couldn't find a job, and his prospects here have not improved in the time since. But in my newfound awareness, I've leaned into hope: *Reinvent yourself professionally*, I've counseled myself. *Learn marketable writing skills. Build up a writing portfolio. You don't have to stay an ESL instructor forever. Be adaptable to the changing times.* I think of our people, who assimilated as slaves under Pharaoh's rule, and how they struggled with their newfound status as a freed nation. They too, had to reinvent themselves, had to learn to liberate their imprisoned minds and hearts.

Our guide talks more in-depth about the destruction of the Second Temple—discusses the Romans, the Crusaders. But to me, all that matters is that one wall that's still standing. The testimony that God's presence rests there. Looking past the thing that threatened to destroy me, the crumbling walls of my family's finances, I see that my inner holiness is fully intact.

We walk through the narrow alleyways and cobblestone streets of the Old City, making our way to the *Kotel*, the Western Wall. The time is eight o'clock in the morning on Thursday, January 4, 2018. Exactly twenty-five years have passed since I was released from the Israel Defense Forces. There's such synchronicity in this moment—observing new rites of passage, saying good-bye to old ones. As a newly released IDF soldier, I wondered about the next chapter. I was nervous about reentering civilian life and letting go of the support system I'd built over the previous three years. Now I wonder about my son—who is becoming a man—and the Jewish values we have tried to model for him, like the responsibility of *tzedakah*, giving to others, and putting on *tefillin*.

Ivry stands tall, with pride, distinguished and handsome at thirteen; his hair flames red in the golden glow of the early-morning sun. My son takes to the cobblestone streets like he belongs here. Every stone here is holy. How many times have I traveled this route in my mind?

We've hired a photographer to take some family shots. We follow his lead, and with each step I'm letting my guard down, easing into a more elevated state. I feel that God has granted me this moment after so much suffering from my longings. We're coming together as a family in my heart home, my evolving spiritual center. My inner holiness is manifested by the stones, the streets, the people, and, yes, the love that surround us. I belong here.

A passerby smiles at us and shouts, "Mazal tov!" Others hear and it's as if the entire city has been summoned and is now bearing witness to our happy and significant event. My boy is about to be Bar Mitzvahed. Through narrow alleyways, we go under arches toward the *Kotel*, a parade met by greetings at every turn. We round a bend and Chassidic Jews, men and women, accompany us in merry-go-round fashion. Here on the crowded streets of Jerusalem, our photoshoot is drawing attention. Our private moment has now become a public spectacle.

When the walk is complete, we find ourselves in a smallish courtyard. As quickly as the fanfare began, it ends, and we descend under the last of the series of archways before making our grand appearance on the steps leading to the *Kotel*. I'm rediscovering my city, the Jewish capital of the world.

In his double-breasted navy-blue suit and sparkling red tie, Ivry adopts a stately stance next to his grandparents, his red hair glimmering gold in the sun. I remember how our family held him in our kibbutz living room days after his birth, our firstborn, awed by his thick crop of red hair and his tiny movements. His name, Ivry—which means, literally, "the Hebrew"— tells me who he is— the first born, the first Hebrew-speaking child and, literally, the first Hebrew.

When the Israelites were slaves in Egypt, Pharaoh dehumanized the Children of Israel by un-naming them. He felt threatened by the presence of the children of Israel flourishing in his land, so he began a multi-staged plan of isolation and oppression in order to estrange the Jews from Egyptian society. This is why the opening of Shemot (Exodus) lists each tribal head and every person. The grand takeaway: Every Jew matters, beginning with one's name. The Israelites kept their Hebrew names during the period of enslavement, and that prevented their total assimilation into Egyptian culture—allowed them to preserve their identity.

Shortly after we arrived in Pittsburgh, I decided I didn't want Ivry to be just another American but someone whose name had essence and meaning. *Ivry Anochi.* Now my son, weighted by the big, silver-plated Torah he's carrying in his arms, leads his family from the inner sanctuary toward the open space of the men's section at the *Kotel,* and I sense how the holy and the cultural parts of his name come together. His heritage. *And he said unto them, Ivri anochi (I am a Hebrew); and I fear Hashem, Elohei HaShomayim, which hath made the yam (sea) and the yabashah (dry land)* (Bereshis 1:9; Genesis).

With the help of the rabbi, Ivry opens the Torah to The Book of Names and begins reciting the story of his people. In this open space, we bear witness—slices of moments. Women climb on chairs on one side of the divider, men on the other. Ivry starts the Torah reading while men crowd around, including passersby. My son. The Hebrew. The Jew. In Israel.

My Israeli-born father bears witness too—his arms and head tightly wrapped in *tefillin,* thanks to the help of the rabbi. My heart is wrapped in love. The unity, the generations. Later, he will tell the rabbi and other family members about the last time he put on *tefillin,* when he was just a boy. He, too, is the first Hebrew, *Ivry Anochi.*

Ayala, in her red woolen coat, leans into me and we bounce up and down for warmth. An old friend from my teaching days procures a pair of black gloves for her and I'm touched. I want to bottle this moment so I can access these feelings wherever I go.

Ivry reaches the part of his Torah reading when he mentions the seventy names of his own Parashah. His lineage. Our ancestors. One connected tribe.

The morning slowly warms up. From beginning to end of the Torah reading, Ivry speaks effortlessly, as if he's been doing this for years, leaving us all in amazement. A veteran Hebrew teacher mentioned how gifted he was at Torah reading, but even so, his fluency surprises me.

Toward the end of the Torah reading, we the women, still standing on chairs and armed with fistfuls of candies, talking among ourselves about our Ivry, all of us filled with pride for the man, the Jew, he's becoming. I observe the way he looks at the rabbi with his humorous, engaged expression, as well as his jocular tone as he speaks Hebrew with his uncles and aunts. I admire the way he relates to everyone.

How many times has Ivry whisked off his kippa and stuffed it in his pocket before and after services in Pittsburgh? *I don't want to be seen as a Jew. I want to assimilate. Nobody cares.* Each time I've urged him to put his kippa on, to never forget where he came from, to appreciate his unique name. "You're Ivry Anochi!" I've said, to which he's simply rolled his eyes. "C'mon, Mom. Enough already."

A turtle dove circles around and nestles in a crevice of the Wall. On the other side of the partition, my Ivry stands tall, the center of love and attention. I keep my footing on two imbalanced chairs, weighed down by my candy-filled pockets. Today I am surrounded by my family and my people. In less than a week we will go back to the dark world of the Diaspora, to our minority-in-a-minority status. But for now, I soak up the present moment. This is where I belong.

It's Jewish tradition to shower the Bar Mitzvah boy with candies, and so we now fire them at him in bucket loads. They catch glints of sun, filling the air with sparkling color. "Mazal tov, Mazal tov!" we shout in joy. Ayala fills her tiny coat pockets with candies that fall to the ground. She looks up and gives me an immense grin. She's pleased with herself.

Ivry is attacked from all angles, smothered with love and congratulatory words. My heart warms a thousand times over. He is lifted high into the sky and as he rises, he lifts his hands into the air in profound joy, as if to say, *I am the king.*

As we make our way to the taxi that will take us to the lunch reception, my son says, "Now I know what a Bar Mitzvah feels like."

I reach for Haim's hand. I feel the same way.

23

LETTING GO

Christmas trees on rooftops. Mosques and minarets. Over the course of a two-mile, uneven walk in search of a hard-to-find rock wall-top, a gem hidden from locals and tourists alike, the familiar disappears and my feet ache. The walk will end soon, and we'll need to decide whether to take the long way back to our Airbnb or take the shortcut through the Muslim Quarter. As I delight in the views of the Christian Quarter with its numerous churches and other Vatican buildings below the walls leading to the Muslim Quarter of the Old City, I try to not notice the stiffness in my husband's body, his uneven gait, his labored expression. We've just left our comfort zone. The Jewish Quarter's behind us.

"You see why the guard said this side of the wall was not *sympatie*—welcoming?" he says.

When we walked through the Jewish Quarter, I wanted to grab my phone and snap photos of Jews and Arab-Israelis walking side by side, but in the Muslim Quarter that diversity is not overly apparent.

Invisible boundaries separate the four quarters of this enchanting holy city. There are Armenian, Muslim, Jewish, and Christian neighborhoods. This place has a difficult history, marked by wars, uprisings, conflicts. The choice to view the Muslim Quarter or any of the neighborhoods through a lens of coexistence is ours. I've experienced tolerance and connection firsthand: my Arab Christian family on my father's side; studying with Israeli Christian Arabs, Israeli Muslim Arabs, Israeli Druze, Israeli Cherkesim, and Israeli Jews. Emotions and faith have roots as deep as the ancient olive trees of the Old City.

While we walked along the wall, we were at the same height as many of the rooftops, had an elevated perspective. But now, at the end of the walk, we're back down with other people. Haim turns to me with a look on his face: *What do we do now?* He's anxious to get back to the Jewish Quarter. Back to his comfort zone.

We meet up with two German tourists and Haim consults with them. Left, we go down to Damascus Gate. Right, we descend to the Shuk that goes through the Muslim Quarter.

"Or we can go back the way we came," Haim murmurs.

"Right," I say, "but that's the longer way. Not so good for Ayala." The rocky ground is uneven and she's already complaining. Haim would have to carry her for the entire two-mile walk back, and he's already tired himself.

Comfort zones. I mull over this concept in my mind. As Israeli Jews, we were sheltered by life on the kibbutz. I've never seen Haim exercise as much caution as he does right now. His unease is palpable.

Haim grew up speaking Arabic with his Iraqi grandmother, Savtah Majodah, and knows four Arabic dialects: Syrian, Egyptian, Lebanese, and Modern. He's used Arabic in the IDF. A lesser-known fact: Jews—specifically, Jews from the Arab world, like our Iraqi grandmothers—have been speaking Arabic for over a millennia. But Haim also fought in the Israel–Lebanese war in 1982 for eighty-two days straight when he was twenty-three years old. I can only assume he's triggered, that this is some form of post-traumatic stress surfacing. Here's a tight-lipped man who I've always known to be strong and fiercely independent. He's not used to feeling vulnerable, and I know that's part of what's going on. Perhaps his reluctance to walk through the Shuk is about never having gotten over seeing the people who live here as "the other." Right now, I imagine, his emotions are getting in the way of him thinking practically. But we can't just go back the way we came; we don't have the energy.

He stops another group of German tourists, and they reassure him a few times that it's safe to go through the Muslim Quarter. I can see that he needs a second opinion and is depending upon their responses to make a decision. I can't help but notice that he doesn't ask me. Perhaps he thinks I'm not objective enough.

I start to imagine Haim's experience as a young soldier. His brigade commander orders his platoon to infiltrate the border into Lebanon. Armed with Uzis and M16s, they enter abandoned villages. He is so tired as he strains to distinguish between the bodies of soldiers and civilians. "*Kod, kod!*" they shout to one another on communication devices while sirens blast around them.

Although he's clearly tense, I consider this might be an opportunity to ask my husband some questions about that time in his life, things I've always wanted to know but have never asked. I've relied on his strong, impenetrable shell over the years, but that's also sometimes come at a cost. Now I wonder, *How vulnerable is he, really?* This moment is mine to seize. These triggers are presenting themselves right now, in the holy land, for a reason.

The young German tourists descend toward Damascus Gate, leaving us once again alone and Haim once again to deal with his fears. I look around and see no other tourists. Perhaps his fears have been amplified because of how deserted this side is. Could it be that he isn't the only one who has been triggered by this place? That people have noted how this side passes by the Lion's Gate and the Dome of the Rock, the Islamic shrine located on Temple Mount, and gotten cold feet?

Like Ivry, I'm anxious to move on, but I'm also compelled to piece together Haim's frayed emotions, like a detective.

"Conquer your fears," I tell him. "You can go through the Shuk. It'll be okay." I say these words mostly to reassure myself and am relieved that he listens thoughtfully.

"C'mon dad. What are you scared about?" Ivry asks matter-of-factly.

How do you explain to a thirteen-year-old boy what it means to defend your country?

Haim eyes the Shuk like a vulture. The market teems with people. His face begins to morph—cheeks, eyes, chin, and forehead tensing up again—and I wonder if he'll be able to push through. He seems bent on controlling the situation.

"You can do it." My words float. I'm going to wait for him to make the decision that seems so clear to me.

He takes a first step down the stone steps and toward the Shuk and I'm relieved. *There you go.*

"Just don't speak any Hebrew," he whispers fiercely as he takes the lead. "Only English."

I look at Ayala. We've been mostly speaking Hebrew on this trip, so I wonder if she'll slip if we try to tell her she can't have too much candy and sweets in English. I recognize that speaking English in the Muslim Quarter is Haim's way of protecting himself. I'm happy to comply if that will make him feel more comfortable.

We descend slippery and rocky steps. They seem to sway. We enter the Shuk, and Ayala, as I anticipated, already wants candy, but Haim pulls her along. *Soon, soon.* I take in the scenes, the same as in other quarters: the scent of fresh pita wafting on the air, colorful scarves and handbags hanging. The only difference here is that you hear more Arabic than Hebrew, and I see an old, dilapidated sign to Hebron in green.

Walking through the Muslim Quarter is like navigating a maze. There are signs to the Via Dolorosa and a black imprint on the corner wall that's twice as big as Haim's hand.

When we finally pause for a moment, Haim surprises me by speaking Arabic with a shop owner who's selling socks and purses. I'd been looking for a replacement for my old, beat-up purse, and my socks are dirty, so I take this moment as good timing. Ivry watches closely and listens to Haim haggling over the price. *There you go, Haim. Let your guard down. Show your kids that you can overcome your fears.*

We stop a few more times—at one point at a ceramics store where the owner makes us Turkish coffee. I'm afraid that Ayala might break a piece of pottery, but the shop owner takes no notice. He's engrossed in casual conversation with Haim, who seems to be back in his element and over whatever was bothering him at the beginning of this adventure. I'm noticing how his words flow. He's clearly more comfortable. I listen to the Arabic all around us and think about the teacher's college where I learned so much from Arab-speaking students about their culture, food, and history. Whatever was triggering Haim, I'm proud of him now for pushing through his fears.

As we complete the last leg of the walk to our Airbnb in the Jewish Quarter, the familiar arch appears, the same one where I first noticed Arabs and Chassidim walking side by side, and Ivry asks his *Abu* Haim questions for his Jewish studies project about the pogroms in Iraq, the story of Haim's family's migration. It turns out this experience is giving them a chance to have a conversation they wouldn't have otherwise had—about Ivry's roots and where he comes from. Our personal experiences and histories. Not separated into quarters after all.

※

Evening falls and the Western Wall turns a beautiful shade of rosy pink. The night before traveling back to the States, I tuck one last prayer note into the wall's crevices, my eyes misty and teary. I locate the glove from Ivry's Bar Mitzvah in my pocket and use it to dab at my eyes since I don't have any tissues. I've been praying for IDF soldiers, for family and friends, to find a job, for my Pittsburgh community, and for clarity on whether I'm meant to be in Israel or the States. My job search has been on hold during this trip. I'm not eager to go back to the States and an uncertain future. My heart still belongs in Israel.

But I already know what Haim will say if I ask him about staying, because he's said it a thousand times before. *Dorit, it's not practical. No one in Israel hired me at forty-four. Who's gonna hire me now, at fifty-eight?* So I don't tell him that last night I sat with a former colleague and Pittsburgher who returned to Jerusalem to teach English, and she shared different ways I could earn money.

"You'll make more money tutoring in English than classroom teaching," she told me.

"Really?" I asked. "Jerusalem's saturated with so many native English speakers."

"Yes," she responded. "But there's a need for the really good ones who know what they're doing."

Know what they're doing. If anything, this trip has made me consider how little I know.

Pigeon poop falls on my coat just as I settle into my cozy, familiar corner, smack up against the Wall, close to the male-female divide. I'm a tiny speck on the live webcam sponsored by Simcha Hall, but my longing has escalated and become enormous. I know what I'm about to give up once again—my country. I turn around and take in the panorama of the Western Wall, a place I've visited almost every day for the past twelve days: Israel flags waving against the background of the Jerusalem stone buildings of various heights, the constant milling of visitors and prayer goers. Just a few meters away, my father and stepmother and in-laws witnessed Ivry's proud moment.

A woman cries out, bringing me back to the present moment. From nowhere, it seems, a strong, boisterous, male voice with a Yemenite accent shouts something. I strain to hear. It's the opening line from Psalm 121: "A song for ascents. I shall raise my eyes to the mountains, from where will my help come?" Next he moves to Kaddish, the mourner's prayer, the evening prayer.

At the conclusion of each Shabbat during the past year, I've headed to the nearest coffee shop and pulled up a YouTube video of a well-known Israeli singer singing these opening lines in order to transport myself here. And now here I am. I take it all the way in.

There's structure to what may sound like one big mish-mash. Words spoken with real *kavannah*, intention, that I lean into for strength. In between words, the man sobs. Some of us on the women's side are already sobbing as well.

In the background, groups of children sing various renditions of well-known prayers. When he says Kaddish, the mourner's prayer, everyone says, "Amen." I allow his voice to buoy and lift me. He finally stops as if the waters have quieted, parted. Who is this man?

I turn to see if the man is really Yemenite and there, he is— faced away from me, short and righteous, at least seventy years old, hobbling with a cane and shrouded with a tallit. A group of people escort him out. God must have sent him as the messenger to uplift our prayers.

Take in his strength, Dorit. You're gonna need it.

Before checking in for our return flight to the States, I post a picture of the check-in terminal on Facebook: "Someone please hold me because I do not want to get on that plane." This is my plea, my last cry for help.

The country I thought I'd outgrown is once again the country I don't want to leave. This kind of longing is about a desire to be connected to some place or something when you cannot. This kind of longing is about deep loss. If I were to grab an Israeli on a street and initiate a random conversation about living abroad, regardless whether he had lived abroad, ultimately, the conversation would intersect various pain points: first the highs—the adventure, the fun—and then the somber, the longing, loss. *I see you. I feel you.* This imaginary Israeli would look me in the eye in a way that no American or Israeli in Pittsburgh has ever done and say in Hebrew, "It's so difficult living abroad," and we would both internalize what that means, our hearts quickly coming alive.

As I pull our suitcases closer to the check-out counter with Ivry and Ayala by my side, my throat tightens up and my eyes brim with tears. My glasses start fogging up. Haim leads the way, turning around periodically to make sure the kids aren't making any trouble, and making just enough eye contact with me to help steady me.

We've both had a long day of packing squeezed around last-minute souvenir shopping and a last visit to the Western Wall. I'm afraid to check in with him. So much to say. So little time. I don't want to distract him from his current target: getting home.

The couple in front of us finishes checking in and Haim approaches the next available clerk, motioning for me to follow.

Go, go, he seems to say, but without the accompanying pep talk I am looking for.

A Pittsburgh-based friend quickly responds to my post of angst with the comment, "New adventures await you." As an Israeli-American herself, I can see her point. Leave one country. Cross the ocean to get to the other. An act of formality that involves so much risk and heartache. I take her response as a kind of internal push. *Look what you'd be giving up in the States if you don't leave Israel now,* I remind myself. Weighing the loss against the gain is perhaps the hardest challenge for an expat.

I hand over our Israeli passports to the clerk with a shaky hand. Haim places the suitcases on the scale while my phone pings with messages from family. On the other side of the ocean waits uncertainty.

We walk through the final security check, my legs like jelly. Our Hebrew gives way and bit by bit, English creeps in. Our mouths crunch down on syllables and we start pounding out familiar words and sentences that put the States back on the map again in my head, though not yet in my heart.

When we arrived not even a fortnight ago, even from the tarmac there was the pulse of familiar energy that I associate with Israel— the body language of the workers, the police cars in the distance. I couldn't hear anything from inside the plane, but I was eager and anxious to leap out of my seat and head straight to our kibbutz home.

Leaving Israel, perhaps like leaving anything one holds dear to the heart, has been one long exercise in learning to gather faith and trust, like a farmer preparing not just for one harvest but for every day of the year, for years on end.

I slowly start the final walk to the plane as if my shoes are filled with stones. We arrive at the gated area. *This is it.* Ayala and Ivry rush to look at the sparkling white planes in the dark lit by floodlights. I take in their excitement, my eyes resting on an EL AL plane in the distance. Even in the dark, I can still make out the Israel flag. After years of Diasporic living, my heart now understands that flag's meaning: It's a giant reminder of the sovereign land of the Jewish nation after thousands of years of exile. A free land for all religions. A promised land. And regrettably, a land I'm leaving again today, not knowing when I'll return.

24

COMING TOGETHER

At around 10:15 a.m. on October 27, 2018, Kanako, our fifth Japanese homestay, makes her way down the stairs, cell phone in hand. As she reads message after message, I'm jerked into the outside world on a Shabbat. Everything about this moment feels off, including the madly chirping birds outside in the foliage. The blue light of the phone reflects in her glasses and eyes, which are glued to the screen.

Then her usually peaceful face cringes.

"Somebody killed in Squirrel Hill?" She pauses between each word, trying to understand the unnerving reality. I give her a ghostly look. On a holy day that's typically set aside for prayer and introspection, I am being pulled into chaos, a formidable black hole that will soon enough engulf not only our quiet Squirrel Hill enclave but all of Pittsburgh and the whole country.

In a matter of seconds, Ivry's phone is vibrating with a flurry of text messages. "Mommy, there's been a shooting!" he cries, holding the phone in midair like a mannequin.

Outside, birds are still madly chirping.

More vibrations.

"At the Tree of Life synagogue."

"What? No way," I cry. "Can't be."

Just when I've allowed myself to feel at peace here, this news of more shootings and violence in our community shatters that bubble. In the last few years, I thought I was on the safe side of the bright line, even as I witnessed the way hate was blooming in this country, my country of origin and now my chosen home. Now, I'm terrified.

Hatred has been growing in this country like a poison, fueling people to target minority groups. Initially, I reasoned that hate is geographic, restricted to big places, large cities; but clearly it's everywhere—and no place is truly safe.

This event feels an ominous sign of the times we live in, like some terrible shadow taking over the world. I look at the images streaming in on both Ivry and Kanako's phones in a pool of unfiltered blackness, and like a thunderbolt I see how this terror will become everyone's terrible, combustive reality. I decide not to engage with my phone, which would be a violation of Shabbat. Like a spectator, I stay on the sidelines, trying to process what's occurring.

We are moving targets. My thoughts turn immediately to Haim, who is on his way to our synagogue—located just a few minutes away from the Tree of Life synagogue—with five-year-old Ayala. Tree of Life is where my son and his classmates formed a prayer minyan each Wednesday last year. Some of my son's friends and their families attend that synagogue.

"Mom, I'll stay at home," Ivry tells me as I start to gather my things. The game of chess he was supposed to play at the library before going to services will not be happening. News outlets are already calling this incident out as a "hate crime." We have been warned by the city to avoid the library and the stores on the main intersecting streets, which are closed anyhow.

This moment is deep and dark as a cavern. I make my way to the door. I don't need to say where I'm going. The hollow look on my face expresses my terror that Haim and Ayala are out in this unsafe world.

"Mom, are you going to be okay? Maybe you should go via Darlington."

The latest update on Ivry's cell tells us that the active shooter is still on the prowl.

Outside, the world is on fire, burning up. In the ten-minute walk to the main street, I've already cried for a thousand deaths, for all the countless people who've died for being Jewish, from Israel to Pittsburgh and back again. I'm transcending emotional boundaries that have known true catastrophes. These live in my cells. And even while I'm silently crying for the lives lost, I long to interact, talk, share, engage with others—not even necessarily my fellow Jews but anyone. But I only see stick figures in the wind. Frozen statues. People who look too shell-shocked to slow down. Their thoughts, too, are scattered like sand across a desert, and each of us floats away on our own, scurrying to whatever destination awaits us. To safety.

Even as I go down the main street—against my son's request—past the police brigades and toward our synagogue, sirens continue for a long while. I steadily walk for another ten minutes, wondering if our congregation knows the news or if I will have to be the bearer of that news. I'm aware of a deep stillness within, somewhere underneath the panic and the chaos. I know this tragedy is both communal and individual. I know I will seek peace from my community even as we grieve. These are feelings I know well from catastrophes witnessed in Israel. Our community has gone through something profoundly terrible, but it's too early to verbalize any emotions just yet.

When I reach our synagogue, sirens still ring in my ears.

A newish congregant opens the door only to those he recognizes, his bearded face full of grave concern. As he holds the door for me, he tells me he knows, everyone knows. These are difficult times, I say. We talk out our emotions for a few moments. The most vulnerable of emotions find their way to my lips. This beast has infringed itself on our city. My darkest fears have been realized. By and by another congregant joins us from the main sanctuary, where men wrapped in *tallits* work through the prayers of the morning service. We talk some more where we are, quietly so as not to disturb the prayers.

Through the double doors, Haim catches sight of me. He approaches me to say that he knows, that a doctor's beeper was the bearer of the awful news. Then he goes back to the sea of prayer goers, along with our rabbi, who sings and prays loudly, with pride. It's almost time to open the ark and begin the Torah-reading portion of the service. I'm still on my guard and deeply triggered, but I've found comfort and strength enough here at our synagogue to finally enter the main sanctuary.

Men and a few women present steady their gazes on the Torah ark. No one is talking, just praying. I immediately think to myself how vulnerable they've become; here, silent and still, we are all sitting ducks. *It could have been us*, I think. *It was us*, I remind myself.

The colors in the stained glass window are limp, lifeless. I see Ayala quietly playing in the adjoining room, unaware of my presence. In my head, I conduct a low-scale reconnaissance of the two adjoining sanctuaries in my mind—Where are our exit doors? How quickly could everyone escape if a shooter struck?

How odd it feels to be so on guard in this spiritual sanctuary that I've worked so hard to call home. Just as I wanted to protect my young son from an unknown war back in 2006, I now want to protect my children and fellow Jews from this hater of Jews. I look around and feel utterly helpless.

Forty-five minutes in, our rabbi gives his sermon, signaling the end of the services, and I shudder at this thought: at ten o'clock in the morning, almost two hours ago, while Haim and his fellow congregants were probably reciting the *Shemah*, the most essential prayer in all of Jewish liturgy, with their hands covering their eyes to affirm God's omnipotence, a murderer was on the rampage, killing Jews, our brethren, just a few blocks away.

Immediately following the attack, our little enclave of Squirrel Hill becomes a media jungle. There are still reporters and officials everywhere. We have made international headlines for all the wrong reasons. We're on the map.

It's been three days since the tragedy. Today, I go to our Jewish Community Center and try to pull myself together at the gym. On CNN, Jeffrey Meyers, president of the Tree of Life congregation, talks about our communal suffering and the need for healing. Like me, regular community members work out their pain and suffering on the treadmill and elliptical trainer with a sense of urgency. Despite our ferocious need to work out, there's a deep heaviness in the air.

Next to me, a gym member shouts, "Robert Bowers was an evil Nazi!" in a voice full of fury and anger. Others question why we wait longer to bury our dead; they want to bypass the twenty-four hour rule that is customary in Israel. I try to make eye contact with those around me—*I see you, I understand you*—but everyone seems too consumed by grief to connect. Regardless of background, everyone in this gym has been affected by our communal tragedy.

For me this event is reflective of an age of growing anti-Semitism, not just in our community, but the world at large. Even more so than in the past, I crave a safe haven. Everyone I know contends with a version of some kind of longing and tries to escape it. But grieving in our Jewish community is a longing in and of itself—an awkward stab at feeling whole, feeling alive again. I'm hoping we'll find a way through this dark, uncertain period and become strong again, connect and take upon ourselves the principles of

Ethics of the Fathers—to love our fellow Jew as ourselves—but perhaps it's too early to have that kind of expectation here.

Israel, however, quickly gets it: on the walls of Jerusalem's Old City, colored lights are projected to form the Israeli and American flags, along with the words, "We're with you, Pittsburgh."

Have I misunderstood the purpose of my longings? For the last eleven years, I have managed to convince myself that the only way through them is by fighting them off, only to eventually surrender to the pain they evoke. Rebelliously, desperately, I want to discharge myself of these self-imposed beliefs and replace them with a new intention: being the community connection I'm seeking in the Diaspora. I want to bridge the gaps between longing and true connection. The time has come.

An opportunity lurks in the back of the gym, where a neighbor from our street works out with alacrity on one of the elliptical trainers. I gather the courage to talk to him. We've never spoken before. I discover he is a New Yorker, like me, and that his cousin, Naftali Bennet, an Israeli politician, texted him with questions about our small town before speaking to thousands at the peace rally that happened one day ago in Pittsburgh, another global event where thousands stood together in solidarity and garnered worldwide media attention. I invite his family to come over for a Shabbat dinner sometime soon.

I am experiencing something I know to be true of catastrophes—that they bring communities closer together. Seeing how the entire city of Pittsburgh and the world at large is standing in solidarity with those beloved souls we lost is unlocking a deeper connection in me, one I've not felt since I lived in Israel. This senseless tragedy has connected me to the fact that I have become part of this community.

Out of the eleven funerals this tragic week, I will attend five.

On Friday, I attend the funerals for Sylvan and Bernice Simon, a loving older couple who were regular synagogue-goers at the Tree of Life, and my heart breaks as family members tell stories about them. The Torah reading of *Kedoshim* in Leviticus is the great dictum in which the esteemed sage, Rabbi Akiva, refers to the cardinal principle of Torah, "Love your fellow Jew as yourself."

It's standing room only. I go alone, during the day, when the kids are at school and Haim's at work. I huddle in the back, hanging my head and making small talk with a few neighbors. I try to wrap my head around the sorrowful idea of dying *al kiddush Hashem*—sanctifying God's name in a house of worship—as I take in the stories, and feel my connection to this community grow, despite the fact that I never knew these people.

A well-known community member turns around, her eyes wet with tears. How is it that we never got a chance to know these beautiful *neshamas*, souls?

I make my way out of the funeral home alone. I cross to the other side of the street, thinking I will wait for the hearse, but then I decide not to wait and head home instead. As I'm pondering whether or not to take a bus, a friend tells me she's parked nearby, and she'll give me a ride.

We make our way to her car via the street that Tree of Life Synagogue is on. The street is still piled with hundreds of bouquets. A woman dressed in a hijab sobs, "How can they do something like this? This doesn't make sense." I take a photo of the entire block and upload it to Instagram—a memorial, a shrine of sorts, to preserve this moment. As I do, a sequence of related images uploads to my mind like butterflies trying to nestle on a sunny rock. They capture for me the feeling of communal grieving in Israel. Where have I seen this image before?

As we near the car, we happen upon members of a rabbinical organization who've flown in from Los Angeles and New York for the week of funerals.

When I express my gratitude, one of them says, "I trust you'd come for us if, God forbid, something like this were to happen in our Jewish community, wouldn't you?"

I let the question—which feels like a request—sink in. This is what building a community within a larger Jewish community feels like. Instantly, I feel as if I'm back in Israel, my powerful little country that always bands together with support and love. I'm astounded by the generosity I'm witnessing here in the Diaspora, despite our differences in culture and background, and it fills me with pride to know I've become part of this.

Moish—a proud, Pittsburgh-born, observant Jew—and his wife invite us, along with other community members, to a Shabbat meal at their home, the first Shabbat after the attack, in an attempt to bring our community closer together. He's one of many members of our local Pittsburgh *Chevra Kadisha*, Jewish burial society, who is preparing to bury our Jewish martyrs with their blood, an age-old tradition. This past week, along with the entire Pittsburgh community, I'm becoming part of this Jewish history.

When I learn of Moish's holy "side job," I have questions. Lots of them. In Judaism, blood is life and cannot simply be washed away and disposed of; it needs to be buried with the dead. So someone has to collect it. I'm aware of the fact that this isn't particularly an easy topic, but I know Moish well enough to know he'll be receptive to my questions. I also know he is still processing everything, and perhaps this will be an opportunity for him to speak of his experience.

He is level-headed, calm, and rational. He's knows I'm a storyteller and, like him, an observer and processor. I admire his ability to share his experiences about such a horrific scene. Perhaps he trusts my ability to handle his story because of my years serving in the IDF and living in Israel.

Still, with his traditional Hasidic garb and full black beard, Moish is a private person; I know he won't share what he's seen and experienced in the last week with just anyone. I'm honored by his willingness to talk to me, and I feel it's my duty to bear witness to his stories.

"So, I'm curious, " I say in a low voice. "The FBI—I mean, were they watching you the whole time? What were they doing? Taking notes?"

He tugs his beard. "The FBI was involved in the whole process. They watched how I knelt and bent over in the main sanctuary and other areas of the building using backlight to scrape and search for blood."

Luminol, he explains, is used by forensic investigators to detect traces of blood at crime scenes, as it reacts with the iron in hemoglobin and hydrogen peroxide.

The blood. All of it. The life force energy of our beloved people whose memories are now absorbed by carpets and the walls. Whispers, words, and floating images. In Judaism, the blood needs to be accounted for, but what about their names? Will they be remembered?

Talking about this "secret" group confirms for me the intricacies of our religion. There is teamwork involved, but also feelings of abandonment and loss. We may bury our dead but not ourselves. As he powerfully recollects what it has felt like to be at the Tree of Life during these recent, dark days, I feel how Judaism, my religion, takes care of its people.

At some point during his twenty-six-hour shift, Moish recounts, he was left alone in the blackness of the night. Other members had retired for a much-needed respite from the gloomy and tiring job, and he lay under the steps and pews on his back, all by himself, cleaning what had not been found during earlier searches. He says it was eerie and overwhelming at times, but he felt as if the souls of the recently departed were with him and watching over him during his attempt to honor their holy remains.

At some point, though, the work became too overwhelming. The echoing sounds of everyday noises and the ghostly, whirring sound of the hot water boiler down the hall got to him, and he ran out of the building to breathe some fresh air and clear his head. Standing out there, he says, he was comforted by the sight of two police cars parked outside, protecting the crime scene.

"Your courage. Your strength. I admire you," I say.

I look at this man, a Hassidic Jew in charge of taking care of the dead. Our dead. Eleven holy martyrs killed for being Jews. Eleven Jewish brothers and sisters—all of whom could have been my grandmothers and grandfathers, neighbors and uncles. I have never heard a man, let alone a Hassidic man, humanize the process of death so eloquently. I have never heard a man of my faith speak about death so vulnerably that it ushered in the presence of our Creator. I imagine that God was looking over Moish and the other men as they completed their holy work.

In his quiet telling of the moment, I witness how he becomes even more subdued. I don't need to hear about how, during the early hours of cleanup, the Tree of Life was a site of carnage. I do sense, however, that at some point, even as Moish was focused on the holy motivation for doing the work, he was still struggling to understand why someone would do this kind of evil to his community.

An hour into our conversation, most of the guests around the table have turned to other matters. It's just Moish and me in quiet conversation now.

"God will avenge their blood," he whispers. People like Moish, who has witnessed these victims' blood firsthand, will forever be moved from any kind of complacency. He speaks with the assertiveness Israelis are born with.

"I wasn't just cleaning blood and accounting for the victims and their burial, but I was actually cleaning where the victims were shot down," he says. "It was so eerie. That darkness. I was really scared to think what their last thoughts were as I looked at the scene from their point of view, staring at the ceiling as I lay on the floor where one of their holy bodies once lay.

"It felt as if the soul of that person was hovering. It felt like I was getting it ready for the *olam haba-ah*—the world to come."

All in all, we talk for about forty minutes about the details, his lack of sleep, the physicality of it all. I've never felt so connected to this behind-the-scenes process as I do now.

"So, for the entire night and the entire next day, all the eleven souls were hovering, lingering, waiting?" I'm getting goosebumps. These are not just any souls. These are now Tree of Life souls.

"Yes, that's right, I could definitely feel their presence," he says.

He and the other members of the *Chevra Kadisha* wouldn't take off their bodysuits and gloves until every ounce of blood had been collected and reunited with the dead. During the cleanup, a slew of Jewish guards watched over the bodies to ensure that the dead would not be alone until their burial.

On this almost-peaceful Shabbat, it feels good to bear witness to the story of one righteous Jewish man who just happens to be my neighbor, giving me a snapshot of what it means to bury the blood of these precious Jewish souls.

The souls we lost have been laid to rest. All that is left now is for this community—my evolving community—to heal.

We have a long way to go. But we will do this work together, and each time we make that effort, I will feel as if I'm bridging the gaps between my longing for Israel and my need for community in Pittsburgh.

EPILOGUE

For the first year following the Tree of Life attack, our local paper will continue referencing related incidents, people, places—culminating with the one-year commemoration we hold in October 2019. Our community, myself included, will have a hard time letting go, accepting this trauma. Community weddings and Bar Mitzvahs will serve as happy distractions, but my fear will continue to be triggered each time a siren wails, and all over again I'll remember the turn of events of October 27, 2018, as if they had just happened.

As we approach the High Holidays in Pittsburgh, I am again coming to terms with the cycle of my longings. As always, they are heightened during these times. But I'll try giving myself a bit of grace, trying not to think it's better there. I'll use my time in the synagogue during these Twelve Days of Awe that fall between Rosh Hashana and Yom Kippur to cement a deeper, more spiritual connection. We'll sit among unfamiliar faces in our synagogue's *succah*, a dwelling for God, and my heart will unfold as I experience being here, surrounded by Jewish unity and unity in general. Though I still feel as if I'm giving up one home for the other, I've realized that it's possible to find a home here, so long as my heart stays open to connections.

Shortly before the High Holidays, I'll eagerly speak Hebrew with an Israeli woman at our synagogue. There's the far-off look in her eyes, the disconnect from the actions. She's not a regular, and I wonder if she even notices the *siddur* in my hands. *We won't rest until we've connected with every single Jew.* This was the Rebbe's mission, and those words speak to me even more deeply now, at this moment when Jewish and Israeli identities come together.

The woman will at first politely decline when I ask if she'd like to follow along with the Torah reading together, reminding me of my own hesitations when I lived in Israel. After a few more minutes, however, she will turn to me and ask for the page and we'll bend over the pages together.

I live for these human connections. They help me stay connected to my heart home. My longing for Israel will continue to simmer like a pot of chicken soup, and it will continue to erupt into a boil on the High Holidays, leaving me to find creative ways to come to terms with my feelings.

This is exactly the opposite of what happened when I saw a photo of my son on his school blog, his red hair being dunked into the Jordan River, on his long-awaited middle school graduation trip to Israel. Just ten minutes away from our kibbutz, his birthplace, he wore a red T-shirt that read: "Dunk It!" Seeing the photo, my longings were calmed; as he traveled the entire country from north to south with his classmates, taking in his homeland on his own terms, I felt my son was like a proxy.

Before the High Holidays of 2019, I'll make a pact with myself not to let longings completely take over—not to play that mental game where I try to convince myself I'm better off in Israel. New Jewish year, new me. Will this push-pull be eased now that my stepmother and dad are back in the States? I see their reverse immigration playing out like a movie and I'm reminded of our own journey back, when we first came to Pittsburgh, thrown by the reverse culture shock. I managed to convince myself all those years that coming to Pittsburgh was one big mistake. I'm relieved to no longer feel that way. Yet having my dad here, surprisingly, doesn't quell my longings. If anything, my longings intensify, most likely because I have one less home to return to in Israel—one less tie to the country I willingly gave up.

Home is where you find strength, community, connection. But all of that only happens when you learn to adapt. Here, I've had to do that—had to embody the qualities of sand. I've had to learn when to interact as an Israeli and when as an American Jew. Sometimes one surges to the forefront at the expense of the other. But no matter which identity is in control, all my actions are driven by a motivation to feel more settled, to find belonging, to feel at home.

⋰⋰

Home is where moments unfold, where memories are made, where love abounds. In this post–Tree of Life era, the strength of our community is a reminder that here I have the best of both worlds—the resolve of steel and the malleability of sand. How well I connect determines the extent to which I am at peace in my heart, regardless of where my physical home lies.

When our rabbi talks about the strength of our community, I think back to the moment when our kibbutz community first started to disintegrate—back in 2002, when we first got married. Then I think back to fifteen years later, in 2017, when we sat at the pool at our old kibbutz during a visit.

At first, we didn't engage with anyone; there were too many unfamiliar faces. But then, as the sun set and the heat of the day slowly died down, Moshe, a veteran kibbutz member, approached me. His head hung low, but he still met my gaze straight on.

What he said caught me off guard: "We really let you down. We let Haim down. We lost out on you all, but especially Haim."

These words bowled me over. I was speechless. At that moment, Haim walked over, and Moshe repeated what he'd just said: "We lost you. I'm so sorry."

To hear this from a kibbutz member—that Haim's dedication and devotion weren't in vain, that he was worth something even after greed took over—was a balm to my soul. And yet I was angry, too. To push through the hurt, which still felt tall as a mountain, I had to speak out against the injustice of the kibbutz's past actions.

"So why didn't anyone do anything to help Haim find a job?"

Moshe didn't have a good response. He commiserated with us, though, and I realized that would have to be enough. Maybe the kibbutz wasn't privy to how troubled and torn we felt about leaving. Maybe they were too consumed by greed, didn't know how to help members like Haim. Maybe they didn't know how vulnerable our position was—how we were forced into a decision about whether to leave or to stay.

Whatever the reason for their failure to come through for us all those years earlier, I couldn't confide in any of our former kibbutz family about the longings that weighed on my heart or the anger over how they'd let Haim down. But if there was any kind of consolation prize, this conversation with Moshe was it. At least I knew now that people—or at least one person in the kibbutz—did care. That we were missed.

Home is the love you have for a place, the pride you have for a country. Home is creating new routines that will eventually become familiar. Home is the people who make up your community, even when they test you—your character, your resilience, and maybe even your faith and ability to surrender. Through Moshe, I considered what might have been, and for the first time, I saw the path we took—to America to raise our children in Pittsburgh—as a choice I probably would have made again.

Our kibbutz home, where we once built a life, and memories, and the home of our hearts now feels like a far-away exit on the highway. Maybe I've outgrown our kibbutz, whose members, intentionally or unintentionally, destroyed the place that had once nurtured us, making our familiar home unfamiliar and uncomfortable.

Moshe appeared to recognize the restraint in my face. I'm sorry, his face seemed to say. A kind of homelessness ignited from within—a momentary feeling of being untethered. It was as if all the homes I'd ever known were knocking heads with each other like tectonic plates.

When we took our leave of Moshe that hot summer evening, I wondered if we'd ever see each other again.

We hopped into our oven-hot rental car and passed tired-looking parched fields shimmering with silvery waves of heat. We made our way around the perimeter of the kibbutz until we reached the entrance. This rhythm I knew well. We'd wait at the guard's quarters for someone to hit the button to open the gate.

I glanced at Haim. "You wanna go in?" I asked jokingly.

A slim man emerges from the guard quarters and for a moment, he could almost be Haim. We quickly learn he's a kibbutz renter, filling in for one of the regulars. Our exchange of hellos is made even more prolonged by the heat; we're all moving in slow motion. But we need to be on our way. In just a few minutes, we'll be on Route 90, headed toward the center of the country. Later tonight, we'll cross the mighty Atlantic back again to our cold Diasporic home.

Once again, I wondered how badly we were needed in Pittsburgh.

I looked in the rearview mirror and smiled at how my husband had managed to snuggle in between our children in the backseat. They, too, were facets of home.

Home is everywhere you feel and think, no matter how far away you've drifted. My journey has been one of reconciling the many versions of home—Pittsburgh, Israel, New York—from childhood and beyond. The definition of home is always changing because we're always changing, and that's okay.

There in the car, as I once again prepared to leave the country I still hold most dear in my heart, I turned up the soul-stirring Hebrew music on the radio, wondering if anyone but me was still listening. When the song ended, our car went quiet, and the only noise was the blast of the air-conditioning. And in those few seconds, it felt as if the Earth made revolutions around us.

DEAR READER:

Now that you've made it to the end of this book (thank you!), I have two requests.

1. If you enjoyed this memoir, could you please hop over to Amazon or Goodreads and post a review? Something short and sweet, nothing fancy. Even the words, "short and engaging story" would be perfect!
    Why are reviews hugely important for authors?
    They serve a purpose beyond the feedback of a story. They demonstrate social proof—a way for authors like myself to promote our books and ultimately our platforms so we can reach those vast online audiences. Without reviews, a book just collects dust on a shelf or gets lost in the digital ocean of ebooks. I don't want *Sand and Steel* to be a forgotten book. I want its message to continue touching the hearts and minds of readers everywhere.
2. Please sign up for my monthly ezine at DoritSasson.com. This would be the best way for us to continue staying in contact. Authors need readers and readers need authors. Each month you'll receive updates of any new works in progress, articles and essays I've written, book tours, classes or workshops, and other events. And I hope to see you either at a future online or local author event.

Thank you so much. I'm utterly grateful to you for your support. Continue being the great big-hearted reader that you are!

Dorit Sasson

ACKNOWLEDGMENTS

I owe a huge debt of gratitude to the team who brought *Sand and Steel* into the world.

Brooke Warner and Krissa Lagos—you make me feel the luckiest. You are the editorial dream team and I'm so fortunate to work with you once again.

To Judy Siegel Henn for your proofreading prowess. I am so grateful for our connection.

To Michelle Webber, who was more than just Mascot's marketing manager. Michelle, you're a real confidant, author advocate, and team player. Thank you for all your support these past few years.

To the team at Mascot who believed in the book's idea and message, beginning with Maria Abrams.

Teri Case, my first reader, who offered me amazing feedback and insights.

To Lee Constantine, for your guidance in helping me crowdfund *Sand and Steel* through Publishizer so I could attract the right publisher for this book. Having the financial backup of numerous crowdfunders at the very beginning instilled in me the vote of confidence I needed to push this book to the finish line. Thank you so much for your patience. I hope the wait was worth it.

Writing any book is a long road, but this one felt especially long—maybe in part because at the onset of writing, I suddenly found myself dealing with unanticipated hurdles which significantly delayed the writing and production process. There were days when the writing felt hard and out of reach. Every now and then, I'd share the book's idea with members of online groups such as Power Hours for Freelance Hours and The Jewish Binders. Having the support of the online camaraderie kept me going.

Writing and marketing a book pre- and post-COVID-19, this historic global pandemic, is a challenge within itself. As I got closer to production, I wondered if I'd ever have the chance to market to a traditional bookstore audience. I am grateful to all my sisters through She Writes Press for helping me stay sane and supported with marketing ideas and assistance. I love what our tribe has become.

Big warm thanks to Rabbi Sruly and Chani Altein for helping us stay connected. We are grateful to be a part of the Chabad family.

Thank you to my husband, Haim Sasson, for sharing with me this crazy author life and for living it together with even more joy and love.

To my family, near and far—you are always in my heart.

To Ayala and Ivry, my precious gems. This book is for you too, because you have helped me come home.

ABOUT THE AUTHOR

Dorit Sasson is an Israeli-American writer and the award-winning author of *Accidental Soldier: A Memoir of Service and Sacrifice in the Israel Defense Forces*. Following her military service and graduate studies in English literature in Israel, Dorit taught English before returning to the United States in 2007 with her family. Her work has been featured in *The Writer*, *Kveller*, *The Philadelphia Inquirer*, *Ravishly*, *The Wisdom Daily*, *SheKnows*, and, most recently, *HuffPost*.

She is an Author SEO Specialist with Author Branding Solutions. She also supports small businesses, companies, and organizations with their SEO copywriting needs. She teaches for Writer's Digest University and does training on SEO for companies, non-profits, and small businesses. Become part of Dorit's community by signing up for her monthly ezine at DoritSasson.com.

BOOK DISCUSSION QUESTIONS

An online version of these questions is available at DoritSasson.com, under the reading group guide for *Sand and Steel*.

1. In the memoir, the author reconciles with the many versions of home, including the Israeli and American ones. Compare her feelings toward the Israeli and American emotional and physical homes. How does she reconcile with the various versions of home?

2. The author grapples with the security of leaving the kibbutz to find her United States home. What do you think helps her to find a sense of belonging again in the United States after living so many years in Israel?

3. In a COVID-19 era, where people have been literally forced to at stay at home, meaningful human connection has never been so important. How do you see the definition of home and human relationship changing in a crisis?

4. What do you think is more important in the psychology of home—the external or the internal home, or both? Does one's psychology, consciousness, and subjectivity depend on the place where you live?

5. How can you make your home an extension of yourself either physically or emotionally or both? What elements and facets are important to consider?

6. In what way do we outgrow certain homes? Is it also possible to destroy the security and safety of a home? In what way?

7. How does building roots help strengthen one's identity in a new place?

8. What kind of mindset is required for building roots and finding nurturing connections in a new place? Do you think it's easier to find a home as we age? Why or why not?

9. Do you think the author did the right thing by encouraging her husband to leave the kibbutz for an unknown future in the States? What would you have done?

10. Initially, the author sees social media as a way to satisfy her unsatisfied longings for Israel. Do you think these attempts are in vain? How, if at all, can social media satisfy an individual's longings?

11. Have you ever experienced unsatisfied longings? What did you do to satisfy them?

12. In the memoir, the author has to figure out unique and creative ways of dealing with the loss of giving up her country as a result of the misunderstood condition of Reverse Culture Shock—the psychological, emotional and cultural aspects of returning home. What are some ways she turns her longing for Israel into something useful for the greater good of others in her new community?

13. What kinds of groups can you think of who have been suffering from alienation and isolation? Do you think there's space in our culture to have conversations about unsatisfied longings?

14. How is social media helping people cultivate meaningful relationships that many people are desperately seeking? Has the impact of COVID-19 helped people connect more deeply and find their digital wellbeing?

15. What did you already know about Reverse Culture Shock before you read this book? How has this book changed your understanding of finding home and building roots?

16. What aspects of the author's story could you most relate to?

17. Upon her arrival in Pittsburgh, the author is overwhelmed by the differences in size between Israel and America. How does she overcome this emotional displacement? What do her actions tell you about her character and what it feels like to experience Reverse Culture Shock as a returning American?

18. Do you think it's important for people to read the author's story of emotional displacement and Reverse Culture Shock? Why or why not?